Maths Progress

International 11–14

Contributing editors: Dr Naomi Norman and Katherine Pate

8

Pearson

Published by Pearson Education Limited, 80 Strand, London, WC2R 0RL.

www.pearsonschoolsandfecolleges.co.uk

Text © Pearson Education Limited 2020
Project managed and edited by Just Content Ltd
Typeset by PDQ Digital Media Solutions Ltd
Original illustrations © Pearson Education Limited 2020
Cover illustration by Robert Samuel Hanson

The rights of Nick Asker, Jack Barraclough, Sharon Bolger, Gwenllian Burns, Greg Byrd, Lynn Byrd, Andrew Edmondson, Keith Gallick, Sophie Goldie, Bobbie Johns, Catherine Murphy, Amy O'Brien, Mary Pardoe, Katherine Pate, Harry Smith and Angela Wheeler to be identified as authors of this work have been asserted by them in accordance with the Copyright, Designs and Patents Act 1988.

First published 2020

24

14

British Library Cataloguing in Publication Data
A catalogue record for this book is available from the British Library.

ISBN 978 1 292 32717 4

Printed in Great Britain by Bell and Bain Ltd, Glasgow

Acknowledgements
The publisher would like to thank the following for their kind permission to reproduce their photographs:

123RF: tristan3d 26, Richard Semik 69, Vasiliy Vishnevskiy 84, Comaniciu Dan Dumitru 86, Brian Jackson 110, Ingrid Balabanova 182, orangeline 186, kbuntu 227, bryljaev 230, Ashwin Kharidehal Abhirama 248, timurpix 251; **Alamy Images:** EThamPhoto 29, petographer 81, Hero Images Inc. 137, John White Photos 140, MediaWorldImages 142, Design Pics Inc 146, John Birdsall 176, Justin Kase zsixz 178, WaterFrame 233; **Getty Images:** stocksnapper 1, skynesher 31, Rafal Olechowski 47, Alexis Boichard 130, Mike Watson Images 132, Jeffrey Coolidge 135, RainervonBrandis 144, Getty images 180, Harvepino 198, 36clicks 202; **Shutterstock:** Alexander Raths 7, dibrova 9, Baloncici 23, Boris Rabtsevich 45, Dario Sabljak 49, IM_photo 51, Pagina 54, GEORGII MIRONOV 72, Johan Swanepoel 75, Africa Studio 78, FOTOGRIN 89, Claudio Divizia 104, Air Images 107, Mopic 113, Lisa S. 116, ESB Professional 159, Brian Goodman 162, Kekyalyaynen 184, Joachim Wendler 206, NAN728 221, pixeldreams.eu 224.

All other images © Pearson Education

The publisher would like to thank Diane Oliver for her input and advice.

Note from the publisher
Pearson has robust editorial processes, including answer and fact checks, to ensure the accuracy of the content in this publication, and every effort is made to ensure this publication is free of errors. We are, however, only human, and occasionally errors do occur. Pearson is not liable for any misunderstandings that arise as a result of errors in this publication, but it is our priority to ensure that the content is accurate. If you spot an error, please do contact us at resourcescorrections@pearson.com so we can make sure it is corrected.

Contents

8

Maths Progress International

Confidence • Fluency • Problem-solving • Progression

Confidence at the heart

Maths Progress International is built around a unique pedagogy that has been created by leading educational researchers and teachers. The result is an innovative learning structure based around 10 key principles designed to nurture confidence and raise achievement.

Pedagogy – our 10 key principles

- Fluency
- Problem-solving
- Reflection
- Mathematical reasoning
- Progression

- Linking
- Multiplicative reasoning
- Modelling
- Concrete - Pictorial - Abstract (CPA)
- Relevance

This edition of Maths Progress has been designed specifically for international students and provides seamless progression into Pearson Edexcel International GCSE Mathematics (9–1), as well as complete coverage of the Pearson Edexcel iLowerSecondary Award and the UK National Curriculum.

Student books

 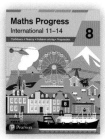 

The **Student books** are based on a single well-paced curriculum with built-in differentiation, fluency, problem-solving and reasoning so you can use them with your whole class. They follow the unique unit structure that has been shown to boost confidence and support every student's progress.

Workbooks

The **Workbooks** offer extra practice of key content. They provide additional support via guided questions with partially-worked solutions, hints and QR codes linking to worked example videos. Confidence checkers encourage students to take ownership of their learning, and allow them to track their progress.

Progress with confidence

This innovative 11–14 course builds on the first edition KS3 Maths Progress (2014) course, and is tailored to the needs of international students.

Take a look at the other parts of the series

*Active*Learn Service

The *Active*Learn service enhances the course by bringing together your planning, teaching and assessment tools, as well as giving students access to additional resources to support their learning. Use the interactive Scheme of Work, linked to all the teacher and student resources, to create a personalised learning experience both in and outside the classroom.

What's in *Active*Learn for Maths Progress International?

- ☑ **Front-of-class Student books** with links to PowerPoints, videos and animations
- ☑ **Over 40 assessments and online markbooks,** including end-of-unit, end-of-term and end-of-year tests
- ☑ **Online, automarked homework activities**
- ☑ **Interactive Scheme of Work** makes re-ordering the course easy by bringing everything together into one curriculum for all students with links to resources and teacher guidance
- ☑ **Lesson plans** for every Student book lesson
- ☑ **Answers** to the Student books and Workbooks
- ☑ **Printable glossaries** for each Student book contain all the key terms in one place.
- ☑ **Student access to glossaries, videos, homework and online textbooks**

*Active*Learn Progress & Assess

The Progress & Assess service is part of the full *Active*Learn service, or can be bought as a separate subscription. This service includes:

- assessments that have been designed to ensure that all students have the opportunity to show what they have learned
- editable tests that mimic the style of Pearson Edexcel International GCSE exams
- online markbooks for tracking and reporting
- baseline assessments for Year 7 and both tiers of International GCSE.

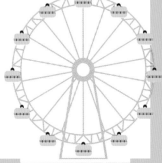

Welcome to Maths Progress International
Student books

 Confidence • Fluency • Problem-solving • Progression

Starting a new course is exciting! We believe you will have fun with maths, while at the same time nurturing your confidence and raising your achievement. Here's how:

Learn fundamental knowledge and skills over a series of *Master* lessons.

Some questions are tagged as *Finance* or *STEM*. These questions show how the real world relies on maths.

Literacy hints (explain unfamiliar terms) and *Strategy hints* (help with working out).

You can improve your ability to use maths in everyday situations by tackling *Modelling*, *Reasoning*, *Problem-solving*, and *Real* questions. *Discussions* prompt you to explain your reasoning or explore new ideas with a partner.

Clear objectives show what you will cover in each lesson.

Why learn this? shows you how maths is useful in everyday life.

Improve your *Fluency* – practise answering questions using maths you already know.

The first questions are *Warm up*. Here you can show what you already know about this topic or related ones...

...before moving on to further questions, with *Worked examples* and *Hints* for help when you need it.

Key points explain key concepts and definitions where you need them.

Your teacher has online access to *Answers*.

A printable *Glossary* containing all the key mathematical terms is available online.

Topic links and *Subject links* show you how the maths in a lesson is connected to other mathematical topics and other subjects.

Explore a real-life problem by discussing and having a go. By the end of the lesson you'll have gained the skills you need to start finding a solution to the question using maths.

At the end of each lesson, you get a chance to *Reflect* on how confident you feel about the topic.

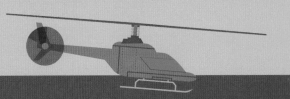

At the end of the Master lessons, take a **Check up** test to help you decide to Strengthen or Extend your learning. You may be able to mark this test yourself.

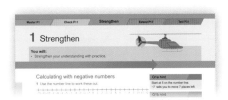

Choose only the topics in **Strengthen** that you need a bit more practice with. You'll find more hints here to lead you through specific questions. Then move on to *Extend*.

Extend helps you to apply the maths you know to some different situations. Strengthen and Extend both include Enrichment or Investigations.

When you have finished the whole unit, a **Unit test** helps you see how much progress you are making.

STEM lessons

These lessons focus on STEM maths. STEM stands for Science, Technology, Engineering and Maths. You can find out how charities use maths in their fundraising, how engineers monitor water flow in rivers, and why diamonds sparkle (among other things!).

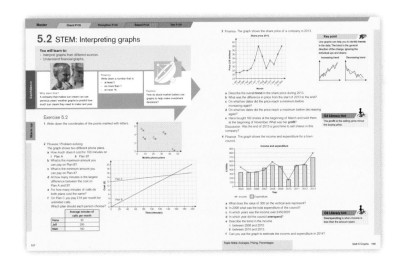

Further support

You can easily access extra resources that tie into each lesson by logging into *Active*Learn. Here you will find online homework clearly mapped to the units, providing fun, interactive exercises linked to helpful worked examples and videos.

The workbooks, full of extra practice of key questions, will help you reinforce your learning and track your own progress.

1.1 Calculating with negative integers

You will learn to:
- Add, subtract, multiply and divide positive and negative numbers.

Confidence

Why learn this?
Calculating with negative numbers is a critical skill for anyone working in finance.

Fluency
- What is the difference between 3 and 12?
- The temperature is −5 °C and rises by 8 °C. What is the new temperature?
- What is the fall in temperature from −7 °C to −13 °C?

Explore
What is the difference in the surface temperature of the Moon between midday and midnight?

Exercise 1.1

Warm up

1 Use a number line to work these out.
   a Subtract 10 from 6
   b Subtract 4 from −2
   c Add 3 to −9
   d Add 20 to −5

2 Work out
   a 11 − 5   b 4 − 7   c −2 + 5
   d −2 − 3   e 0 − 7   f −12 + 3

3 Work out
   a 12 + −15   b 12 − −15   c 12 − 15
   d −12 + 15   e −26 + −18   f −26 − −18
   g −26 − 18   h −18 + −26
   Discussion Which questions give the same answers? Explain why.

4 Work out the **difference** between each pair of numbers.
   a 8 and 15   b −3 and 6   c −2 and 8
   d −4 and −10   e 7 and −7   f −2 and −12

> **Key point**
>
> To find the **difference** between two numbers, subtract the lower number from the higher one.

5 **STEM** When hydrogen gas is cooled, it becomes a liquid at −253 °C and freezes solid at −259 °C.

   a Hydrogen gas at −160 °C is cooled by 100 °C.
      After cooling, is it a gas, liquid or solid?

   b In a science lab, hydrogen has a temperature of 20 °C.
      By how many degrees do you need to cool it so that it becomes a liquid?

> **Q5b hint**
>
> 6 − −3 = ☐

1

Topic links: Priority of operations, Averages and range, Formulae, Square numbers and roots

Subject links: Science (Q5)

6 **Real / Finance / Problem-solving** The table shows Mrs Prestwick's **bank balance** each time she made a **deposit** (+) or **withdrawal** (−) in May.

Date in May	1	2	13	19	20	25	31
Deposit/Withdrawal (£)		+20	−37	+200	−12	+55	−25
Balance (£)	−128						

Q6 Literacy hint

A **bank balance** is the amount of money in a bank account. A **negative bank balance** (or **overdraft**) is an amount owed to the bank.
When you put money into a bank account, this is a **deposit**. When you take money out, this is a **withdrawal**.

  a Copy and complete the table.
  b Work out the difference in her bank balance between 1 May and 31 May.

7 a Copy the tables and continue the patterns to complete the answers.

Calculation	Answer
3 × 4	12
3 × 3	9
3 × 2	
3 × 1	
3 × 0	
3 × −1	
3 × −2	
3 × −3	

$\big)$−3

Calculation	Answer
4 × −3	
3 × −3	
2 × −3	
1 × −3	
0 × −3	
−1 × −3	
−2 × −3	
−3 × −3	

  b Copy and complete the rules.
  positive × positive = positive   positive × negative = ...
  negative × positive = ...   negative × negative = ...
  Discussion What is an easy way to remember these rules?

8 Work out
  a −2 × −4   **b** 8 × −3   **c** −6 × 6   **d** 5 × (−9)
  e (−3) × (−3)   **f** −20 × 6   **g** −4 × (−9)   **h** (−12) × 5
  i −10 × 0.5   **j** 100 × (−0.1)   **k** −2 × −3 × −4   **l** 2 × −4 × 5

Q8d hint

(−9) is another way of writing the negative number −9.

9 a Fill in the missing number facts. The first one has been done for you.
     i 2 × −3 = −6, so −6 ÷ 2 = −3 and −6 ÷ −3 = 2
     ii −3 × −4 = 12, so 12 ÷ −3 = ☐ and 12 ÷ −4 = ☐
     iii −2 × 5 = −10, so −10 ÷ −2 = ☐ and −10 ÷ 5 = ☐
  b Look at the signs of the division facts in part **a**.
  Copy and complete the rules.
  positive ÷ positive = positive   positive ÷ negative = ...
  negative ÷ positive = ...   negative ÷ negative = ...

10 Work out
  a −8 ÷ −2   **b** 15 ÷ −3   **c** −18 ÷ 6   **d** (−20) ÷ 5
  e 40 ÷ (−8)   **f** (−6) ÷ (−6)   **g** −1000 ÷ (−10)   **h** 132 ÷ −11
  i 200 ÷ −25   **j** 0.8 ÷ −2   **k** −12.4 ÷ 2   **l** 16 ÷ (−2) ÷ 2

11 Expand the brackets to work these out.
  Check your answers using the priority of operations.
  a 6 × (−2 − 1)   **b** 3 × (−1 + 4) − 13   **c** −2(−3 + 5)
  d −3(−4 − 1)   **e** −5(3 − 4)   **f** −4(−3 + 5) − 2

Q11a hint

6 × (−2 − 1) = 6 × −2 + 6 × −1 = ☐
Check: 6 × (−2 − 1) = 6 × −3 = ☐

12 Real / STEM A house has solar panels to generate electricity.
When it doesn't generate enough it uses electricity from the national grid. When it generates too much it sends electricity back to the national grid.
The table shows the electricity sent to the national grid every 10 minutes for one hour.

Time	14 00	14 10	14 20	14 30	14 40	14 50
Electricity (power, W)	−130	220	−1395	640	−1565	−290

Discussion Why is the power negative sometimes?
Work out
a the median   b the range   c the mean.

13 Substitute the values into each formula and work out the answers.
a $m = 2n - 1$ when $n = -7$
b $v = u + at$ when $u = -8$, $a = -10$ and $t = 6$
c $A = 3a - 4b$ when $a = -2$ and $b = -5$
d $T = k(e - f)$ when $k = -3$, $e = 4$ and $f = -2$
e $L = a - (2b + c)$ when $a = -10$, $b = -8$ and $c = 4$

Q13a hint

Use the priority of operations.

14 Work out these calculations. The first one is started for you.
a $(-2)^2 = -2 \times -2 = \square$ b $(-3)^2$ c $(-4)^2$ d $(-5)^2$
e $(-6)^2$ f $(-7)^2$ g $(-8)^2$ h $(-10)^2$

15 Reasoning
a What do you notice about the answer when you square a negative number?
b Is it possible to square a negative number and get an answer that is also negative? Explain.

16 Write the positive and negative square roots of these numbers.
a 25   b 64   c 81
d 1   e 121   f 144

Key point

$3^2 = 9$ and $(-3)^2 = 9$.
The **positive square root** of 9 is 3.
The **negative square root** of 9 is −3.
The $\sqrt{\ }$ symbol is used for the principal square root, which is always a positive number.
For example, $\sqrt{9} = 3$

Investigation   **Problem-solving**

1 a Work out -2×-3.
b Use your answer to work out $-2 \times -3 \times -4$.
c When you multiply three negative numbers together, is the answer positive or negative?
2 Is the answer positive or negative when you multiply these? Write some calculations for each.
a positive × negative × negative
b positive × positive × negative

17 Explore What is the difference in the surface temperature of the Moon between midday and midnight?
Is it easier to explore this question now that you have completed the lesson?
What further information do you need to be able to answer this?

18 Reflect Look back at what you have learned in this lesson about negative numbers.
What is different and what is the same about positive and negative numbers?
Copy this table and list all the things you know about positive and negative numbers.

Same for positive and negative numbers	Different for positive and negative numbers
When you multiply two negative numbers, or two positive numbers, you always get a positive answer.	As you move away from zero, negative numbers get lower, but positive numbers get higher.

Explore

Reflect

*Active*Learn   Homework, Year 8, Unit 1

1.2 Prime factor decomposition

You will learn to:
* Write the prime factor decomposition of a number.
* Use prime factor decomposition to find the HCF or LCM of two numbers.

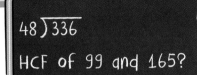

48) 336

HCF of 99 and 165?

Why learn this?
Writing a number as a product of its prime factors can help you work out divisions, HCFs and LCMs.

Fluency
Which of these numbers are prime?
* 12, 7, 9, 2, 5, 4, 1
Write using powers
* 3 × 3 × 3 × 3
* 2 × 2 × 2 × 2 × 2

Explore
Can you make every number just by multiplying prime numbers?

Exercise 1.2

1 Work out the product of 4, 6 and 2.

2 **a** Write the factors of 18 and 30 using this Venn diagram.
   b What is the highest common factor (HCF) of 18 and 30?

Factors of 18 | Factors of 30

3 **a** List the first 8 multiples of 9 and 12.
   b What is the lowest common multiple (LCM) of 9 and 12?

4 **a** Copy and complete this factor tree to find all the prime factors of 90.

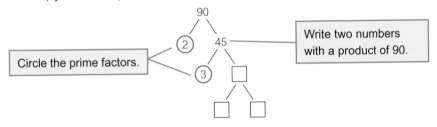
Circle the prime factors.
Write two numbers with a product of 90.

   b Write down the **product** of the prime factors.
   90 = 2 × 3 × □ × □
   Discussion Draw a different factor tree for the number 90. Does it matter which two factors you choose first?

5 Write each number as a product of its prime factors.
   a 32   **b** 75   **c** 54   **d** 36
   Discussion How can you use the **prime factor decomposition** of 36 to quickly work out the prime factor decomposition of 72? What about 18?

Warm up

Key point
You can write a number as a product of prime number factors. This is called **prime factor decomposition**.

Q4b Literacy hint
Product means the answer when two of more numbers are multiplied.

6 Write each number as a product of its prime factors.

   a **i** 225

      ii 450

   b **i** 140

      ii 420

Q6a ii hint

$450 = 225 \times \square$

Investigation

Reasoning

  1 Write 48 and 336 as a product of their prime factors.

  2 Explain how you can tell by looking at the prime factor decomposition that 48 divides exactly into 336.

  3 Use your answers to part 1 and part 2 to write down the answer to 336 ÷ 48. Use a calculator to check your answer.

  4 Use prime factor decomposition to test whether these divisions have exact answers.
     If they have, write down the answer. Check your answers with a calculator.

     a 840 ÷ 56   **b** 576 ÷ 64   **c** 594 ÷ 108   **d** 468 ÷ 39

  5 Write two division questions of your own that have exact answers. Test them on a partner to see if
     they can work out the answer using prime factor decomposition, not a calculator.

---

7 **Problem-solving** Here are some prime factor decomposition cards.

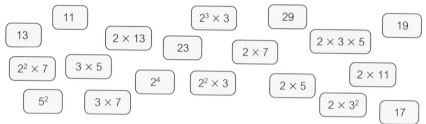

Key point

You can use prime factor decomposition to find the HCF of two or more numbers.

The cards represent the numbers from 10 to 30.

Two of the cards are missing.

What is the prime factor decomposition on the missing cards?

Worked example

Find the highest common factor of 90 and 252.

$90 = 2 \times 3^2 \times 5$

$252 = 2^2 \times 3^2 \times 7$

                → Write each number as a product of prime factors.

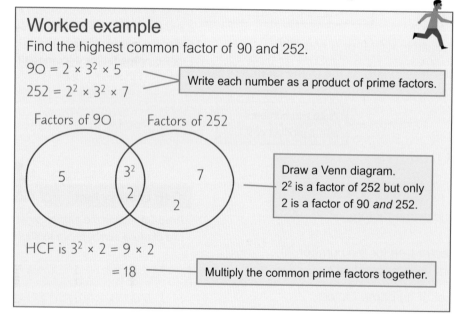

Draw a Venn diagram.
2^2 is a factor of 252 but only 2 is a factor of 90 *and* 252.

HCF is $3^2 \times 2 = 9 \times 2$

           $= 18$ Multiply the common prime factors together.

---

8 Use prime factor decomposition to find the HCF of each pair of numbers.

   a 60 and 84

   b 90 and 210

   c 42 and 105

   d 99 and 165

9 **Problem-solving** Kyle works out that the HCF of two numbers is
$2^2 \times 3^2 = 36$.
What two numbers might Kyle have been using?
Discussion What method did you use to solve this problem?

10 **Reasoning**
a Write the prime factors of 12 and 18 in this Venn diagram.

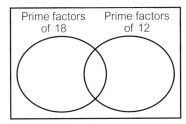

b Write 36 as a product of prime factors.
c The lowest common multiple (LCM) of 12 and 18 is 36.
Show how you can use the Venn diagram from part **a** to work out
the LCM of 12 and 18.
Discussion What method did you use to answer part **c**?

11 **Reasoning** Use prime factor decomposition to show that the LCM
of 21 and 45 is 315.

Q11 hint
Draw a Venn diagram.

12 Use prime factor decomposition to find the LCM of each pair of
numbers.
a 8 and 36
b 18 and 66
c 28 and 42
d 30 and 75

13 **STEM / Problem-solving** Two weather satellites pass over the
London Eye at 11 am. It takes one satellite 100 minutes to orbit the
Earth and it takes the other satellite 120 minutes to orbit the Earth.
At what time will both of the satellites next pass over the London Eye
at the same time?

Q13 Strategy hint
Work out the LCM first.

14 **Explore** Can you make every number by just multiplying prime
numbers?
Choose some sensible numbers to help you explore this situation.
Then use what you've learned in this lesson to help you answer the
question.

15 **Reflect** Write down your own short definition for each of these
mathematics words.
• Prime
• Factor
• Decomposition
Use your definitions to write down (in your own words) the meaning
of prime factor decomposition.

Q15 hint
Compose means to make or create
something. What do you think
decompose means?

Explore

Reflect

1.3 Using indices

Confidence

You will learn to:
- Work out the laws of indices for positive powers.
- Show that any number to the power of zero is 1.
- Use the laws for indices for multiplying and dividing.

Why learn this?
Knowing the rules for indices can speed up complicated calculations that scientists, engineers and doctors need to do.

Fluency
What is the missing power?
- $3 \times 3 \times 3 \times 3 \times 3 = 3^\square$
- $4 \times 4 \times 4 = 4^\square$
- $5 \times 5 \times 5 \times 5 \times 5 \times 5 \times 5 = 5^\square$
- $16 = 4^\square$
- $25 = 5^\square$
- $27 = 3^\square$

Explore
What expressions will simplify to 9^6?

Exercise 1.3

Warm up

1 Work out
   a $\dfrac{2 \times 2}{4 \times 5}$ b $\dfrac{4 \times 9}{6 \times 2}$ c $\dfrac{8 \times 5}{6 \times 4}$

2 Work out
   a 4×4^2 b $5^2 \times 5$ c $3^2 \times 3^2$ d $2^2 \times 2^3$

3 Work out
   a 2^6 b 3^5 c 10^7 d 5^4

4 **Reasoning** Penny works out
   $2^2 \times 2^3$
   $2 \times 2 \times 2 \times 2 \times 2 = 2^5$
   How can you quickly find $2^2 \times 2^3$ without writing all the 2s?

5 Write each product as a single power.
   a $3^4 \times 3^2$ b $4^3 \times 4$ c $5^4 \times 5^2$ d $7^3 \times 7^3$
   e $4^8 \times 4^6$ f $3^9 \times 3$ g 6×6^{12}

6 **Problem-solving** Tam multiplies three powers of 8 together.
   $8^\square \times 8^\square \times 8^\square = 8^{15}$
   What could the three powers be if
   a all the powers are different
   b two of the powers are the same
   c all three powers are the same?

7 **Reasoning**
   a i Work out $\dfrac{4 \times 4 \times 4 \times 4 \times 4}{4 \times 4 \times 4}$ by cancelling. Write your answer as a power of 4.
      ii Copy and complete $4^5 \div 4^3 = 4^\square$
   b Copy and complete $2^5 \div 2^2 = \dfrac{2^5}{2^2} = \dfrac{2 \times 2 \times 2 \times 2 \times 2}{2 \times 2} = 2^\square$
   c Work out $5^4 \div 5^3$
   Discussion How can you quickly find $4^8 \div 4^3$ without writing all the 4s?

Q3 hint
Use the $\boxed{x^y}$ button on your calculator.

Q4 hint
Look at the indices in the question and the answer.

Key point
When you multiply numbers written as powers of the same number, you add the indices.

Q5b hint
$4 = 4^1$

Q5 Literacy hint
A single power means one number with a power. For example, 5^7.

8 Write each of these as a single power.

  a $6^8 \div 6^2$ **b** $5^7 \div 5^3$ **c** $9^9 \div 9^8$

  d $2^9 \div 2^4$ **e** $4^{15} \div 4^9$ **f** $12^5 \div 12$

Key point

When you divide numbers written as powers of the same number, you subtract the indices.

9 **Problem-solving** Su divides two powers of 3.

  $3^{\square} \div 3^{\square} = 3^2$

  What could the two numbers be if

  a both numbers are greater than 3^{20}

  b both numbers are smaller than 3^{20}

  c the power of one number is double the power of the other number?

10 **STEM** The diameter of Saturn is approximately 2^{17} km. The diameter of the dwarf planet Ceres is approximately 2^{10} km. How many times larger is the diameter of Saturn than the diameter of Ceres?

Q10 hint

$2^{10} \times \square = 2^{17}$

11 **Reasoning** Write each of these as a single power.

  a $(2^4)^2$ **b** $(5^2)^2$ **c** $(3^2)^3$ **d** $(6^2)^4$

  Discussion How can you find the values of parts **a–d** using the indices?

Key point

When you work out the power of a power, you multiply the indices.

12 Write each of these as a single power.

  a $(4^3)^4$ **b** $(7^2)^5$ **c** $(3^6)^3$ **d** $(8^5)^7$

13 **Reasoning** **a** Write each of these as a single power.

    i $2^5 \times 2^3$ **ii** $3^5 \times 3^3$ **iii** $p^5 \times p^3 = p^{\square}$

  b Copy and complete this general rule for any number p with positive integer powers a and b. $p^a \times p^b = p^{\square + \square}$

  c Write each as a single power.   **i** $2^5 \div 2^3$ **ii** $3^5 \div 3^3$ **iii** $p^5 \div p^3$

  d Copy and complete this general rule for any number p with positive integer powers a and b. $p^a \div p^b = p^{\square - \square}$

  e Copy and complete   **i** $(2^5)^3 = 2^{\square}$ **ii** $(3^5)^3 = 3^{\square}$ **iii** $(p^5)^3 = p^{\square}$

  f Copy and complete this general rule for any number p with positive integer powers a and b. $(p^a)^b = p^{\square \times \square}$

Q13 hint

A general rule is a rule that works for any numbers. Using letters shows that any number can be substituted.

14 **Reasoning**

  a **i** Work out the answers to these divisions: $\dfrac{5}{5}$ $\dfrac{7}{7}$ $\dfrac{12}{12}$ $\dfrac{100}{100}$ $\dfrac{3^4}{3^4}$ $\dfrac{9^5}{9^5}$

    ii What do you notice about dividing a number by itself? Test with a few more numbers.

  b **i** Copy and complete this pattern.

    $\dfrac{9^5}{9^1} = 9^4$ $\dfrac{9^5}{9^2} = 9^3$ $\dfrac{9^5}{9^3} = 9^{\square}$ $\dfrac{9^5}{9^4} = 9^{\square}$ $\dfrac{9^5}{9^5} = 9^{\square}$

    ii What do you notice about your answers to $\dfrac{9^5}{9^5}$ in part **ai** and part **bi**?

    iii Complete this statement: 'Any number to the power of zero = $\square$'.

  Discussion $2^0 = 1$. Does this mean that 4^0 is twice as big?

15 Write each calculation as a single power.

  a $\dfrac{4^2 \times 4^8}{4^3}$ **b** $\dfrac{7^{12}}{7^2 \times 7^6}$ **c** $\dfrac{5^6 \times 5^6}{5^7 \times 5}$

16 **Problem-solving** Write each calculation as a single power.

  a $16 \times 32 \times 8$ **b** $\dfrac{4^9}{64}$ **c** $\dfrac{27 \times 81}{3^2}$

Q16a Strategy hint

Start by writing each number as a power of 2.

17 **Explore** What expressions will simplify to 9^6? Choose some sensible numbers and use what you've learned in this lesson to help you explore this situation.

18 **Reflect** Lana says, 'Mathematics is often about spotting (noticing) patterns.' Do you agree with Lana? Explain. Why does it help to spot patterns in mathematics? Explain.

Q18 hint

Look back at this lesson. Can you find questions where you were spotting a pattern? Where else in mathematics have you used pattern spotting?

Explore   Reflect

1.4 Priority of operations

You will learn to:

* Carry out calculations involving powers, roots and brackets following the priority of operations.

Why learn this?
When engineers calculate the forces acting on bridges, they need to combine more than one calculation. The order in which they carry out the calculation will affect the value.

Fluency
Work out:
15 ÷ 3
3 × 8
8 + 3
8 − 3

Explore
How can you calculate all the numbers from 1 to 10 using only the numbers from 1 to 4, indices and brackets?

Confidence

Warm up

Exercise 1.4

1 Work out
  a 3^2 **b** 9^2 **c** 10^2 **d** 20^2
  e $\sqrt{9}$ **f** $\sqrt{81}$ **g** $\sqrt{100}$ **h** $\sqrt{400}$

2 Work out
  a $(4 + 3) \times 5$ **b** $3 + 4 \times 2$
  c $6 - 4 + 5$ **d** $4 \times 5 - 2 \times 3$

3 Reasoning Afsa works out $20 - (4 \times 3)$
  $4 \times 3 = 12$
  $12 - 20 = -8$
  a Explain what she has done wrong.
  b Work out the correct answer.

4 Work out
  a $4^2 - 12$ **b** $10 + 3^2$ **c** 9×1^3 **d** $12^2 - 100$
  e $\sqrt{81} \times 3$ **f** $12 - \sqrt{100}$ **g** $4 \times \sqrt[3]{8}$ **h** $12 \div \sqrt[3]{1}$

5 a $(5^2 - 13) \times 2$
  b $5^2 - 13 \times 2$
  c $5^2 - (13 \times 2)$
  d $(8 + 1)^2 - 5$
  e $(8 + 1 - 5)^2$
  f $8 + (5 - 1)^2$
  g $8^2 + 5 - 1$
  h Check your answers to parts **a–g** with a calculator by typing in the whole calculation.
    Does your calculator follow the priority of operations?

Investigation

Reasoning

Does putting a set of brackets into a calculation always change the value?
Are there any calculations that have the same value with and without brackets?
Try different calculations (e.g. $4 + 3 - 5$ and $5 \times 6 \div 2$).

6 Problem solving / Reasoning Make the calculations correct by putting in a set of brackets.

a $3 + 4 \times 7 = 49$

b $5 + 6^2 - 9 = 112$

c $8 + 4 \times 5 - 3 = 16$

7 Work out:

a $100 - 3^3$

b $4 \times 2^3 - 10$

c $\dfrac{\sqrt[3]{1000}}{2} + 3^2$

8 Work out:

a $(6 - 4)^5$

b $100 - (6 - 4)^5$

c $6^5 - 4^5$

Q8 hint

Use the $\sqrt[3]{\ }$ and x^y buttons on your calculator.

9 Work out:

a $2^5 + 3 \times 7$

b 2×5^4

c $34 - \sqrt[3]{729}$

10 Problem-solving

a Match each calculation card with the correct answer card.
Check your answers using a calculator.

| $(7 - 5)^4$ | $7 \times 5 - 1^4$ | $2 \times (5 - 1)^3$ | $(2 \times 5)^5 - 4^2$ |

| 128 | 34 | 56 | 99 984 | 16 |

b There is one answer card left over.
Write a calculation card to go with this answer card.
The calculation must include index notation.

11 Write the answers to these calculations in ascending order.

| $2^6 - \sqrt[3]{125}$ | $\sqrt{49} + 2^4$ | $\dfrac{\sqrt{121} + 5}{2^2}$ | $\dfrac{7^2 - 3^2}{\sqrt[3]{8}}$ |

12 Explore How can you calculate all the numbers from 1 to 10 using only the numbers from 1 to 4, indices and brackets?
Look back at the maths you have learned in this lesson.
How can you use it to answer this question?

13 Reflect In this lesson you used the priority of operations:
Brackets → Indices → Multiplication/Division → Addition/Subtraction
Think of a method for remembering this, for example, you might want to remember the word BIDMAS.

Explore

Reflect

1 Check up

Calculating with negative numbers

1 Work these out.
  a $6 - -2$
  b $-5 - 3$
  c $-8 + 12$
  d $-3 + 2 - 5$
  e 4×-2
  f $15 \div -5$
  g $12 \div -4 - 8$
  h $-5 \times (4 - 7)$

2 Write these in order from smallest to largest.

  -2×-3 $-2 + -3$ $-3 \div -2$ $-3 - -2$ $-2 \div -3$ $-3 + -2$

3 The temperature in Moscow is $-12°C$. The temperature in Florida is $27°C$.
  Which calculation correctly calculates the difference in temperature between Moscow and Florida?
  A $-12 + 27$
  B $27 - -12$
  C $12 + 27$

Prime factors

4 Draw a factor tree for the number 72.

5 Write 300 as a product of its prime factors.

6 Use prime factor decomposition to find
  a the highest common factor of 135 and 180
  b the lowest common multiple of 32 and 40.

Indices and priority of operations

7 Write each calculation as a single power.
  a $3^4 \times 3^3$ **b** $5^2 \times 5$ **c** $6^7 \times 6^2 \times 6^9$ **d** $2^6 \div 2^2$
  e $5^8 \div 5$ **f** $(3^4)^2$ **g** $4^3 \div 4^3$

8 Evaluate $\dfrac{3 \times 2^9}{2^6}$

9 Work out
  a $(-5)^2$
  b $30 - 3^2 - (-4)^2$
  c 6^0

10 Write each calculation as a single power.

a $\dfrac{6^4 \times 6^5}{6^3}$

b $\dfrac{2^5 \times 2^2}{2 \times 2^3}$

c $27 \times 3 \times 9$

11 Which two calculations give the same answer?

A $(2 \times 5)^2$ **B** 2×5^2

C $2^2 \times 5^2$ **D** $2^2 \times 5$

12 Evaluate $\dfrac{(3 \times 2)^3}{2 \times 18}$

13 Copy and complete these statements.

$a^x \times a^y = a^{\square}$ $a^x \div a^y = a^{\square}$ $(a^x)^y = a^{\square}$

14 Work out:

a $3 \times 4 + 7$ b $9 + 14 \div 7$

c $(8 + 11) \times 4$ d $3^2 - 5 \times 8$

e $(3 + 4)^2 - 12 + 7$ f $7 \times (2 + 1)^3 - 9$

15 Put a pair of brackets in this calculation to make it correct.

$7 + 8 \times 3 - 2 = 15$

16 **How sure are you of your answers? Were you mostly**
😞 **Just guessing**   😐 **Feeling doubtful**   🙂 **Confident**
What next? Use your results to decide whether to strengthen or extend your learning.

Challenge

17 a Choose your own numbers to make these calculations correct.

$5^{\square} \times 5^{\square} = 5^{18}$

$5^{\square} \div 5^{\square} = 5^{18}$

$(5^{\square})^{\square} = 5^{18}$

b Repeat part **a** using different numbers.

18 Ellen is working out the prime factor decomposition of a number. She draws this factor tree.

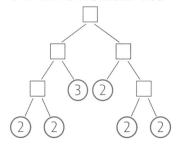

What is Ellen's number?

19 Hassan writes a number as a product of its prime factors like this:

$2^3 \times 3 \times 7^2$

What number did Hassan start with?

1 Strengthen

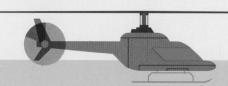

You will:
• Strengthen your understanding with practice.

Calculating with negative numbers

1 Use the number line to work these out.

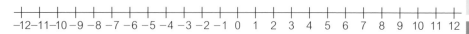

$$-12\ -11\ -10\ -9\ -8\ -7\ -6\ -5\ -4\ -3\ -2\ -1\ \ 0\ \ 1\ \ 2\ \ 3\ \ 4\ \ 5\ \ 6\ \ 7\ \ 8\ \ 9\ \ 10\ 11\ 12$$

  a $5 - 7$
  b $5 - (-7)$
  c $-5 + 7$
  d $-5 - 7$

> **Q1a hint**
> Start at 5 on the number line.
> −7 tells you to move 7 places left.

> **Q1b hint**
> Start at 5 on the number line.
> − −7 is the same as + 7.

> **Q1c hint**
> Start at −5 on the number line.
> +7 tells you to move 7 places right.

> **Q1d hint**
> Start at −5 on the number line.
> −7 tells you to move 7 places left.

2 Work out
  a $10 + -5$ **b** $8 - -4$ **c** $-2 - -8$ **d** $-5 + -2$

> **Q2 hint**
> Replace different signs with minus (−).
> Replace same signs with plus (+).

3 The answer to each of these questions is 6 or −6. Write down the correct answer.
  a -3×2 **b** 3×-2 **c** 3×2 **d** -2×-3
  e 1×6 **f** -1×-6 **g** -1×6 **h** -6×1

4 Reasoning Write down three different pairs of numbers that multiply to give −10.

5 The answer to each of these questions is 5 or − 5. Write down the correct answer.
  a $10 \div 2$ **b** $-10 \div -2$ **c** $-10 \div 2$ **d** $10 \div -2$
  e $15 \div -3$ **f** $-15 \div -3$ **g** $-15 \div 3$ **h** $15 \div 3$

6 Reasoning Write down three different pairs of numbers that divide to give −10.

7 Work out.
  a $-12 \div -2$ **b** -8×-3 **c** -4×3
  d $3 \times -2 \times 4$ **e** $-2 \times 5 \times -7$ **f** $-3 \times -4 \div -2$

> **Q7 hint**
> For multiplying and dividing:
> same signs give a positive answer;
> different signs give a negative answer.

Prime factors

1 Write each product using index notation (powers).
The first one has been done for you.
  a $11 \times 11 \times 11 \times 7 \times 7 \times 7 \times 7 \times 2 = 11^3 \times 7^4 \times 2 = 2 \times 7^4 \times 11^3$
  b $2 \times 2 \times 2 \times 2 \times 5 \times 5 \times 3$
  c $5 \times 5 \times 5 \times 5 \times 5 \times 3 \times 3 \times 3 \times 2 \times 7$

> **Q1a hint**
> Write the factors in numerical order:
> 2s, then 7s, then 11s.

2 a Copy and complete the factor tree for the number 630 until you end up with just prime factors.

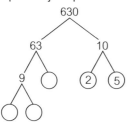

Q2a hint

Choose an easy factor pair to start with (630 = 63 × 10).
2 and 5 are prime factors of 630.

b Use index notation to write 630 as the product of its prime factors.

3 Use a factor tree to write each number as a product of its prime factors.
  a 92
  b 160
  c 156
  d 195
  e 441

Q3a hint

92 is an even number, so start by dividing by 2.

Q3d hint

195 is an odd number, so try dividing by 3 or 5.

4 This is how Yona works out the HCF of 12 and 30.

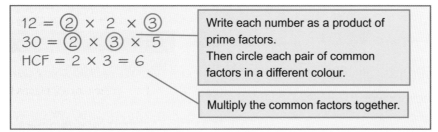

$12 = ② × 2 × ③$
$30 = ② × ③ × 5$
$HCF = 2 × 3 = 6$

Write each number as a product of prime factors.
Then circle each pair of common factors in a different colour.

Multiply the common factors together.

Q4 hint

First work out the prime factor decomposition.

Work out the HCF of each pair of numbers.
  a 32 and 36   **b** 45 and 72   **c** 132 and 180

Q5 hint

First find the prime factor decomposition.

5 This is how Simon works out the LCM of 12 and 30.

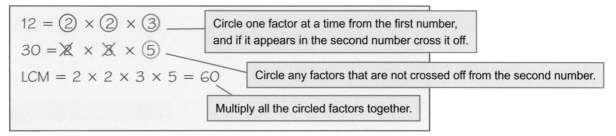

$12 = ② × ② × ③$
$30 = ✗ × ✗ × ⑤$
$LCM = 2 × 2 × 3 × 5 = 60$

Circle one factor at a time from the first number, and if it appears in the second number cross it off.

Circle any factors that are not crossed off from the second number.

Multiply all the circled factors together.

Work out the LCM of each pair of numbers.
  a 27 and 45   **b** 36 and 54   **c** 135 and 225

Indices and priority of operations

1 Copy and complete this table showing the powers of 4.

4^0	4^1	4^2	4^3	4^4
	4	16		

×4 ×4 ×4 ×4

2 Write each calculation as a single power.
  a $3^2 × 3^5 = 3^{\square + \square} = 3^{\square}$ **b** $4^3 × 4 = 4^{3 + \square} = 4^{\square}$
  c $9^6 × 9^3 = 9^{\square + \square}$ **d** $5^4 × 5^5 × 5^2$

Q2a hint

$$3^2 × 3^5 = \underbrace{3 × 3}_{2} × \underbrace{3 × 3 × 3 × 3 × 3}_{5}$$
$$\square$$

3 Write each calculation as a single power.

  a $4^6 \div 4^3 = 4^{\square - \square} = 4^\square$ **b** $3^5 \div 3 = 3^{\square - \square} = 3^\square$

  c $7^7 \div 7^5$ **d** $9^{12} \div 9^4$

4 Write each calculation as a single power.

  a $(4^3)^2 = 4^3 \times 4^3 = 4^\square$ **b** $(3^2)^5 = 3^2 \times 3^2 \times 3^2 \times 3^2 \times 3^2$

  c $(6^4)^2$ **d** $(8^5)^6$

5 Copy and complete these statements.

  $2^4 \times 2^3 = 2^{\square + \square}$ $2^x \times 2^y = 2^{\square + \square}$ $n^x \times n^y = n^\square$

  $2^4 \div 2^3 = 2^{\square - \square}$ $2^x \div 2^y = 2^{\square - \square}$ $n^x \div n^y = n^\square$

  $(2^4)^3 = 2^{\square \times \square}$ $(2^x)^y = 2^{\square \times \square}$ $(n^x)^y = n^\square$

6 Copy and complete this table showing the powers of 2.

2^0	2^1	2^2	2^3	2^4	2^5	2^6	2^7
	2	4					

$\times 2 \quad \times 2 \quad \times 2 \quad \times 2 \quad \times 2 \quad \times 2 \quad \times 2$

7 Work out

  a i $\dfrac{2^8}{2^5}$ **ii** $\dfrac{3 \times 2^8}{2^5}$ **b i** $\dfrac{5^6}{5^4}$ **ii** $\dfrac{5^6 \times 4}{5^4}$

8 a Work out

  i $(-3)^2$ **ii** $(7)^2$ **iii** $(-7)^2$

  b Work out

  i $(-4)^2$ **ii** $20 + (-4)^2$ **iii** $20 - (-4)^2$

9 Write each calculation as a single power.

  a $\dfrac{8^6 \times 8^5}{8^4} = \dfrac{8^\square}{8^4} = 8^\square$ **b** $\dfrac{3^7 \times 3^4}{3^6 \times 3} = \dfrac{3^\square}{3^\square} = 3^\square$

  c $\dfrac{6^2 \times 6^5}{6^7}$ **d** $\dfrac{10^4 \times 10^7}{10 \times 10^5}$

10 Write each calculation as a single power.

  a $64 \times 4 \times 8 = 2^\square \times 2^\square \times 2^\square = 2^{\square + \square + \square} = 2^\square$

  b $27 \times 81 \times 9 =$

  c $\dfrac{3^{10}}{9 \times 27} = \dfrac{3^{10}}{3^\square \times 3^\square} = 3^{10 - \square - \square} = 3^\square$

11 Work out

  a $3 \times 4 + 2$ **b** $2 + 3 \times 4$

  Discussion What do you notice about your answers to parts **a** and **b**?

12 Work out

  a $12 \div 4 + 5$ **b** $5 + 12 \div 4$

  Discussion What do you notice about your answers to **a** and **b**?

13 Copy and complete.

  a $3 + 5 \times 2 - 7$ **b** $7 - 12 \div 4 + 1$ **c** $12 + 8 - 2 \times 6$

  $= 3 + \ldots\ldots - 7$ $= 7 - \ldots\ldots + 1$ $= 12 + 8 - \ldots\ldots$

  $= \ldots\ldots$ $= \ldots\ldots$ $= \ldots\ldots$

Q3a hint

$4^6 \div 4^3 = \dfrac{\overbrace{4 \times 4 \times 4 \times 4 \times 4 \times 4}^{6}}{\underbrace{4 \times 4 \times 4}_{3}}$

Q5 hint

Some answers will need to be written in terms of x and y.

Q7aii hint

$\dfrac{3 \times 2^8}{2^5} = 3 \times \dfrac{2^8}{2^5}$

Q8 hint

Negative $\times$ negative $= \square$

Q10 hint

Use the powers of 2 from your table in Q6.

Q11 hint

Multiplication **before** addition.

Q12 hint

Division **before** addition.

Q13 hint

Multiplication and division **before** addition and subtraction.

14 Copy and complete.

a $5^2 - 12$

$= \ldots\ldots - 12$

$= \ldots\ldots$

b 7×2^3

$= 7 \times \ldots\ldots$

$= \ldots\ldots$

c $15 - 3^2$

$= 15 - \ldots\ldots$

$= \ldots\ldots$

Q14 hint

Indices before multiplication and division and addition and subtraction.

15 Copy and complete.

a $(3 + 7) \times 5$

$= \ldots\ldots \times 5$

$= \ldots\ldots$

b $8 - (2 \times 4)$

$= 8 - \ldots\ldots$

$= \ldots\ldots$

c $4 + (9 \times 2) - 3$

$= 4 + \ldots\ldots - 3$

$= \ldots\ldots$

d $(2 + 3)^2$

$= \ldots\ldots^2$

$= \ldots\ldots$

e $52 + \sqrt{100}$

$= 52 + \ldots\ldots$

$= \ldots\ldots$

f $4 \times 5^2 - 7$

$= 4 \times \ldots\ldots - 7$

$= \ldots\ldots - 7$

$= \ldots\ldots$

Q15 hint

Brackets, then indices, then multiplication and division and then addition and subtraction.

Enrichment

1 Use the numbers from the cloud to complete these calculations. You can only use each number once.

$7^{\square} \times 7^{\square} = 7^{\square}$

$7^{\square} \div 7^{\square} = 7^{\square}$

$(7^{\square})^{\square} = 7^{\square}$

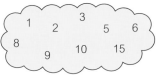

2 It takes Aisha 84 seconds to run one lap of an athletics track. It takes Brenda 96 seconds to run one lap of the athletics track. They set off from the start line at the same time.

a After how many seconds will they cross the line together for the first time? (Assume they keep running at the same speed.)

b They set off at 2 pm. At what time will they cross the line together for the first time? Give your answer in hours, minutes and seconds.

c When they cross the line together for the first time,

   i how many laps will Aisha have run

   ii how many laps will Brenda have run?

One lap is 400 m.

d When they cross the line together for the first time,

   i how far will Aisha have run

   ii how far will Brenda have run?

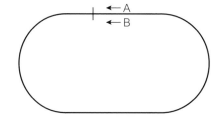

3 **Reflect** Helen says, 'Working with indices is all about adding, subtracting, multiplying and dividing.'

Look back at the questions you answered in these Strengthen lessons. Describe when you had to:

   • add   • subtract   • multiply   • divide.

Do you agree with Helen's statement?

Give some examples to explain why.

Reflect

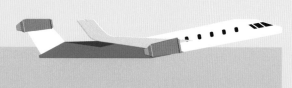

1 Extend

You will:
* Extend your understanding with problem-solving.

1 **Problem-solving / Reasoning** Here is the prime factor decomposition of a number.
The number is less than 100.
□ = $2^2 \times$ □ $\times 7$
What is the number? Explain how you made your decision.

Q1 hint
Start by working out $2^2 \times 7$.

2 **Problem-solving** Work out the missing numbers in this prime factor decomposition.
□ = $2^3 \times 3^{\square} \times$ □

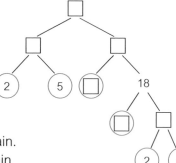

3 **Reasoning**
  a Is $(-2)^2 \times (-2)^3$ equal to $(-2)^5$? Explain.
  b Is $(-3)^5 \div (-3)^2$ equal to $(-3)^3$? Explain.
  c Write with a single power.
      i $(-4)^4 \times (-4)^6$
      ii $(-7)^8 \div (-7)^3$

Q3a, b hint
Show your working.

4 **Reasoning** The area of this square is 2^6 cm².
What is the length of one side?
Write your answer as a power of 2.

2^6 cm²

5 a Work out the prime factor decomposition of these numbers.
      i 165
      ii 180
      iii 210
  b What is the HCF of 165, 180 and 210?
  c What is the LCM of 165, 180 and 210?

6 Substitute the values into each formula and work out the answers.
  a $m = 2n - 1$ when $n = -7$
  b $v = u + at$ when $u = -8$, $a = -10$ and $t = 6$
  c $A = 3a - 4b$ when $a = -2$ and $b = -5$
  d $T = k(e - f)$ when $k = -3$, $e = 4$ and $f = -2$
  e $L = a - (2b + c)$ when $a = -10$, $b = -8$ and $c = 4$

Q6a hint
Use priority of operations.

7 **Real** Gaerwyn recorded these outside temperatures at midnight on the first day of each month.
  11.2 °C −1.7 °C 3 °C 4.8 °C −7.3° −0.9 °C
  a Find the median temperature.
  b Estimate the mean temperature.
  c Work out the range.

8 The formula $C = 0.56(F - 32)$ converts temperatures measured in Fahrenheit (F) to Celsius (C). Use an estimate to convert $-11.8°$F to Celsius. Check your estimate using a calculator.

9 **STEM** The approximate power intensity I watts/m^2 at a distance r metres from a radio transmitter of power P watts is estimated using the formula

$$I = \frac{P}{12r^2}$$

Use your calculator to find the power intensity I from
a a wireless router of power 0.5 watts at a distance of 2 metres
b a smart meter of power 2.5 watts at a distance of 5 metres.

10 The first term of a sequence is 4 and the term-to-term rule is 'multiply by -2'.
a Write the first five terms of the sequence.
b Work out the difference between the second and fourth terms.
c Write the fifth term using index notation.

11 Work these out. Check your answers using a calculator.

a $\dfrac{5^2 - 1}{\sqrt[3]{64} - 1}$

b $\sqrt[3]{100 - 36}$

c $\sqrt{19 + 5^3}$

d $\sqrt[3]{11^2 + 2^2}$

e $\dfrac{20 + 50}{\sqrt[3]{20 \times 50}}$

f $\dfrac{11^2 - 1}{2^3 + 2}$

12 Work out $\sqrt{a^2 + b^2}$ where
a $a = 3$ and $b = 4$
b $a = 6$ and $b = 8$
Discussion Can you find any other values for a and b that give whole number answers?

13 Copy and complete these calculations.
a $3^3 \times 3^\square = 3^{10}$
b $7^9 \times 7^\square = 7^{15}$
c $5^4 \times 2^3 \times 5^\square \times 2^\square = 5^{10} \times 2^7$

14 Write each of these as a product of prime numbers.
a $6^3 \times 2^5 \times 3^2$ **b** $5^4 \times 10^5 \times 2^6$ **c** $6^4 \times 18^3 \times 9^7$

Q14a hint

First write 6^3 as $(2 \times 3)^3$.

15 Evaluate these. Give each fraction in its simplest form.

a $\dfrac{12 \times 3^{10}}{3^{13}}$

b $\dfrac{15 \times 5^7}{5^9}$

c $\dfrac{2 \times 8^9}{8^{10} \times 3}$

d $\dfrac{20 \times 4^{12}}{4^7 \times 4^9}$

Q15a hint

$\dfrac{12 \times 3^{10}}{3^{13}} = \dfrac{12}{3^3}$

16 Use the formula $F = mg - 3t^2$ to work out the value of F when
  a $m = 5$, $g = 8$ and $t = 5$
  b $m = 7$, $g = 10$ and $t = -2$

17 **Problem-solving** The numbers in this diagram follow this rule.

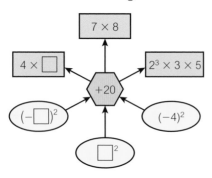

Input + 20 = Output

Work out the missing numbers in the diagram.

18 Evaluate
  a $\dfrac{(2 \times 4)^3}{8 \times 4} = \dfrac{8^3}{8 \times 4} =$
  b $\dfrac{(5 \times 3)^2}{9 \times 5} = \dfrac{15^2}{3 \times 3 \times 5} = \dfrac{15 \times 15}{3 \times 15} =$
  c $\dfrac{24 \times 6^3}{(3 \times 4)^2} = \dfrac{24 \times 6 \times 6 \times 6}{12^2} =$

19 Work these out. Give each answer in its simplest form, as a mixed number or a fraction.
  a $\dfrac{(2 \times 5)^2}{15 \times 2^3}$
  b $\dfrac{(3 \times 7)^3}{21 \times 14}$
  c $\dfrac{6 \times 5^2}{(4 \times 3)^3}$
  d $\dfrac{(3 \times 2 \times 4)^3}{9 \times (6 \times 2)^2}$

20 **Problem-solving** In these multiplication pyramids, the number in a brick is the product of the two bricks below it.
Work out the missing entries. Write each answer in index form.

  a

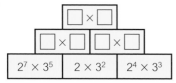

  b

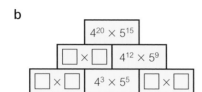

  c Make your own multiplication pyramid like the ones above, for a partner to work out.

Investigation

1 Copy and complete these number patterns.

a $2^2 = 4$

$2^2 + 2^2 = \square$

$2^2 + 2^2 + 2^3 = \square$

$2^2 + 2^2 + 2^3 + 2^4 = \square$

$2^2 + 2^2 + 2^3 + 2^4 + 2^5 = \square$

b $2^2 = 4$

$2^3 = \square$

$2^4 = \square$

$2^5 = \square$

$2^6 = \square$

2 What do you notice about the answers to part 1**a**?

3 What do you notice about the answers to part 1**a** and **b**?

4 Write down the missing numbers in this statement.

$2^2 + 2^2 + 2^3 + 2^4 + 2^5 + 2^6 = \square = 2^{\square}$

5 Use your answer to part 4 to write down the answer to $2^1 + 2^2 + 2^3 + 2^4 + 2^5 + 2^6$

6 Copy and complete

$2^1 + 2^2 + 2^3 + 2^4 + 2^5 + 2^6 = 2^{\square} - 2$

$2^1 + 2^2 + 2^3 + 2^4 + 2^5 + 2^6 + 2^7 = 2^{\square} - 2$

$2^1 + 2^2 + 2^3 + 2^4 + \ldots + 2^x = 2^{\square} - 2$

Investigation hint

Compare $2^1 + 2^2 + 2^3 + 2^4 + 2^5 + 2^6$
with $2^2 + 2^2 + 2^3 + 2^4 + 2^5 + 2^6$

21 **Reasoning** Copy and complete these general rules using your answers to Q20 to help you.

a $x^a \times y^b \times x^c \times y^d = x^{\square} \times y^{\square}$

b $\dfrac{x^a \times y^b}{x^c \times y^d} = x^{\square} \times y^{\square}$

22 **Reflect** Look back at the questions you answered in these lessons. Find a question that you could not answer straight away, or that you really had to think about.

• Why couldn't you immediately see what to do?

• How did this make you feel?

• Did you keep trying or did you give up?

• Did you think you would get the answer correct or incorrect?

Write down any strategies you could use when answering challenging questions.

Compare your strategies with those of your classmates.

Reflect

1 Unit test

1 The temperature in Moscow was $-8\,°C$ at 6 am and $2\,°C$ at midday.
  a Work out the difference in temperature.
  b By midnight, the temperature had fallen by $14\,°C$ compared with midday.
    i What was the temperature at midnight?
    ii What is the difference in temperature between 6 am and midnight?
  c Work out $-4 - 6$.

2 Write each number as a product of prime factors.
  a 76
  b 648

3 Write each calculation as a single power.
  a $8^5 \times 8^4$ b $3^{11} \times 3$ c $9^3 \times 9^7 \times 9^6$
  d $7^7 \div 7$ e $12^{10} \div 12^5$ f $(6^3)^6$

4 Write each calculation as a single power.
  a $(-3)^5 \times (-3)^2$ b $(-8)^7 \times (-8)^3$

5 a Work out the prime factor decomposition of
    i 144
    ii 180
  b Work out the HCF of 144 and 180.

6 Ardem has two lights.
  One flashes every 15 seconds, the other flashes every 42 seconds.
  They start flashing at the same time.
  After how many seconds will they next flash at the same time?

7 a Calculate the HCF of 180, 189 and 600.
  b Calculate the LCM of 180, 189 and 600.

8 Evaluate $\dfrac{2 \times 5^7}{5^4}$

9 Write each of these as a product of primes.
  a $5^3 \times 2^5 \times 10^2$ b $3^3 \times 15^3 \times 5^6$

10 Match each red card to the correct blue card.

  A $(m^p)^q$ D m^{p-q}

  B $m^p \times m^q$ E m^{p+q}

  C $m^p \div m^q$ F m^{pq}

11 Work out
  a $-4 \times 5 + 1$ b 9^2 c $\sqrt{25}$ d 5^3
  e 2×5^2 f $13 + \sqrt{49}$ g $\sqrt{4 + 9 \times 5}$ h $\sqrt[3]{64}$

12 Work out

    a $(-7)^2$ **b** $10^2 - (-2)^2 - (3)^2$

13 Use the formula $F = mg - 3t^2$ to work out the value of F when

    a $m = 4$, $g = 6$ and $t = 2$

    b $m = 6$, $g = 11$ and $t = -4$

14 Work out

    a $5 - -8$ **b** -3×8

    c $16 \div -8$ **d** $6 + 15 \div -3$

    e $(-6)^2$ **f** $3^2 \times 2^3$

    g $\sqrt[3]{1000} - \sqrt{121}$ **h** $-10 \times (7 - 12)$

15 Work out

    a $5^2 - \left(10 - \sqrt[3]{64}\right)$ **b** $\sqrt[3]{6^2 - 3^2}$

16 Work out each calculation as a single power.

    a $\dfrac{15^3 \times 15^8}{15^6}$ **b** $\dfrac{4^7 \times 4}{4^2 \times 4^4}$ **c** $25 \times 5 \times 125$ **d** $\dfrac{2^{10}}{32 \times 8}$

17 Which calculation does not give the same answer as the others?

    A $(3 \times 4)^2$ **B** 3×4^2 **C** $3^2 \times 4^2$ **D** 12^2

18 Evaluate

    a $\dfrac{(7 \times 4)^2}{8 \times 14}$ **b** $\dfrac{6 \times 15}{(3 \times 5)^3}$

Challenge

19 The aim of this puzzle is to fill in the white squares on a 5×5 grid with as many integers as possible.

This diagram shows how you can move from one square to the next. The example grid starts at the number 8.

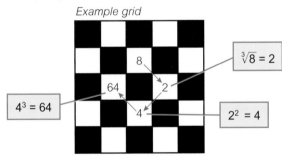

Example grid

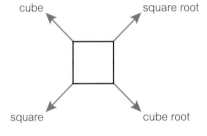

    1 Draw your own copy of the grid.

    2 Write any positive integer in a white square and circle it.

    3 Start filling in the adjacent squares. Use arrows to show where you move to.

    4 Continue until you cannot fill in any more squares.

    5 Try again. Work out a strategy to fill in more squares this time.

    6 Try again. This time start with a negative integer.

    7 Try again. This time you can only use each operation twice.

2.1 Solving one-step equations

You will learn to:
- Write and solve simple equations.
- Solve problems using equations.

Why learn this?
Police collision (accident) investigators use an equation to work out the speed at which a car was travelling before it crashed. The equation uses the length of the skid and the final position of the car.

Fluency
Work out
- $3 + -6$
- $-5 + 2$
- -2×7
- $12 \div -6$

Explore
How far can a car travel in 10 seconds?

Confidence

Exercise 2.1

Warm up

1 When $x = 6$ and $y = 3$, what is

   a $x - y$ b $3x$ c $2y$

   d $\dfrac{x}{y}$ e $\dfrac{2y}{x}$ f xy

2 Jack is 3 years older than Adele. Write an expression for Jack's age when Adele is x years old.

3 Write an expression for the cost of 5 cinema tickets at £y each.

4 Work out the outputs for each **function** machine.

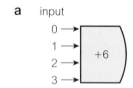

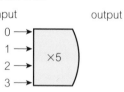

Key point

A **function** is a rule.
The function +3 adds 3 to a number.
The **inverse function** is −3, because it reverses the effect of the function +3.

$$2 \rightarrow \boxed{+3} \rightarrow 5$$
$$2 \leftarrow \boxed{-3} \leftarrow 5$$

5 Use the **inverse function** to find each missing input.

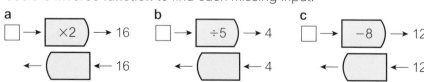

Topic links: Negative numbers, Angles in a triangle and on a straight line

Subject links: Science (Q9, Q16)

6 Copy and complete the function machines to solve these **equations**.

a $x - 6 = 4$

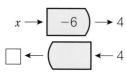

$x = \square$

b $4x = 12$

$x \rightarrow \boxed{\times 4} \rightarrow 12$

$\square \leftarrow \bigcirc \leftarrow 12$

$x = \square$

c $\dfrac{x}{3} = 7$

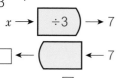

$x = \square$

d $x + 11 = 8$

$x \rightarrow \boxed{+11} \rightarrow 8$

$\square \leftarrow \bigcirc \leftarrow 8$

$x = \square$

Key point

An **equation** contains an **unknown** number (a letter) and an '=' sign. To solve an equation means to work out the value of the unknown number.

7 Draw function machines to solve these equations.

a $3x = 18$ b $n + 15 = 21$ c $\dfrac{m}{5} = 2$ d $p - 0.7 = 2.1$

Discussion Do you always need to draw a function machine to solve an equation?

Q7 hint

You can use any letter to stand for an unknown value.

Worked example

Solve the equation $x + 5 = 12$

$x + 5 - 5 = 12 - 5$

$\qquad x = 7$

Check: $7 + 5 = 12$ ✓

Visualise the function machines to decide which inverse to use.

$x \rightarrow \boxed{+5} \rightarrow 12$

$\square \leftarrow \bigcirc{-5} \leftarrow 12$

Check by replacing x in the equation with your solution.

Balance the equation by subtracting 5 from each side.

Key point

In an equation, the expressions on both sides of the equals sign have the same value. You can visualise them on balanced scales.

$x + 3 \quad = \quad 8$

To stay balanced, do the same operation to both sides.

$x + 3 - 3 \quad = \quad 8 - 3$

This is called the **balancing method**.

8 Solve these equations.

a $z + 15 = 27$ b $4x = 36$ c $\dfrac{y}{7} = 3$

d $1.2 + c = 4.6$ e $3a = 2.7$ f $\dfrac{k}{0.5} = 6$

g $x + 5 = 1$ h $7 + y = -10$ i $-5n = 15$

j $3p = 0$ k $-2 + x = -3$ l $-x = 7$

Q8 hint

Remember to check each solution.

9 **STEM** Substitute the values given into each formula. Solve the equation to find the unknown value.

a $x - 2 = e$ Find x when $e = 9$

b $\dfrac{m}{4} = d$ Work out m when $d = 2$

c $6t = u$ Work out t when $u = 30$

d $d = \dfrac{m}{v}$ Work out m when $d = 7$ and $v = 2$

e $V = IR$ Find R when $V = 6$ and $I = 3$

f $s = \dfrac{d}{t}$ Find d when $s = 4$ and $t = 10$

Discussion What is the difference between an equation and a formula?

10 Real / Modelling An online retailer adds £3 post and packing to each order.
  a Write a formula for the total cost C for an order of £x.
  b Work out the value of the order £x when the total cost is £36.50.

Q10a hint

$C = \square + \square$

11 Modelling
  a Write an equation for these three angles.

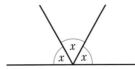

  b Solve your equation to find the value of x.

Q11a hint

What do the angles on a straight line add up to?

12 Modelling
  a Work out the value of m.
  b Work out the sizes of the three angles.

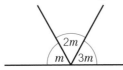

Q12a Strategy hint

Write an equation and solve it.

13 Work out the sizes of the missing angles in the triangle.

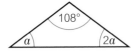

Q13 hint

What do the angles in a triangle add up to?

14 Problem-solving / Modelling One week Craig spent 12 hours on his PlayStation.
He spent the same length of time each weekday, and twice as much each day at the weekend.
How long did he spend on his PlayStation on Saturday?
Give your answer in hours and minutes.

Q14 hint

Use n to stand for the number of hours each weekday.

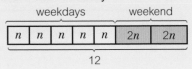

15 Problem-solving / Modelling Tickets for 2 adults and 3 children at the zoo come to £28. An adult ticket costs twice as much as a child ticket.
Work out the price of an adult ticket.

16 Explore How far can a car travel in 10 seconds?
Is it easier to explore this question now that you have completed the lesson? What further information do you need to be able to answer this?

17 Reflect Write down the steps you take to solve equations like the ones in this lesson.
Beside each step, show if you found that step OK (😊) or difficult (☹).
Ask a friend or your teacher to help you with any difficult steps.

Q17 hint

Look at the equations you solved for Q6, 7 and 8.

2.2 Solving two-step equations

You will learn to:
- Write and solve two-step equations.
- Write and solve equations that have brackets.

Why learn this?
By writing and solving equations, John Couch Adams and Urbain Le Verrier both, independently, calculated the position of Neptune, which was first seen by telescope in 1846.

Fluency
$t = 5$
Work out
- $3t$
- $4t + 3$
- $3(t + 1)$
- t^2
- $2t^2$

Explore
You think of a number, multiply it by 10 and then subtract another number.
Your answer is 8. What number could you have chosen? What number did you subtract?

Exercise 2.2

1 Solve these equations.

   a $y - 8 = 6$ **b** $\dfrac{a}{4} = -2$ **c** $-x = 3$

2 Expand the brackets.

   a $2(x + 4)$ **b** $3(y - 2)$ **c** $5(3 - z)$

3 Work out the outputs for these two-step function machines.

   a input → ×2 → +4 → output (inputs 1, 3, 5)

   b input → ÷3 → −1 → output (inputs 3, 9, 12)

Discussion Does it matter which function you use first?

4 Use inverse function machines to find the value of the input of each two-step function machine.

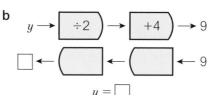

   a $x →$ ×2 → −3 → 7; □ ← (← +3 ← 7; $x = □$

   b $y →$ ÷2 → +4 → 9; □ ← (← (← 9; $y = □$

   c $z →$ ×5 → +2 → 32

   d $m →$ ÷4 → −1 → −6

Discussion How could you write these as equations?

5 Draw function machines to solve these equations.

   a $2x + 3 = 11$ **b** $3y - 4 = 17$ **c** $\dfrac{r}{2} - 1 = -4$

Discussion What do you notice about the order of the operations in the function machine and the order in the inverse function machine?

Warm up

Worked example

Solve $4x + 7 = 27$

$4x + 7 - 7 = 27 - 7$ — Balance the equation by subtracting 7 from each side.

$\div 4 \overset{4x = 20}{\underset{x = 5}{\curvearrowright}} \div 4$ — Balance again by dividing both sides by 4.

Check: $4 \times 5 + 7 = 27$ ✓

Check by replacing x in the equation with your solution.

Visualise the function machines to decide which inverses to use.

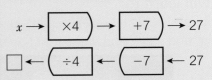

6 Solve these equations.

a $2x + 11 = 19$ b $3x - 2 = 10$ c $8 + 4x = 16$

d $12 + 2x = 24$ e $\dfrac{x}{3} - 2 = 2$ f $\dfrac{9x}{2} = 36$

g $\dfrac{5x}{4} = 10$ h $2(x - 1) = 8$ i $\dfrac{x + 5}{2} = 4$

Q6f hint

$x \rightarrow \boxed{\times 9} \rightarrow \boxed{\div 2} \rightarrow 36$

Q6h hint

Expand the brackets first.

Investigation   Reasoning

Here are two ways of solving the equation $6(x + 2) = 30$.

Method 1

Balance the equation by dividing both sides by 6 and then subtract 2:

$6(x + 2) = 30$

$x + 2 = \dfrac{30}{6}$

$x + 2 = 5$

$x = 3$

Method 1 hint

$x \rightarrow \boxed{+2} \rightarrow \boxed{\times 6} \rightarrow 30$

$\square \leftarrow \boxed{-2} \leftarrow \boxed{\div 6} \leftarrow 30$

Method 2

Expand the brackets, then balance by subtracting 12 and dividing by 6:

$6(x + 2) = 30$

$6x + 12 = 30$

$6x = 30 - 12$

$6x = 18$

$x = 3$

1 Use both methods to solve $4(x + 5) = 28$.
Which method do you prefer? Why?

2 Which method would you use to solve $2(x - 3) = 7$? Explain why.

Discussion When is it easiest to expand the brackets first?

---

7 STEM Substitute the values given into each formula. Solve the equation to find the unknown value.

a $P = 2v + r$ Find v when $r = 6$ and $P = 28$

b $y = mx + c$ Work out x when $y = 11$, $m = 3$ and $c = -1$

c $D = \dfrac{w}{8} + v$ Work out w when $v = 5$ and $D = 15$

d $A = \dfrac{(a + b)h}{2}$ Work out h when $a = 3$, $b = 4$ and $A = 10.5$

e $v = u + at$ Find a when $u = 0$, $t = 10$ and $v = 45$

f $s = ut + \dfrac{1}{2}at^2$ Work out u when $t = 2$, $a = 10$ and $s = 30$

8 Solve

a $-3x + 5 = -7$ b $8 - x = -2$ c $\dfrac{-x}{5} + 11 = 7$

Q8b hint

Addition can be done in any order.
You could rewrite this as $-x + 8 = -2$

Topic links: Angles, Factors, Polygons   **Subject links:** Science (Q7)

9 **Modelling** Pia says, 'I think of a number, multiply it by 6 and add 3. My answer is 21.'
   a Write an equation to show Pia's calculation. Use n for the number she thinks of.
   b Solve your equation to find Pia's number.

10 **Modelling** Write and solve equations for these 'think of a number' problems.
   a I think of a number, divide it by 4 and subtract 10. My answer is 1.
   b I think of a number, add 7 and multiply by 6. My answer is 54.
   c I think of a number, double it and add 12. My answer is 42.
   d I think of a number, subtract 3 and then halve it. My answer is 5.

11 **Modelling** Work out the value of each letter.
   a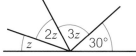
   b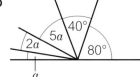

Q12c hint

What do you know about the blue angle?

12 **Modelling** Work out the sizes of the angles.
   a
   b
   c
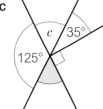

13 **Modelling / Real** Match tickets for 2 adults and 1 senior citizen cost a total of £31. A senior citizen ticket is £5 less than an adult ticket.
   a Write an equation for the cost of the tickets.
   b Work out the cost of an adult ticket.

Q13a hint

An adult ticket costs £x. Write an expression for the cost of a senior citizen ticket.

14 **Explore** You think of a number, multiply it by 10 and then subtract another number.
   Your answer is 8. What number could you have chosen? What number did you subtract?
   Look back at the maths you have learned in this lesson.
   How can you use it to answer this question?

15 **Reflect** Look back at the steps you wrote down for solving equations at the end of lesson 2.1.
   In this lesson you have solved more complex equations.
   Choose an equation from this lesson.
   Do the steps solving equations that you wrote at the end of lesson 2.1 work for this equation too? If not rewrite your steps.
   Check that they work for another equation from this lesson.

Explore

Reflect

2.3 More complex equations

Confidence

You will learn to:
* Write and solve equations with letters on both sides.

Why learn this?
The flight path of an aircraft can be plotted using an equation. Air traffic control can equate two flight paths to find out where the planes would meet and prevent accidents.

Fluency
Expand the brackets
* $2(x + 7)$
* $3(10 - x)$
* $4(3x - 5)$

Explore
Can $x + 2$ ever be equal to $x - 2$?

Exercise 2.3

Warm up

1 Write an expression for each 'think of a number' problem.
  a I think of a number and add 5.
  b I think of a number, double it and add 10.
  c I think of a number, add 4 and multiply by 7.

Q1 hint

Use n for the number each time.

2 Solve these equations.
  a $5x - 2 = 18$
  b $3 + 6x = 21$
  c $4x + 11 = -5$

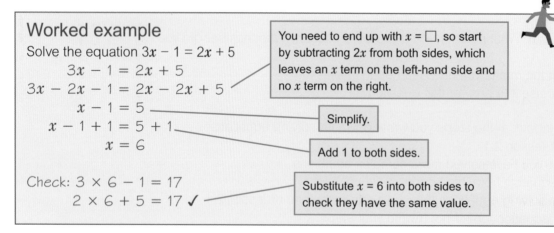

Worked example

Solve the equation $3x - 1 = 2x + 5$
$$3x - 1 = 2x + 5$$
$$3x - 2x - 1 = 2x - 2x + 5$$
$$x - 1 = 5$$
$$x - 1 + 1 = 5 + 1$$
$$x = 6$$

Check: $3 \times 6 - 1 = 17$
$2 \times 6 + 5 = 17$ ✓

You need to end up with $x = \square$, so start by subtracting $2x$ from both sides, which leaves an x term on the left-hand side and no x term on the right.

Simplify.

Add 1 to both sides.

Substitute $x = 6$ into both sides to check they have the same value.

3 Solve these equations.
  a $3x - 2 = 2x + 1$ **b** $8x - 10 = 6x$
  c $5y - 3 = 2y + 18$ **d** $6m + 11 = 5m + 8$
  e $3(x - 4) = 2x$ **f** $8(x - 3) = 7x - 13$
  g $5(x + 4) = 4(x + 7)$ **h** $7(m - 5) = 2(m + 5)$
  i $4(r + 3) = 2(r + 9)$ **j** $6(t - 5) = 5(t + 1)$

Q3 hint

Remember to check your solutions.

Q3e hint

Expand the brackets first.

4 **Modelling** Solange says, 'I think of a number, double it and add 4. When I start again with the same number, multiply it by 5 and subtract 20, I get the same answer.'
  a Write an expression for each of Solange's calculations.
  b Write an equation to show that both calculations give the same answer.
  c Solve your equation to find the number Solange was thinking of.

> **Key point**
>
> The **coefficient** of x is the number that is multiplying x.
> In the term $4x$, the coefficient of x is 4.

5 **Reasoning** Write a 'think of a number' problem like Q4 for one of the equations in Q3.

Investigation   Reasoning

Solve the equation $3x + 6 = 7x - 2$ in two ways.
1 $3x + 6 = 7x - 2$ First subtract $7x$ from both sides
2 $3x + 6 = 7x - 2$ First subtract $3x$ from both sides
Did you get the same answer both ways?
Was one way easier than the other? If so, explain which one was easiest and why.
What would you do first to solve $2x + 6 = 9x - 8$?
Discussion How does looking at the **coefficients** of x help you to decide which step to do first?

---

6 Solve these equations.
  a $2x + 5 = 3x - 1$ **b** $5x + 8 = 7x - 4$
  c $3(y + 6) = 5y + 12$ **d** $6(x - 5) = 3(x - 2)$
  e $12(m + 3) = 10(m + 4)$ **f** $5(y + 6) = 3(y + 12)$

> **Q6a hint**
>
> Subtract $2x$ from each side first, as it has the smallest coefficient of x.

7 **Problem-solving / Reasoning** Write an equation and solve it to find the size of each angle.

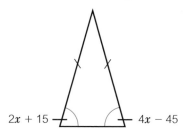

$2x + 15$ $4x - 45$

8 **Reasoning / Problem-solving**
  a Look at this equation:
  $$x + 5 = y - 3$$
  Which is larger, x or y? How much larger?
  b Look at this equation:
  $$5 - r = 7 - s$$
  Which of r and s is greater? By how much?

> **Q8a Strategy hint**
>
> Rearrange the equation so that one letter is 'on its own' on one side of the equals sign.

9 **Explore** Can $x + 2$ ever be equal to $x - 2$?
  Look back at the maths you have learned in this lesson. How can you use it to answer this question?

10 **Reflect** Do the steps you wrote for solving equations at the end of lesson 2.2 work for equations with an unknown (a letter) on both sides of the = sign?
  If not, rewrite them.

Explore

Reflect

2.4 Working with formulae

Confidence

You will learn to:
- Find numbers which satisfy an equation with two unknowns.
- Solve problems by writing and using formulae.

Why learn this?
Formulae can be programmed into computers. This enables them to make complex calculations very quickly. It allows you to solve complex problems that would otherwise take years to solve.

Fluency
If $a = 5$ and $b = 7$ what is the value of $2a + 3b$?

Explore
How many values of x and y are there that satisfy the equation $x + y = 10$?

Exercise 2.4

Warm up

1 Solve these equations.

 a $2a - 4 = 2$

 b $10 - 2x = 5$

 c $\dfrac{3y}{5} = -6$

 d $2(3m - 4) = 22$

 e $4x - 7 = 2x + 8$

 f $8(y - 3) = 10 - 2y$

2 If $a = 3$ and $b = -2$ find
 a ab
 b $a + b$
 c $3a - 2b$
 d $a(2 + b)$.

3 $a + b = 10$
 a If $a = 1$, what is the value of b?
 a and b are both positive **integers**.
 b List all the possible values of a and b.

> **Key point**
>
> Integers are whole numbers, for example, 1, 2, 3 etc. are **integers**.

> **Q3b hint**
> A systematic approach will ensure that you list all the possible values: for example, $a = 1$, $b = \square$
> $a = 2$, $b = \square$

Investigation

Reasoning

A rectangle has perimeter 24 cm.
The length and width of the rectangle are integers.
 a List all the possible dimensions of the rectangle.
 b Which dimensions give the maximum possible area?

4 **Problem-solving** $3n - m =$ 'a multiple of 4.'
 a Find three possible values of m and n.
 b What do you notice about your values of n and m?

5 a Convert 3 m into cm.
  b Copy and complete the **formula** for converting a length in metres (M) to a length in cm (C).
  $$C = \square$$

6 Real / Reasoning Write a formula for converting
  a kg (K) into grams (g)
  b grams (g) into kg (K)
  c litres (L) into ml (m)
  d ml (m) into litres (L).

7 Here is a regular pentagon.
  The length of one of the sides is x.

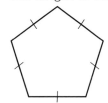

  a Write down a formula for calculating the perimeter, P.
  b Use the formula to calculate the perimeter when
    i $x = 12$
    ii $x = 0.4$
  c Work out the value of x when
    i $P = 24$
    ii $P = 7$
  Give your answers as mixed numbers.

8 Real / Problem-solving To calculate the time (T) needed to cook a chicken, multiply the mass in kg (m) by 40 and add 20.
  a Write a formula that connects T and m.
  b Use the formula to work out the value of T when
    i $m = 3$
    ii $m = 1.5$
  c Use the formula to work out the value of m when
    i $T = 100$
    ii $T = 150$

9 Explore How many values of x and y are there that satisfy the equation $x + y = 10$?
  Choose some values for x and y that satisfy the equation. Will it be possible to list all the values?

10 Reflect Look back at what you've learned in this lesson. What skills did you need to use to answer all the questions? List at least five different skills.

Explore

Reflect

2 Check up

Solving equations

1 Solve these equations.

   a $x - 7 = 12$ **b** $4 + n = 15$

   c $\frac{s}{3} = 5$ **d** $6y = 24$

   e $8m = 0$ **f** $-2p = 8$

2 a $V = IR$ is a formula used in science.
     Work out I when $V = 18$ and $R = 9$

   b Use the formula $s = \frac{d}{t}$ to find the value of d when $s = 7$ and $t = 3$.

3 Solve these equations.

   a $3x + 5 = 17$ **b** $4x - 1 = 19$

   c $\frac{n}{3} + 2 = 4$ **d** $5(m + 4) = 30$

   e $4x + 15 = 3$ **f** $13 - 2x = 7$

4 A taxi driver uses this formula to work out the cost of a journey:
   $C = 5 + 3m$
   where C is the cost of a journey in £ and m is the number of miles.
   A journey costs £29. Work out how many miles it is.

5 Solve these equations.

   a $2x + 5 = 3x - 5$ **b** $5x + 7 = 3x + 13$

6 Solve $4(n + 2) = 5(n + 1)$.

Writing equations and formulae

7 a Write an equation for these angles.

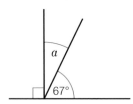

   b Solve your equation to find the value of a.

8 Work out

   a the value of x **b** the size of each angle.

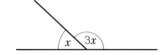

9 Work out the size of the angles.

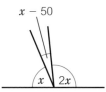

10 Work out the length of each side of the equilateral triangle.

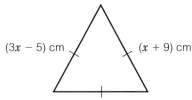

11 Match tickets for 4 adults and 7 children cost a total of £45.
An adult ticket is twice the price of a child's ticket.
   a Write an equation for the cost of the tickets.
   b Work out the cost of an adult ticket.

12 Zoe thinks of a number. She multiplies it by 3 and adds 4.
She gets the same answer when she adds 5 to the number
and then multiplies the result by 2.
   a Write an equation, using n for Zoe's number.
   b Solve your equation to find Zoe's number.

13 To calculate the time it takes to walk to his friend's house, Latif
multiplies the number of miles by 20 and adds 8.
   a Write down a formula for calculating time (T) given the distance in
      miles (m).
   b Use the formula to work out the length of time it will take Latif to
      get to his friend's house 1.5 miles away.
   c If Latif takes 58 minutes to walk to Khog's house. How far did he
      walk?

14 $3x + y = 12$
List three possible pairs of integer value for x and y.

15 **How sure are you of your answers? Were you mostly**
   ☹ **Just guessing**   😐 **Feeling doubtful**   🙂 **Confident**
   What next? Use your results to decide whether to strengthen or
   extend your learning.

Challenge

16 Write an equation with solution $x = 6$.
   Step 1. Write a calculation that includes 6 and work out the answer.
       $4 \times 6 + 2 = 26$
   Step 2. Replace 6 with x.
       $4x + 2 = 26$
   Write four more equations with solution $x = 6$.
   You can use $+$, $-$, $\times$, $\div$ and brackets.

17 Choose another value for x. Write two equations for it – one easy
one and one difficult one. Swap with a partner and solve each
other's equations.

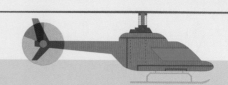

2 Strengthen

You will:
- Strengthen your understanding with practice.

Solving equations

1 Work out the value of each symbol.
  a $3 + \square = 8$
  b $5 \times \triangle = 30$
  c $10 - \lozenge = 7$
  d $\dfrac{\square}{2} = 9$

Q1 hint

Use number facts and times tables.

2 **Problem-solving** Which of these is the correct solution to $3x - 2 = 16$?

$\boxed{x = 4}$　$\boxed{x = -5}$　$\boxed{x = 6}$

Q2 hint

Substitute each value into $3x - 2$ to check.

3 Solve these equations.
  Check each answer by substituting back into the equation.
  a $x + 7 = 11$　　**b** $m + 15 = 29$
  c $28 = 12 + n$　　**d** $x - 3 = 6$
  e $y - 9 = 2$　　**f** $13 = s - 22$

Q3a hint

Draw a bar model.
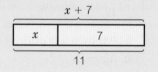

4 Solve these equations.
  Check each answer by substituting back into the equation.

  a $5x = 35$　　**b** $6y = 48$

  c $9p = 63$　　**d** $36 = 4q$

  e $5s = -15$　　**f** $\dfrac{n}{4} = 10$

  g $4 = \dfrac{h}{2}$　　**h** $\dfrac{y}{3} = 5$

  i $\dfrac{m}{4} = -2$　　**j** $\dfrac{n}{7} = -8$

Q4f hint

Draw a bar model.
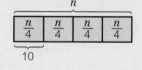

5 Substitute the values given into each formula.
  Solve the equation to find the value of the **unknown**.

  a $L = m - 5$　　　Find m when $L = 17$

  b $y = x + 4$　　　Find x when $y = 13$

  c $R = A + B$　　　Find A when $R = 7$ and $B = 2$

  d $y = 3x$　　　Find x when $y = 21$

  e $y = kx$　　　Find x when $y = 27$ and $k = 9$

  f $v = at$　　　Find a when $v = 30$ and $t = 10$

  g $T = \dfrac{P}{2}$　　　Find P when $T = 11$

  h $m = \dfrac{d}{r}$　　　Find d when $m = 5$ and $r = 4$

Q5 Literacy hint

The **unknown** is the letter in an equation.

Q5a hint

$L = m - 5$
$\square = m - 5$

Q5f hint

$\square = a \times \square$

Topic links: Using formulae, Conversions

6 a Shireen solves the equation $4m - 3 = 5$ like this.

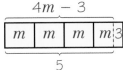

$4m - 3 = 5$

$+3$ on both sides

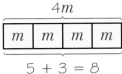

$4m = 8$
$\div 4$ on both sides
$m = 2$ $8 \div 4 = 2$

Substitute $m = 2$ into $4m - 3 = 5$
Did Shireen get the correct solution?

b Solve these equations.
Check each answer by substituting back into the equation.

  i $7x - 10 = 32$

  ii $8n + 9 = 25$

  iii $\frac{x}{5} + 3 = 7$

  iv $\frac{y}{6} - 4 = 1$

7 Solve these equations.
  a $15 - 2x = 5$
  b $11 - 3x = 2$
  c $6x + 7 = -5$

8 Use the formula $m = vt - g$ to find the value of v when $t = 3$, $g = 7$ and $m = 5$.

9 a Copy and complete the balancing to solve the equation.
$2x + 5 = 3x - 3$

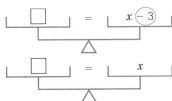

Subtract $2x$ from both sides.

Add 3 to both sides.

b Solve these equations.
  i $5x + 4 = 6x + 1$
  ii $6x - 7 = 2x + 1$

10 a Expand the brackets on both sides of the equals sign.
$4(n + 2) = 5(n + 1)$
  b Solve your equation.
  c Solve $3(x - 2) = 7(x - 6)$

Q6bi hint

You don't have to draw the bar model.
Add 10 to both sides.
Divide both sides by 7.

Q6biii hint

Subtract ☐
Multiply by ☐

Q7a hint

$\dfrac{-10}{-2} = + \square$

Q9bii hint

Subtract $2x$ from both sides first.

Writing equations and formulae

1 Modelling

a Copy and complete: $x + 95 = \square$

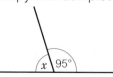

b Solve to find x.

2 Modelling Write an equation for these angles

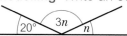

Work out the size of the two missing angles.

Q2 hint

Find n. Then work out $3n$. Make sure you write down the sizes of both angles.

3 Problem-solving / Modelling Here is Billy's answer to the question, 'Work out the lengths of the sides of this rectangle.'

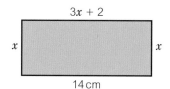

$3x + 2 = 14$
$3x = 12$
$x = 4$

Tom said, 'You haven't answered the question.'
Finish Billy's working to answer the question.

4 Problem-solving / Modelling Work out the lengths of the sides of this rectangle.

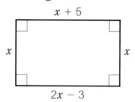

Q4 hint

Write an equation. Find x, then use this value to find the length of each side.

5 a How many minutes are there in
  i 2 hours
  ii 3 hours.
  b Copy and complete:
  number of minutes = number of hours × $\square$
  c Which formula converts time in hours (h) to time in minutes (m)?

  $h = m + 60$ $m = 60h$ $h = 60m$ $m = \dfrac{h}{60}$

Q5a hint

What did you do to the values in part **a**?

6 Problem-solving For a party, Hadil allows 10 sweets per guest plus 15 spare sweets.
  a How many sweets should she buy if there are
    i 5 guests
    ii 12 guests?

b Which formula should she use to work out the number of sweets (*S*) she should buy, for *C* guests?

| $S = 15C + 10$ | $S = 10C + 15$ | $C = 10S + 15$ | $C = \frac{S}{10} + 15$ |

Hadil buys 145 sweets.

c How many guests are at her party?

7 Here is a rectangle.

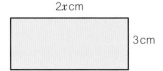

2*x* cm

3 cm

a Write down and simplify an expression for the perimeter of the rectangle.

b Copy and complete the formula for calculating perimeter *P*.
$$P = \square + 6$$

c The perimeter of the rectangle is 34 cm.
Work out the length of the longest side.

Q6c hint

Put S = 145 into the formula and solve it to find C.

Q7a hint

$2x + 3 + \dots + \dots = 4x + \dots$

Q7c hint

Find the value of x first.
To find the length of the longest side, work out the value of $2x$.

Enrichment

1 The sum of two numbers is 20 and their difference is 6.
Use *x* and *y* for the two numbers:
the sum is $x + y = 20$
the difference is $x - y = 6$
Follow the flow diagram to find *x* and *y*.

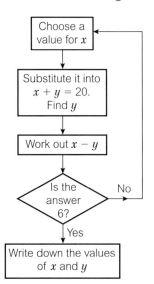

2 Reflect In these strengthen lessons you solved equations using the balancing method and bar models. You may also have used other methods.
Which method do you prefer for solving equations?

Reflect

2 Extend

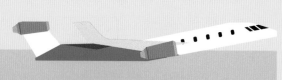

You will:
• Extend your understanding with problem-solving.

1 **Problem-solving** You are given some information about each rectangle. For each rectangle, write an equation and solve it to find the unknown quantity.

a

3 cm

2x

Area = 24 cm²

b

3y

y

Perimeter = 40 cm

2 **Modelling**
  a Two identical regular hexagons are joined along a side to make a shape with perimeter 240 cm.
     Solve an equation to find the length of one side.
  b Three identical regular hexagons are joined at one of their corners to make a shape with perimeter 360 cm.
     Solve an equation to find the length of one side.

3 Use the formula $S = 180(n - 2)$ to work out n when $S = 900$.

4 Solve these equations.
  a $2x + 7 = 1$ b $5m - 20 = -5$ c $-3t + 2 = 17$
  d $-2n + 5 = 11$ e $-3d + 7 = 1$ f $-10e - 30 = 10$

5 Matthew solves equations using inverse operations like this.
   Use Matthew's method to solve
  a $2m + 5 = 21$ b $4u + 3 = 27$
  c $5n - 2 = 23$ d $3w - 4 = 26$
  e $2y + 9 = 5$ f $-4t + 1 = -7$

$$3y + 5 = 17$$
$$(-5) \qquad\qquad (-5)$$
$$3y = 12$$
$$(\div 3) \qquad\qquad (\div 3)$$
$$y = 4$$

6 **Reasoning**
  a Make x the subject of each formula.
       i $3x + 2r = 2x + r$
      ii $5x + 3c = 9c - 4x$
     iii $x^2 = r$
  b Solve these equations.
       i $3x + 4 = 2x + 2$
      ii $5x + 9 = 27 - 4x$
     iii $x^2 = 25$

Q6a Literacy hint

The subject of a formula is the variable on its own on one side of the equals sign.

  c Mariana says, 'Solving equations is a bit like changing the subject of a formula.' Do you agree? Explain.

7 Solve each equation.

  a $6x + 1 = 4x + 13$

  b $5m + 3 = 4m + 5$

  c $3y - 2 = y + 8$

  d $10t - 3 = 7t + 9$

  e $4p + 9 = 2p + 1$

  f $x^2 = 100$

  g $x^2 - 5 = 31$

Worked example

Solve the equation $\dfrac{2a + 1}{3} = 5$.

$$(2a + 1) \div 3 = 5$$

$\dfrac{2a + 1}{3}$ can be written as $\dfrac{(2a + 1)}{3}$ or $(2a + 1) \div 3$.

$$(2a + 1) \div 3 \times 3 = 5 \times 3$$

$$2a + 1 = 15$$

× 3 is the inverse of ÷ 3.

$$2a + 1 - 1 = 15 - 1$$

$$2a = 14$$

$$2 \times a \div 2 = 14 \div 2$$

$$a = 7$$

---

8 Solve these equations. Check your solutions by substituting.

  a $\dfrac{h + 2}{5} = 3$ **b** $\dfrac{m - 5}{4} = 2$

  c $\dfrac{2b + 5}{3} = 7$ **d** $\dfrac{3k - 4}{2} = 4$

9 **Modelling** The mean of the five numbers 21, 25, x, 23 and 18 is 20.

  a Write an expression for the sum of the five numbers.

  b Divide your expression by 5, to give an expression for the mean.

  c Write an equation for the mean.

  d Solve the equation to find x.

10 **Modelling / Problem-solving** The mean of the six numbers
11, 10, 15, y, 19 and 8 is 13.
What is the value of y?

11 **Modelling / Problem-solving** The perimeter of this rectangle is 36 cm.

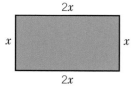

Work out the length and the width.

12 **Modelling / Problem-solving** The length of a rectangle is 3 times
its width.

  a Sketch the rectangle. Label its width w.
  What is the length of the rectangle **in terms of** w?

  b The perimeter of the rectangle is 24 cm.
  Work out the length and the width.

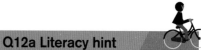

Q12a Literacy hint

An expression **in terms of** w
includes the letter w.

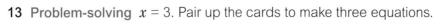

13 **Problem-solving** $x = 3$. Pair up the cards to make three equations.

$2(x + 2)$ $20x + 3$ $3x + 2$

$2x + 5$ $9(x + 4)$ $5(x - 1)$ $3(x + 12)$

14 **Modelling / Problem-solving** Work out the size of each angle in this isosceles triangle.

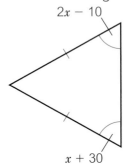

2x − 10

x + 30

Q14 Strategy hint

Write and solve an equation for the two equal angles.
Substitute the value of x into the expressions for the angles.
Solve the equation to find x.
What is the sum of the angles in a triangle? Calculate the third angle.

15 **Modelling / Problem-solving**
When $x = 10\,cm$, work out
a the perimeter of this rectangle
b the area of the rectangle.

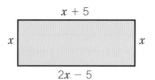

x + 5

x   x

2x − 5

Q15 Strategy hint

Write and solve an equation for two equal sides.
Use the value of x to work out the length of each side.

16 **Modelling** Two **consecutive integers** add to make 315.
Jamal writes expressions for the two integers:
1st number ☐, 2nd number ☐ + 1
a Add Jamal's expressions together.
b The two integers add to make 315. Write this as an equation using your answer to part **a**.
c Solve your equation.
d Write down the two integers.

Q16 Literacy hint

An **integer** is a whole number.
Two **consecutive** integers come one after the other on a number line.

17 **Modelling / Problem-solving** The sum of two consecutive integers is 523.
What are the two integers?

18 **Modelling / Problem-solving** Three consecutive integers sum to 63.
What are the three integers?

19 **Modelling / Real** I am 25 years older than my son.
a My son is m years old. Write an expression for my age.
b Write an expression for our total age.
c Our total age is 57.
Write an equation and solve it to find m.
d How old is my son?
e How old am I?

20 **Modelling / Real** Rose is 28 years younger than her mother.
Their total age is 112.
What are their ages?

21 **Modelling / Problem-solving** Write a problem like Q20 for a friend to solve.
Make sure you know the answer.

22 **Modelling / Real** Train tickets to London for 3 adults and 1 child cost £95.
An adult ticket costs £25 more than a child's ticket.
Work out the cost of each ticket.

23 **Problem-solving** The formula for the area of a trapezium is

$$\text{area} = \frac{(a + b)h}{2}$$

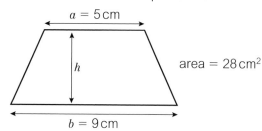

Q23 Strategy hint

Substitute the values for area, a and b into the formula. Solve to find h.

What is the height h of this trapezium?

24 The sum of two numbers is 10. Their difference is 20.
What are the two numbers?

Q24 hint

Write two equations to represent the information you have been given:
for example, $x + y = \ldots\ldots$
$x - y = \ldots\ldots$

25 In the pyramid below, the value in each brick is found by summing (adding) the value in the two bricks below it.

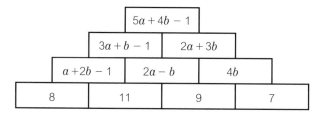

a Work out the values of a and b.
b Hence calculate the value of the top brick.

26 x and y are multiples of 5.
Given that $2x + 3y = 100$, what are the possible values of x and y?

27 I think of a number.
5 less than double the number is equal to three times 1 less than the number.
What is the number that I originally thought of?

Q28 hint

Try different values of y.

28 If $x = \dfrac{1}{y + 2}$ and $y \geqslant 1$, what is the largest value that x could have?

29 If $\dfrac{a}{b} = 1$, what can you say about the values a and b?

30 **Reflect** Look back at Q17–22.
How did you decide what letter to use when you wrote the equation?
Did it make a difference to your final answer?

2 Unit test

1 Solve these equations.

  a $x - 8 = 15$ **b** $5x = 45$ **c** $\frac{x}{7} = 2$

2 Work out the sizes of the three angles.

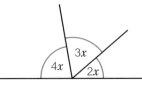

3 Solve these equations.

  a $4x - 5 = 23$ **b** $\frac{x}{6} + 4 = 6$

  c $17 - 3x = -10$ **d** $5(x + 8) = 55$

  e $\frac{5x}{4} = -10$

4 Work out the size of each angle in this triangle.

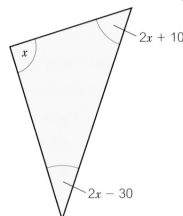

5 Solve $\frac{3x - 1}{5} = 4$

6 Use the formula

$$m = \frac{1}{2} sv - 3s^2$$

to work out the value of v when $s = 4$ and $m = 62$.

7 Solve these equations.

  a $5m + 2 = 7m - 10$

  b $3(n - 4) = 2(n - 1)$

  c $2(x + 5) = 4(x - 2)$

8 These two rectangles have the same area.

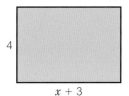 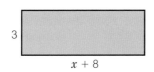

$x + 3$

$x + 8$

Work out the value of x.

9 a Write down a formula for converting hours (h) into days (d).

b Use the formula to convert 480 hours into days.

10 $2x - 4y = 12$

If x and y are both positive integers, give three possible pairs of values for x and y.

11 The formula for calculating the surface area (S) of a cuboid is

$$S = 2(ab + bc + ac)$$

where a = width, b = width and c = height.

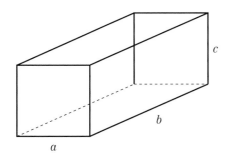

a Work out the surface area of the cuboid when a = 2 cm, b = 3 cm and c = 4 cm.

b A cuboid has surface area 32 cm³. If a = 2 and b = 3, work out the value of c.

Challenge

12 Problem-solving This shape has area 56 cm².
The lengths of the sides are integer values.
Find one set of possible dimensions of the shape.

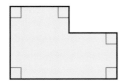

13 Reflect In this unit, you have learned some new vocabulary.
List the new words you have learned, and write a description next to each one.
Ask your friend or teacher to help if you aren't sure what some of the words mean.

3.1 Simplifying expressions

You will learn to:
• Simplify expressions involving powers and brackets.

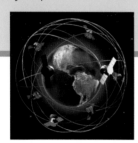

Why learn this?
Scientists simplify expressions involving powers to calculate when and where two objects will collide (hit by accident).

All these expressions simplify to $12x$. What are the missing terms or numbers?
• $8x + \square$
• $\square - 8x$
• $\square \times 4x$
• $\dfrac{24x}{\square}$

Explore
What does the expression x^3*x^2 mean in a spreadsheet program?

Confidence

Exercise 3.1

1 Simplify
   a $3x + 5x$
   b $8y + 2z + 2y + 9z$
   c $7t + 5g - 2g - 5t$
   d $8h + 9j - 15h$
   e $3x^3 + x^2 - x^3$

2 Copy and complete this addition pyramid. Each brick is the sum of the two bricks below it.

| | $9x^2 + 3x^3$ |
| $4x^2 + 2x^3$ | $6x^2 + x^3$ | |

3 Expand
   a $5(x + 7)$ b $-2(a + 3)$

4 Simplify
   a $2a \times 5a$ b $4m \times 3m \times 2m$

5 A tile manufacturer makes two square ceramic tiles. The smaller tile has sides of length x cm. The larger tile has sides that are three times those of the smaller tile.
   a Write an expression, in terms of x, for the length of each side of the large tile.
   b Write expressions for the area of each tile.
   c Write an expression for the total area of a small and a large tile together. Write your expression in its simplest form.

Warm up

6 Write an expression for the perimeter of each rectangle. Write your answers in their simplest form.

a

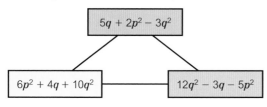

$2x^2 + 3y^2$ $5x^2 + y^2$

$3x^2 + 7y^2$

b

$a^3 - b^2$

$2a^3 + 3b^2$

7 a Add together two of the expressions linked by lines.

$5q + 2p^2 - 3q^2$

$6p^2 + 4q + 10q^2$ $12q^2 - 3q - 5p^2$

b Repeat part **a** in as many different ways as you can.

c Add all three expressions together.

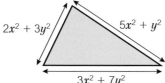

> **Worked example**
>
> **a** Work out $4(x + 5) + 3(x - 6)$.
>
> $4(x + 5) + 3(x - 6)$
>
> $= 4x + 20 + 3x - 18$ —— Expand the brackets.
>
> $= 7x + 2$ —— Collect like terms.
>
> **b** Work out $6(p + 2) - 2(p + 1)$.
>
> $6(p + 2) - 2(p + 1)$ —— Expand the brackets. Multiply terms in the second bracket by -2.
>
> $= 6p + 12 - 2p - 2$
>
> $= 4p + 10$ —— Collect like terms.

8 Expand and simplify

  a $3(x + 5) + 4(x - 2)$ **b** $5(m - 4) - 3(m + 1)$

  c $2(y + 5) - 2(y - 1)$ **d** $2(x + 5) - (3x - 2)$

  e $3(2x + 4) + 2(x - 3)$ **f** $4(3x - 5) - 3(2x - 1)$

9 a Write an expression for the area of the larger rectangle.

  b Write an expression for the area of the smaller rectangle.

  c Write an expression for the shaded area.

$x + 3$

5   $x - 2$ 8

10 Explore What does the expression x^3*x^2 mean in a spreadsheet program?

Is it easier to explore this question now that you have completed the lesson? What further information do you need to be able to answer this?

11 Reflect Write a definition, in your own words, for each of these mathematics words.

  • Expand

  • Simplify

Compare your definitions with those of others in your class.

Can you improve your definitions?

Q11 hint

Look back at questions where you were asked to expand and simplify. What did you do?

Explore

Reflect

3.2 More simplifying

Confidence

You will learn to:
- Use the index laws in algebraic calculations and expressions.
- Simplify expressions with powers.
- Understand the meaning of an identity.

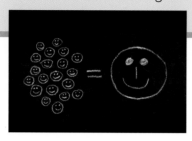

Why learn this?
Solving equations becomes much easier when you can simplify first.

Fluency
What is the value of
- 3^0
- 5^0
- 7^1
- 10^0?

Explore
What is the area of this shape?

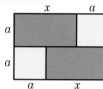

Exercise 3.2

Warm up

1 Write each expression as a single power.
   a $3^2 \times 3^3$ b $5^3 \times 5$ c $4^5 \div 4^2$
   d $(2^2)^3$ e $x \times x$

2 Simplify
   a $2x \times 2x$ b $5a \times 4b$ c $\dfrac{6t}{3}$

3 **Reasoning**
   a Simplify
      i $2^4 \times 2^5$ ii $3^4 \times 3^5$ iii $x^4 \times x^5$
   b Write a rule to explain what you do to indices when you multiply powers of the same **variable**.
   c Copy and complete

   > **Key point**
   > A **variable** is a letter that represents a number.

   i $2^5 \div 2^3 = \dfrac{2^5}{2^3} = \dfrac{2 \times 2 \times 2 \times 2 \times 2}{2 \times 2 \times 2} = 2^\square$

   ii $x^5 \div x^3 = \dfrac{x^5}{x^3} = \dfrac{x \times x \times x \times x \times x}{x \times x \times x} = x^\square$

   d Write a rule to explain what you do to indices when you divide powers of the same variable.
   e Simplify
      i $(2^3)^5$ ii $(3^3)^5$ iii $(x^3)^5$
   f Write a rule to explain what you do to indices when you raise the power of a variable to another power.

4 Simplify
   a $x^7 \times x^9 = x^\square$ b $z^{12} \div z^4 = z^\square$ c $(v^4)^2 = v^\square$

   > **Q4a hint**
   > $x^7 \times x^9 = x^{7+9} = x^\square$

5 Work out the missing power.
   a $y^2 \times y^\square = y^8$ b $n^\square \div n^3 = n^6$ c $(w^\square)^3 = w^{18}$

Topic links: Index laws, Multiplication

6 Multiply each pair of expressions linked by a line.

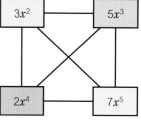

Worked example

Simplify

a $\dfrac{15x^3}{3x}$

$\dfrac{15x^3}{3x}$

$\dfrac{15}{3} = 5$ and $\dfrac{x^3}{x} = x^2$

$= 5x^2$

b $\dfrac{8a^3 \times 6a^2}{3a^3}$

$\dfrac{8a^3 \times \overset{2}{6}a^2}{3a^3}$

$\dfrac{6}{3} = 2$

$\dfrac{a^3}{a^3} = 1$

$= 16a^2$

7 Simplify

a $\dfrac{12a^8}{4a^3} = 3a^{\square}$

b $\dfrac{25b^7}{5b^4}$

c $\dfrac{30n^3}{6n}$

d $\dfrac{18t^5}{3t^4}$

e $\dfrac{3p^5 \times 8p^3}{2p}$

f $\dfrac{5x^3 \times 6x}{3x}$

8 Problem-solving Write two expressions that simplify to give $24x^5$.
One expression must be a multiplication and the other a division.

9 Problem-solving This is part of Teri's homework.
Her pen has leaked ink onto her page.
Work out the numbers underneath the blobs of ink.

Simplify these.

a $\dfrac{5y^5 \times 9y^3}{3y^{\blacksquare}} = \blacksquare y^2$

b $\dfrac{4y^{\blacksquare} \times \blacksquare y^7}{6y^5} = 8y^4$

10 Simplify

a $(4x^2)^2 = 4^2 \times (x^2)^2 = \square x^{\square}$

b $(2y^3)^2$

c $(3z^4)^3$

d $\left(\dfrac{x^2}{4}\right)^3 = \dfrac{(x^2)^3}{4^3} = \dfrac{x^6}{\square}$

e $\left(\dfrac{y^4}{7}\right)^2$

f $\left(\dfrac{z^5}{3}\right)^3$

Discussion Which of these are the same?

$(4x^2)^2 \qquad -4x^4 \qquad -(4x)^4 \qquad (-4x^2)^2 \qquad 4x^4$

11 Decide if these are always true, sometimes true or never true for
positive values of a, b, c and d.
For the statements that are always true, replace the equals sign (=)
with an identity sign ($\equiv$).
For the equations that are sometimes true, state values that make
them true.

a $x^a \times x^b = x^{ab}$

b $x^a \div x^b = x^{a-b}$

c $(x^a)^b = x^{a+b}$

d $y^c \div y^d = y^{d-c}$

e $(y^c)^d = (y^d)^c$

f $y^d \times y^c = y^{c+d}$

12 Explore What is the area of this shape?
Is it easier to explore this question now that you have completed
the lesson? What further information do you need to be able to
answer this?

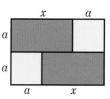

13 Reflect Lucy asks, 'Are the results of $x^2 \times x^2$ and $x^2 + x^2$ the same or
different?' Answer Lucy's question, then explain your answer.

Explore

Reflect

3.3 Factorising expressions

You will learn to:
* Factorise an algebraic expression.

Fluency
What are the common factors of
* 9 and 12
* 25 and 15?

Explore
Is $4x + 7y$ divisible by 2?

Why learn this
Factorising is useful when solving many different types of equations.

Exercise 3.3

1 Expand
a $2(x + 3)$ b $4(3x + 2)$
c $9(2 - x)$ d $5(4 - 7x)$

2 Work out the highest common factor (HCF) of
a 18 and 27   b 20 and 12   c 21 and 35

3 Write the common factors of
a 6 and $2a$ b $12b$ and 3
c $10x$ and 15   d 8 and $12y$

Q3 hint

$2a = 2 \times a$
$6 = 2 \times 3$

4 Write the HCF of
a $16b$ and 8   b 36 and $24x$

Worked example

Factorise $3x + 9$.

$3x + 9$
$= 3(x + 3)$

3 is a common factor of both $3x$ and 9.
Write 3 in front of the bracket.
Divide both terms by 3 to find the values in the bracket.

Key point

Expanding removes brackets from an expression. **Factorising** inserts brackets into an expression.

expand
$6(a + 3) = 6a + 18$
factorise

To factorise $6a + 18$, write the common factor of its terms, 6, outside the brackets. This is called 'taking out the common factor'.

5 Copy and complete
a $4x + 8 = 4(\Box + 2)$ b $12x + 3 = 3(\Box + \Box)$
c $9x - 15 = 3(\Box - \Box)$ d $14x - 21 = 7(\Box - \Box)$
e $12x + 6 = \Box(2x + \Box)$ f $9x - 3 = \Box(3x - \Box)$
g $11x + 33 = \Box(\Box + 3)$ h $10 - 5x = \Box(2 - \Box)$
i $12 + 3x = \Box(\Box + x)$ j $16 + 24x = \Box(2 + \Box x)$

6 **Factorise** each expression.
a $3x + 12$ b $5p - 15$
c $22z - 11$ d $2y - 20$
e $10 + 5m$ f $26 - 13n$
g $14 + 7s$ h $7 - 28t$

Q6 Strategy hint

Check your factorisation by expanding the brackets.

Topic links: HCF

Work in pairs.
a Both of you write an expression with brackets.
b Expand the brackets in your expression.
c Swap the expanded expressions. Factorise the expression you are given.
d Is it the same as the original?
   If not, why?

7 **Problem-solving**   Match the equivalent expressions.

a $2x + 4$
b $5x + 30$
c $2x - 6$
d $6x + 36$
e $5x - 20$
f $6x + 12$

i $6(x + 2)$
ii $2(x - 3)$
iii $5(x - 4)$
iv $2(x + 2)$
v $6(x + 6)$
vi $5(x + 6)$

8 In how many different ways can the expression $12x + 24b$ be factorised?

9 Factorise completely
   a $4x + 8$ b $8y + 12$
   c $14m + 28$ d $12n - 6$
   e $20 - 10s$ f $8 + 20t$
   g $90y + 45$ h $66 + 33z$

Key point

To factorise completely, write the highest common factor outside the brackets.

10 Factorise
   a $4m + 2n + 16$
   b $15 + 10b + 55c$
   c $pq + 2p + 12p$

Q10a hint

$2(\square + \square + \square)$

11 Jim pays £70 deposit for a bike. Then he pays £10 a month.
   Write a formula for the amount paid after m months.

Q11 hint

Use brackets in your formula.

12 Kaz pays £120 deposit for a laptop, then pays £25 a month.
   Write a formula for the amount paid after n months.

13 **Explore** Is $4x + 7y$ divisible by 2?
   Is it easier to explore this question now that you have completed the lesson?
   What further information do you need to be able to answer this?

14 **Reflect** Write down a definition of 'factor'.
   Use your definition to write a definition, in your own words, of 'highest common factor (HCF)'.
   Use your definition of HCF to help you write a definition, in your own words, of 'factorising'. Be as accurate as possible.
   How did your definitions of 'factor' and 'HCF' help you to define factorising?

3.4 Expanding and factorising expressions

Confidence

You will learn to:
- Write and simplify expressions involving brackets and powers.
- Factorise an algebraic expression.

Why learn this?
Scientists factorise expressions to solve equations to find forces, for example the force of a skier coming down a slope.

Fluency
- Which of these are like terms?

  $7x^3$ x^4 $9x^3$ $\dfrac{x^4}{2}$ $11x^2$ $-4x^2$

- What is the highest common factor of
  — 8 and 12
  — 12 and $15x$?

Explore
How many expressions can be simplified to give $12x^2 + 24x$?

Exercise 3.4

Warm up

1 Simplify
  a $5a \times 3b$
  b $2m \times 3m$
  c $4n \times -5n$
  d $7a^2 \times 2a^3$
  e $6p \times -5p^4$

2 Expand
  a $2(3x + 5)$
  b $4(3 - 2y)$
  c $y(y + 3)$
  d $2(x - 1)$
  e $3(10 + p)$
  f $s(10 - s)$

3 Expand
  a $x(x + 5)$
  b $y(8 + y)$
  c $p(2p - 5)$
  d $2q(6 - 3q)$

4 Joe was asked to factorise $12x - 16$ completely.
  His answer is $12x - 16 = 2(6x - 8)$
  Why is this not factorised completely?

5 For each rectangle
  i write an expression for the area of the rectangle
  ii expand the brackets in your expression.

a
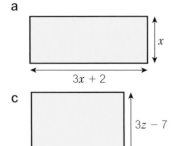
x
$3x + 2$

b
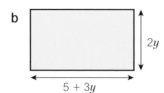
$2y$
$5 + 3y$

c

$3z - 7$
$5z$

Q5a hint
$x(\square + \square)$

Topic links: Perimeter and area of a rectangle, HCF

Worked example

Expand

a $x(x^3 + 3x)$

$x(x^3 + 3x) = x \times x^3 + x \times 3x$
$= x^4 + 3x^2$

b $2x^2(x + 3x^2 - 5)$

$2x^2(x + 3x^2 - 5) = 2x^2 \times x + 2x^2 \times 3x^2 + 2x^2 \times -5$
$= 2x^3 + 6x^4 - 10x^2$

6   Expand
   a $x(x^2 + 4x)$
   b $2x^3(7x^3 - 3x^2)$
   c $5x(x^3 + 2x^2 + 7)$
   d $x^2(x^2 - 5x + 7)$

Q6b hint

$2x^3(7x^3 - 3x^2) = \square x^{\square} - \square x^{\square}$

7   Expand and simplify
   a $2(a + 3b) + 5(a + b)$
   b $x(2x^2 + 5) + 3x(4x^2 + 7)$
   c $3(6 - 2y) + y^2(y - 8)$
   d $5t(t + 2) - 4t^3(t^2 - 2)$

Q7a hint

First expand the two brackets.
Then collect like terms.

8   Write an expression for the total area of this shape.

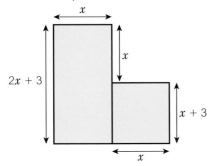

Discussion   Is there another way to answer this question?

Investigation

Reasoning

Start with 2 sticks x cm long. Cut y cm off the end of each stick.

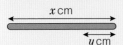

You can arrange the 4 pieces into a rectangle like this.

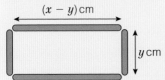

1   Write a simplified expression for the perimeter and for the area of the rectangle.
2   Now start with 4 sticks x cm long and cut y cm off the end of each stick.
   Arrange the pieces to make a rectangle. You don't have to use all the pieces.
   a   How many different rectangles can you make?
   b   How many different expressions are there for the area and for the perimeter?
   c   Work out the perimeter and area of each rectangle when $x = 30$ cm and $y = 10$ cm.

9 Show that an expression for the total area of this shape is $9y^2 + 3y$.

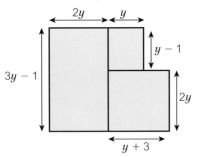

Strategy hint

'Show that' means 'Show your working'.

Worked example

Factorise $18x^2 - 24x$ completely.

$18x^2 - 24x = 6x(3x - 4)$ ← The **HCF** of $18x^2$ and $24x$ is $6x$.

Check:

$6x(3x - 4) = 18x^2 - 24x$ ← $6x \times 3x = 18x^2$ and $6x \times -4 = -24x$

Key point

To **factorise** an expression completely, take out the **highest common factor** (HCF) of its terms.

---

10 Write the **highest common factor** of each pair.

  a x^2 and x^3 **b** p^2 and p **c** y^5 and y^2

  d $8z^3$ and $4z$ **e** $10m^5$ and $15m^3$ **f** pq and p^2q^2

Q10a hint

$x^2 = \boxed{x} \times \boxed{x}$
$x^3 = \boxed{x} \times \boxed{x} \times x$

11 Factorise

  a $15x^3 - 3x$ **b** $32x + 16x^2$ **c** $15x + 21x^2$

  d $3x^3 + 6x$ **e** $y^2 - 7y^4$ **f** $3y^5 + 15y^3$

  g $12y^4 - 4y^3$

12 **Reasoning** For each question, which is the odd one out, A, B or C? Explain why.

  a A $8x(x^2 + 9x + 4)$ B $12x(2x^2 + 6x + 2)$ C $24x(x^2 + 3x + 1)$

  b A $y^2(3y + 1)$ B $y(3y^2 + y)$ C $3y(y^2 + 1)$

  c A $-z^3(3z^2 + 6z - 9)$ B $z^3(6z - 3z^2 + 9)$ C $z^3(9 + 6z + 3z^2)$

13 **Problem-solving / Reasoning**

  a Show that both of these statements are identities.

   i $4x^3 + x(3x^2 + 7x) \equiv 7x^2(x + 1)$

   ii $2b(b^2 + 3b) - b(b^2 + 8b) \equiv 2b^2(b - 1) - b^3$

  b Work out the missing numbers from this identity.

   $\Box y(y^3 - 3) - 2y(2y^3 - \Box) \equiv 2y(y^3 + 3) - 2y$

Q13a Strategy hint

Expand the left-hand side and rewrite it as the right-hand side.

14 **Problem-solving** This expression has been factorised completely.

   $\Box x^2 \Box + \Box \Box y^3 = 6 \Box y^3(2\Box + \Box\Box)$

  Fill in possible missing terms.

15 **Explore** How many expressions can be simplified to give $12x^2 + 24x$? Look back at the maths you have learned in this lesson. How can you use it to answer this question?

16 **Reflect**

  a Write a definition, in your own words, of highest common factor.

  b Use your definition to explain, in your own words, what factorising is.

  c How did the definition you wrote in part **a** help you to write the definition in part **b**?

Explore

Reflect

3.5 Substituting and solving

You will learn to:
- Substitute integers into expressions.
- Construct and solve equations.

Why learn this?
Engineers substitute negative values into expressions when calculating the speed of trains as they are slowing down.

Fluency
Which of these is the correct expression for the perimeter of this rectangle?

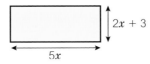

A $7x + 3$ B $10x^2 + 15x$
C $14x + 6$ D $20x$

Explore
How long does it take a car to slow down to enter a speed restriction area?

Exercise 3.5

1 Work out the value of these expressions when $x = 4$ and $y = 5$.
  a $3x + 8$ **b** $2xy$
  c $6(x + y)$ **d** $y^2 - x^2$

2 Solve
  a $3x + 8 = 23$ **b** $5 = 20 - 5x$
  c $8x + 3 = 3x + 33$ **d** $7(x + 8) = 3(x - 4)$

3 Square A has area x cm². Square B has area $(x + 3)$ cm².
The area of square B is four times the area of square A.
  a Write an equation using the information given.
  b Solve the equation to find the value of x.

4 Find the value of these **linear expressions** when $x = 8$, $y = 5$ and $z = -3$.
  a $4x + 3z$ **b** $2(x + 3) + y + x$
  c $5(y - z) - 2x$ **d** $3(x + y) - 2(y + z)$

5 For each shape
  a write an expression for the perimeter
  b simplify the expression
  c work out the perimeter when $a = 3$ and $b = -2$.

A
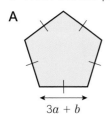
$3a + b$

B
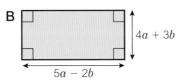
$4a + 3b$
$5a - 2b$

Discussion Is it possible to work out the perimeter of the rectangle when $a = 2$ and $b = -4$?

Warm up

6 Problem-solving These two shapes have the same area. Work out the value of x.

 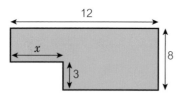

7 Substitute $x = 3$, $y = 4$ and $z = -2$ into
  a $3x(x + y)$
  b $z^2(z + x^2)$
  c $2x(5 + z) + y^2$.

Q7b hint

$(-2)^2 \times (-2 + 3^2)$

8 STEM A formula you can use to work out the distance, s, a car has travelled in metres is

$$s = ut + \tfrac{1}{2}at^2$$

where u is the starting speed in metres per second, a is the acceleration in metres per second² and t is the time in seconds.
Work out the distance the car has travelled when
  a $u = 0$, $a = 2$ and $t = 10$
  b $u = 13$, $a = 3$ and $t = 4$
  c $u = 25$, $a = -4$ and $t = 8$.
Discussion What does it mean when $u = 0$?

9 Problem-solving A square with sides $2x$ is cut out of a rectangle with sides $3x + 8$ and $4x$.
  a Write an expression, in terms of x, for the area of the remaining shape.
  b Use your expression to find the area of the remaining shape when
      i $x = 1$
      ii $x = 2$
      iii $x = 3$
      iv $x = 5$
      v $x = 10$

Worked example

Solve the equation $4(2a - 1) = 32 - 3(2a - 2)$.

$4(2a - 1) = 32 - 3(2a - 2)$ — Multiply out the brackets. Take care with the minus signs.

$8a - 4 = 32 - 6a + 6$

$8a - 4 = 38 - 6a$ — Collect like terms on the right-hand side: $32 + 6 = 38$

$8a + 6a = 38 + 4$ — Rearrange to get like terms on the same side.

$14a = 42$

$a = \dfrac{42}{14} = 3$ — Simplify and then solve.

Topic links: Writing expressions, Perimeter of shapes, Area of composite shapes

Subject links: Science (Q8)

10 Solve
   a $3(x + 5) = 37 - 2(x + 1)$
   b $6(2y + 1) = 46 - 4(3y - 2)$
   c $4(3z - 7) = 65 - 3(4z - 9)$
   d $2(2x + 9) = 4x + 3 - 5(6 - x)$

11 Problem-solving
   a In this diagram the green shapes have the same area.

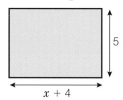
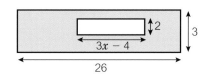

   Work out the value of x.

   b In this diagram the yellow shapes have the same area.

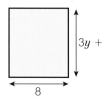
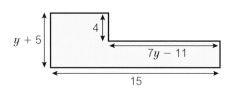

   Work out the value of y.

Q11 Strategy hint
Write an expression for the area of each shape.

12 **Problem-solving** A rectangular piece of card measuring 4 cm by $(x + 5)$ cm has a rectangular hole cut out of it. The hole measures 2 cm by $(x + 3)$ cm. The area of card left over is 24 cm².
   a Work out the value of x.
   b Work out the dimensions of the original piece of card and the hole.

Q12 Strategy hint
Draw a diagram.

Investigation   Problem-solving

Use the values $a = 6$, $b = 8$, $c = -4$ and $d = -3$ to write three expressions that will give an answer of
a 19   b 26   c −30   d −42
For example, $\frac{ab}{2} + c - 1$ is one expression that gives an answer of 19.
At least one of your expressions for each number should involve a square or square root.
Ask a partner to check that your expressions are correct.

---

13 **Explore** How long does it take a car to slow down to enter a speed restriction area?
   Is it easier to explore this question now that you have completed the lesson? What further information do you need to be able to answer this?

14 **Reflect** Safiya says, 'When solving equations, I always check that my solution is correct. If it isn't, first I check my check! Then, I cover my original working and try to solve the equation again.'
   Did you check your solutions to the questions in this lesson?
   If so, what did you do to check?
   What is your strategy if you get an incorrect solution?
   Compare your strategy with those of others in your class.

Explore

Reflect

3 Check up

Simplifying and substituting into expressions

1 Simplify

  a $4x^2 + 6x^2$

  b $8a^2 - 2b^2 - 4b^2 + 3a^2$

  c $9y + 12y^2 + 2y - 7y^2$

2 Copy these statements. Write the correct sign $=$ or $\equiv$ in each empty box.

  a $2x + 5 \,\square\, x + 7 + x - 2$

  b $2x + 1 \,\square\, 4x - 3$

3 Find the value of each linear expression when $x = 3$, $y = -2$ and $z = 4$.

  a $5x + 2y$

  b $6(y + z)$

  c $3(z + 1) + x - y$

  d $4(2z + y) - 3(z - y)$

4 Substitute $x = -1$, $y = -3$ and $z = 5$ into

  a $y^2(z + x^2)$

  b $2xy + z(z + 2y)$

Index laws

5 Simplify

  a $x^3 \times x^2$

  b $\dfrac{y^{12}}{y^2}$

  c $(z^3)^2$

6 Simplify

  a $5x^4 \times 6x^2$

  b $\dfrac{12b^3}{6b}$

  c $(3p^4)^2$

  d $\dfrac{2p^2 \times 6p^4}{3p^3}$

  e $\left(\dfrac{n^3}{5}\right)^2$

Expanding and factorising

7 Expand

  a $x(x^2 + 2x)$

  b $3x^2(2x - 4)$

  c $x^2(3x^2 + 2x - 1)$

8 Expand and simplify
   a $4(x + 3) + 7(x - 1)$
   b $x(x - 6) - x(4x - 2)$
   c $x(3x^2 + 4) + 2x(5x^2 + 9)$

9 Factorise
   a $4x + 20$
   b $6x - 9$
   c $14a - 21b$

10 Factorise completely
   a $6x^2 + 18x$
   b $8y^3 - 2y^4$
   c $16xy - 8x^2y^2$

Solving equations

11 Solve $2(x + 7) = 28 - 3(6 - x)$.

12 The area shaded blue is the same in both diagrams.

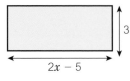
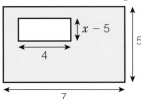

   Work out the value of x.

13 How sure are you of your answers? Were you mostly
   🙁 **Just guessing**   😐 **Feeling doubtful**   🙂 **Confident**
   What next? Use your results to decide whether to strengthen or extend your learning.

Challenge

14 a Choose your own numbers to complete these identities.
   $\square y^{\square} \times \square y^{\square} \equiv 20y^{12}$
   $\square y^{\square} \div \square y^{\square} \equiv 6y^{12}$
   $(\square y^{\square})^{\square} \equiv \square y^{12}$
   b Repeat part **a** using different numbers.

15 a Work out the missing terms from this expression that has been factorised.
   $\square x^2y + \square y^2 + 9\square = 3x\square(\square + 4y + \square)$
   b Is there only one answer to this problem?
   Explain your answer.

16 Work out the whole number values of a and b when $ab = -24$ and $a + b = -2$.

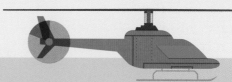

3 Strengthen

You will:
- Strengthen your understanding with practice.

Simplifying and substituting into expressions

1 Copy and complete
  a $2x^2 + 3x^2 = \Box x^2$
  b $7t^3 - 2t^3$
  c $5y^4 + 6y^4 - 2y^4$

> **Q1a hint**
>
> How many x^2 are there altogether?

2 Sort these terms into three groups of like terms.

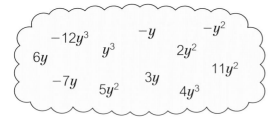

$$-12y^3 \quad -y \quad -y^2$$
$$6y \quad y^3 \quad 2y^2$$
$$-7y \quad 3y \quad 11y^2$$
$$5y^2 \quad 4y^3$$

3 Ryan uses this method to simplify $7y + 5y^2 + 3y - 8y^2$.

> $(7y) (+ 5y^2) (+ 3y) (- 8y^2)$
> $7y + 3y = 10y$
> $5y^2 - 8y^2 = -3y^2$
> Answer: $10y - 3y^2$

> **Q3a hint**
>
> Copy the expression. Circle like terms in different colours.

Simplify
  a $8x + 2x^2 + 4x + 3x^2$
  b $4a^2 + 3b^2 - b^2 - a^2$
  c $9p^3 - 6n^2 - 4n^2 + 2p^3$
  d $2v^3 + 7 + 5v - 2v + 2v^3 - 3$

4 Find the value of each linear expression when $x = 6$, $y = -3$ and $z = 5$.
  a $4x + 2z - 3y$
  b $4z - 2x + y$
  c $4(x + 2) + 5y - z$
  d $3(z + 3x) - 3(z - y)$

> **Q4a hint**
>
>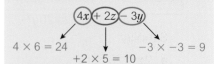
>
> $(4x) (+ 2z) (- 3y)$
> $4 \times 6 = 24$ $-3 \times -3 = 9$
> $+2 \times 5 = 10$
> Add together: $24 + 10 + 9 = \Box$

> **Q4c hint**
>
> Always work out brackets first.
> $4(x + 2) + 5y - z$
> $6 + 2$

5 Find the value of each expression when $a = -4$ and $b = 8$.
  a $a + b^2 = \Box + 8^2 = \Box + \Box =$
  b $3a^2 - b = 3 \times (\Box)^2 - \Box =$
  c $10b + a^3$
  d $(b - a)^2$

> **Q5b hint**
>
> The square of a negative number is positive.

6 Find the value of each expression when $x = -2$, $y = -4$ and $z = 3$.

a $y^2(5z - 3x^2)$

b $z(xy + x^2)$

c $z^2 - yz + xz$

d $3(z - x)^2 - 5y$

Q6a hint

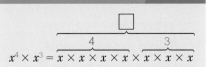

$-4 \times -4 = 16$ $5 \times 3 = 15$ $-3 \times -2 \times -2 = -12$

Work out the brackets first.

Index laws

1 Simplify

a $x^4 \times x^3$

b $y^2 \times y^5$

c $z^8 \times z$

Q1a hint

$$x^4 \times x^3 = \underbrace{\overbrace{x \times x \times x \times x}^{4} \times \overbrace{x \times x \times x}^{3}}_{\square}$$

2 Simplify

a $x^6 \div x^2$

b $y^5 \div y^2$

c $z^8 \div z^3$

Q2a hint

$$x^6 \div x^2 = \frac{\overbrace{\cancel{x} \times \cancel{x} \times x \times x \times x \times x}^{6}}{\underbrace{\cancel{x} \times \cancel{x}}_{2}}$$

3 Simplify

a $(x^3)^2$

b $(y^2)^4$

c $(z^5)^3$

Q3a hint

$$(x^3)^2 = \underbrace{\overbrace{(x \times x \times x)}^{3} \times \overbrace{(x \times x \times x)}^{3}}_{3 \times 2 = \square}$$

4 Mia uses this method to simplify $6y^2 \times 3y^4$ and $\dfrac{6y^5}{3y^2}$

$\cancel{6}y^2 \otimes 3y^4$

$6 \times 3 = 18$

$y^2 \times y^4 = y^6$

Answer: $18y^6$

$\dfrac{6y^5}{3y^2}$

$\dfrac{6}{3} = 2$

$\dfrac{y^5}{y^2} = y^3$

Answer: $2y^3$

Simplify

a $2x^3 \times 3x$

b $4y^4 \times 5y^3$

c $6p^2 \times 3p^5$

d $9q \times 8q^7$

e $\dfrac{16a^6}{8a^2}$

f $\dfrac{12b^4}{4b^3}$

g $\dfrac{15b^9}{15b^5}$

h $\dfrac{10b^7}{5b}$

Q4a hint

Multiply the numbers first. Then multiply the variables (letters).

Q4e hint

Divide the numbers first. Then divide the variables (letters).

5 Copy and complete

a $(5x^3)^2 = 5x^3 \times 5x^3 =$

b $(4m^5)^3$

c $(3n^3)^4$

d $\left(\dfrac{x^3}{2}\right)^2 = \dfrac{x^3}{2} \times \dfrac{x^3}{2} = \dfrac{\square}{\square}$

e $\left(\dfrac{w^6}{6}\right)^2$

Expanding and factorising

1 Miko uses the grid method to expand $y^2(2y - 9)$.

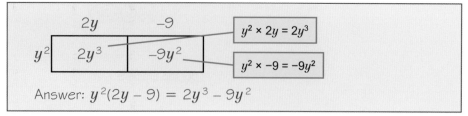

	$2y$	-9
y^2	$2y^3$	$-9y^2$

$y^2 \times 2y = 2y^3$

$y^2 \times -9 = -9y^2$

Answer: $y^2(2y - 9) = 2y^3 - 9y^2$

Expand
a $x^2(x + 3)$ **b** $y^2(y - 5)$
c $2x^3(x - 4)$ **d** $3y^2(2y^2 + 4y)$

2 Expand and simplify
    a $3(x + 2) + 5(x + 1)$
    b $4(a + 3) + 2(a - 1)$
    c $x(x - 1) + x(x + 8)$
    d $3a(a + 2) - 5a(a - 1)$

Q2a hint

Expand each bracket, then collect like terms.

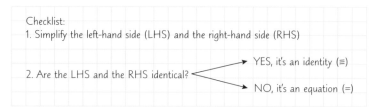

3 Use this checklist to decide whether a statement is an equation or an identity.

Checklist:
1. Simplify the left-hand side (LHS) and the right-hand side (RHS)

2. Are the LHS and the RHS identical?   → YES, it's an identity ($\equiv$)
                                           → NO, it's an equation ($=$)

Copy these statements. Write the correct sign $=$ or $\equiv$ in each empty box.
    a $3x + 2 \,\square\, x + 5 + 2x - 3$
    b $5x + 7 \,\square\, 27$
    c $8p^2 \,\square\, 2p \times 4p$
    d $t + t + t + 8 + 3 \,\square\, 3t + 11$
    e $3x - 9 \,\square\, 2x + 6$
    f $5(x + 3) \,\square\, 3x + 2x + 20 - 5$

4 Copy and complete the working to show that these identities are true.
The first one has been started for you.
    a $2x^3 + 3x^2(4x - 1) \equiv 7x^2(2x - 1) + 4x^2$

LHS $= 2x^3 + 3x^2(4x - 1)$	RHS $= 7x^2(2x - 1) + 4x^2$
$\quad = 2x^3 + 12x^3 - 3x^2$	$\quad = 14x^3 - 7x^2 + 4x^2$
$\quad =$	$\quad =$

    b $3y(y^2 - 5y) + y^2(3 - 2y) \equiv y^2(y - 9) - 3y^2$

5 a What is the highest common factor (HCF) of 3 and 9?
   b Copy and complete
      $3x + 9 = \square(\square + \square)$

Q5b hint

The HCF is outside the bracket.

6 Copy and complete
    a $4x + 8 = 4(\square + \square)$ **b** $2x + 6 = 2(\square + \square)$
    c $15x + 5 = \square(3x + 1)$ **d** $18x - 12 = \square(3x - 2)$
    e $3x + 15 = 3(\square + \square)$ **f** $7x - 14 = 7(\square + \square)$

Solving equations

1 Solve

  a $6(x + 5) = 44 - 2(4 - 2x)$

  b $2(3x - 13) = 40 - 3(x + 4)$

  c $7(x + 1) = 8x + 7 - 2(3x - 5)$

  d $4(3 + 5x) = 16x + 56 - 4(2x - 1)$

2 a Work out the area of the whole large purple rectangle.

  b Write an expression for the area of the small white rectangle.

  c The white rectangle is cut out of the purple rectangle.
    Write an expression for the purple area that is left.

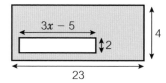

Q1 Strategy hint

Step 1: Expand the brackets on the right-hand side of the = sign and simplify if you can.
Step 2: Expand the brackets on the left-hand side of the = sign and simplify if you can.
Step 3: Solve the equation.
Step 4: Substitute your value of x into the original equation to check.

Enrichment

1 Reasoning Here are four cards.

$3x^2 + 5y^3 - 2z$	$15x^2 - 12y^3 + 8z$	$3y^3 - z - 7x^2$	$7z + 13x^2 - 4y^3$

  a Show that the mean of these expressions is $6x^2 - 2y^3 + 3z$.

  b When $x = 2$, $y = 1$ and $z = 3$

    i work out the value of each card

    ii calculate the mean of the four values

    iii check the mean by working out the value of the expression in part **a**

    iv work out the range of the four values.

2 a Substitute values of x from -4 to 4 in $y = \sqrt{16 - x^2}$

x	-4	-3	-2	-1	0	1	2	3	4
y									

  b Plot the graph of the coordinates in the table.

  c What shape have you drawn?

Q2 hint

Join the points with a smooth curve.

3 Reflect Carla says, 'Algebra is just like arithmetic really, but you use letters when you don't know a number.'
Is Carla's explanation a good one?
Explain your answer.

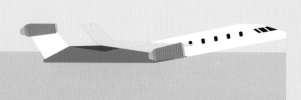

3 Extend

You will:
• Extend your understanding with problem-solving.

 1 STEM / Modelling You can use this formula to calculate the energy, E (joules), in a moving object:

$$E = \frac{1}{2}mv^2$$

where m = mass of object (kg) and v = speed (metres per second, m/s).
Work out the speed, v, of the object when
 a $E = 125$ and $m = 10$
 b $E = 450$ and $m = 16$
 c $E = 1134$ and $m = 7$

2 Reasoning Here are a regular pentagon and a regular octagon.
 a Write an expression using brackets for the perimeter of
  i the pentagon **ii** the octagon.
 b Write an expression, in its simplest form, for the total perimeter of the two shapes.
 c Write an expression, in its simplest form, for the difference in the perimeters of the two shapes when
  i the perimeter of the pentagon is greater than the perimeter of the octagon
  ii the perimeter of the octagon is greater than the perimeter of the pentagon.
 d Explain what you notice about your two answers to part **c**.

$4p^2 + 3pq - 2q^2$ $3q^2 - pq - 4p^2$

3 Reasoning Each rectangle has an area of $12a + 36$.
 a Factorise $12a + 36$ in three different ways to work out the length and width of the three rectangles.
 b i Which rectangle has dimensions that result in the complete factorisation of $12a + 36$?
  ii How could you use the diagrams in part **a** to answer part **b i**?
 c Which rectangle do you think has
  i the greatest perimeter
  ii the smallest perimeter?
  Explain your answers.
 d Write an expression for the perimeter of each rectangle.
 e For $a = 2$
  i work out the dimensions of each rectangle and check that they have the same area
  ii work out the perimeter of each rectangle and check your answers to part **c**.

 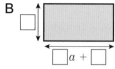 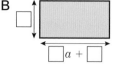 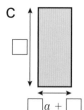

Topic links: Negative numbers, Mean, Range, Perimeter of shapes, Area of a rectangle, Angles in a triangle and kite, Prime factorisation

4 **Reasoning**
  a Show that this statement is **not** true.
     $15a^3 + 6a(3 - 2a^2) \equiv 3a(a^2 + 7)$
  b How can you change the right-hand side of the statement to make it true?

Q4b hint

What do you need to change in the expression $3a(a^2 + 7)$ so that it simplifies to the same as the LHS?

5 Factorise completely
  a $5ab + 10bc - 25ac$
  b $48x^2y - 72y^2 + 120x$
  c $65pt + 39ty - 13yx - 52xp$

6 Factorise completely
  a $16y^3 + 20y^2 + 24y$
  b $12x^2 + 6xy - 2x$
  c $18x^2y - 6x^2y^2 + 30xy^2$
  d $60p^2q^3r^4 - 210p^3q^4r^5 + 54p^5q^4r^3$

7 **Problem-solving** Both of these expressions have been factorised completely. Work out the missing terms.
  a $6xy - 12x^2 + \square x^2\square = 3\square(2y - 4\square + 5xy)$
  b $6\square b + 14a^2\square - 12\square b^2 = 2\square b(3a + 7 - 6a\square)$

8 Find the value of each expression when $x = -2$, $y = -4$ and $z = 3$.
  a $3(z - x)^2 - 5y$
  b $\sqrt{z^3 + x}$
  c $\sqrt{y^2 - 7} + x^2$
  d $\dfrac{2z^2 - x}{5}$
  e $\dfrac{xy - 7y}{z}$

Q8b hint

Work out the value using z and x before taking the square root.

$3^3 + -2$

Q8d hint

Always work out the numerator and the denominator first, before dividing.

$2 \times 3^2 - -2$

9 **Problem-solving** The diagram shows two rectangles. The red rectangle is larger than the yellow rectangle.

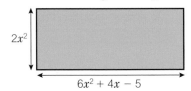
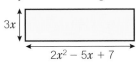

Write an expression to show the difference in the areas of the rectangles.

Q9 hint

Write your expression in its simplest form.

10 **Problem-solving**
  a Match each algebraic expression with the correct value, given the variables in the table below.

a	b	c	d	e	f	g	h	i
4	−3	−6	36	−8	−12	9	−5	13

  b One answer card has not been used.
     Write an expression for this answer card.
     You must use at least three of the letters from the table and your expression must include a power or a root.

Expressions	Values
$5a + 6b - c^2$	2
$\sqrt{d} + h^2$	−9
$\dfrac{g^2 + b^2}{2h}$	−34
$f - 2\sqrt{d} + i$	60
$\dfrac{abc}{d} - e^2$	−26
$\sqrt[3]{e} + a^2 + \dfrac{d}{b}$	−62
	31

11 **Reasoning** Huron is substituting values into the expression $5xy^2 + y^3 + z^2$.
   The values he uses for x, y and z are always negative.
   Can the value of the expression ever be positive?
   Explain your answer.

Q11 Strategy hint

Substitute different negative number values for x, y and z into the expression.

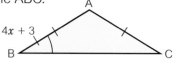

12 Find the value of each expression when $a = \dfrac{1}{2}$ and $b = \dfrac{3}{4}$

a $a^2 - b^2$ **b** $2ab^2$

13 Problem-solving / Reasoning

The diagram shows an isosceles triangle ABC.

a Write an expression for the size of
  i angle BCA
  ii angle BAC.

b Write an equation using the fact that angle BAC = $5(3x - 2)$ and your answer to part **a ii**.

c Solve your equation to find the value of x.

d Work out the sizes of the angles in the triangle. Explain how to check that your answers are correct.

Q13a hint

Angle BAC = 180 − 2 × angle ABC

14 Problem-solving / Reasoning

The diagram shows a kite ABCD.

a Write an expression for the size of
  i angle BCD
  ii angle ADC.

b Write an equation using the fact that angle ADC = $4(2x - 9)$ and your answer to part **a ii**.

c Solve your equation to find the value of x.

d Work out the sizes of the angles in the kite. Explain how to check that your answers are correct.

Q14a hint

What is the total of the angles in a kite?

15 Problem-solving   Here are ages of four friends.

Adrian	Jim	Carl	Rashid
$y + 1$	$2y + 1$	$6y$	$12y + 7$

Twice Jim's age plus Carl's age is the same as Rashid's age take away three times Adrian's age.
Work out the age of each of the four people.

Q15 Strategy hint

Start by using the information given to write an equation that includes brackets.

16 Problem-solving   Ludmilla substitutes $m = -5$ and $n = 3$ into the expression $(2m)^2 + mn - p^2$

She gets an answer of 4.

What value does she use for p?

17 Copy and complete this multiplication pyramid.
Each brick is the product of the bricks below it.

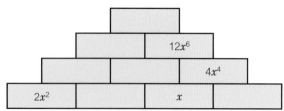

18 Work out

a $w^3 \times w^7 \times w^2$

b $\dfrac{z^8 \times z^4}{z^5}$

c $\dfrac{d^{12}}{d^2 \times d^4}$

d $\dfrac{9s^3 \times 2s^7}{6s^2}$

e $\dfrac{(4b)^3}{(2b)^2 \times (2b)^2}$

f $(n^3)^3 \times (n^2)^2 \times n$

19 Problem-solving The three boxes contain terms involving the letter y.

A $\quad$ $8y^6 \quad 9y^5 \quad 12y^8 \quad 6y^7$

B $\quad$ $6y^3 \quad 10y^6 \quad 8y^9 \quad 12y^5$

C $\quad$ $4y^6 \quad 2y^5 \quad 5y^6 \quad 3y^7$

a Choose one term from each box and simplify $\dfrac{\text{A term} \times \text{B term}}{\text{C term}}$

b Repeat part **a** two more times using different terms each time.

c Which terms from each box will give the answer with the smallest power of y?
What is this answer?

d Which terms from each box will give the answer with the greatest power of y?
What is this answer?

20 Problem-solving In this spider diagram, the six expressions are all equal to the expression in the middle.

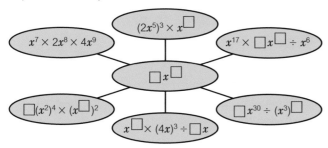

Copy and complete the spider diagram.

21 Problem-solving

a Match each rectangular yellow expression card to the correct circular blue simplified card.

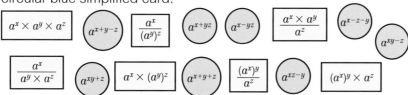

b There is one blue card left over. Write the rectangular yellow expression card that goes with this circular blue card.

Investigation

Reasoning

1 In the expressions below, x can be any positive or negative whole number.
The letters a and b can be any positive whole numbers, with a being greater than b.
Choose values for x, a and b that make these statements true.
a $x^a \times x^b < (x^a)^b$ $\qquad$ **b** $x^a \times x^b > (x^a)^b$
c $x^a \div x^b < (x^a)^b$ $\qquad$ **d** $x^a \div x^b > (x^a)^b$
2 What are the only values of x that you can use to make these statements true?
3 Choose values for a and b to show that these statements are true.
a $x^a \times x^b = (x^a)^b$ $\qquad$ **b** $x^a \div x^b = (x^a)^b$ $\qquad$ **c** $x^a \times x^b = x^a \div x^b$

22 Reflect Which do you find easier: working with expressions, equations or identities?
Explain why.

Reflect

3 Unit test

1 Simplify
  a $12y^2 - 7y^2$
  b $2x + 5x^3 + 3x - 4x^3$
  c $4d^3 - 2 + 3d^3 - 1 + 2d^2$

2 Simplify
  a $x^7 \times x^3$
  b $\dfrac{y^{15}}{y^5}$
  c $(z^2)^5$
  d $m^9 \times m^4 \times m^2$
  e $\dfrac{b^4 \times b^5}{b^2}$

3 Expand
  a $p(p^3 + 2p)$ **b** $2m^2(m - 4)$
  c $2y^2(3y^2 - 2y + 7y^3)$ **d** $3x(8 + 4x - 8x^2)$

4 Expand and simplify
  a $p(8p + 3) + 2p(3p + 5)$ **b** $3v(5v + 2u - 8) + 5v(4 - 2v)$

5 Factorise
  a $2x + 12$
  b $12x - 15$
  c $50 - 20x$

6 Which of these are identities?
  a $3x + 2x + 5 - 2 = 5x + 3$
  b $y + y + y + 6 = 3 + 6y$
  c $2 \times p + 4 \times p - 3 \times 5 = 3(2p - 5)$

7 Show that this identity is true.
  $3y(5y^2 + 4y) + 2y^2(1 + 3y) \equiv 7y^2(3y + 2)$

8 Factorise completely
  a $7y^2 + 28y$
  b $9x - 21x^3$
  c $12w^3 + 20w^2 - 32w$

9 The formula $v^2 - u^2 = 2as$ is used to model a moving object, where u = starting speed (m/s), v = final speed (m/s), a = acceleration (m/s^2) and s = distance travelled (m).
   A car stops at some traffic lights. It then accelerates at 2.3 m/s^2 until it reaches a speed of 13.6 m/s. Find the distance, s, that it has travelled since stopping at the lights. Give your answer correct to 1 decimal place.

10 Find the value of each expression when $x = 6$, $y = -5$ and $z = 8$.
   a $3(z + 2) + 2y$ **b** $4(x - y) - 3(x + y)$

11 Find the value of each expression when $a = 4$, $b = -2$ and $c = 5$.

a $2c^2 + abc$ **b** $a(c + b)^2 - 2a^2$

c $\sqrt{b^2 + 3a}$ **d** $\dfrac{ac - 6b}{a}$

12 Solve $2(x - 5) = 48 - 4(x + 1)$

13 The orange shapes in this diagram have the same area.

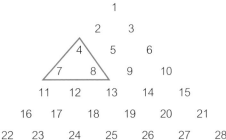

a Work out the value of x.

b What is the area of the orange rectangle?

14 Simplify

a $7y^5 \times 3y^3$ **b** $\dfrac{35b^{10}}{7b^2}$

c $(2g^3)^2$ **d** $\left(\dfrac{q^3}{3}\right)^3$

e $\dfrac{x^5 \times x^3}{x^7}$

Challenge

15 A red triangle is placed over three numbers in this number grid as shown.

```
                    1
               2        3
           4       5        6
         7     8       9        10
       11    12    13     14      15
     16    17    18    19     20     21
   22    23    24    25    26    27    28
```

Using the numbers in the red triangle, this calculation has been done:
top × bottom right − top × bottom left = $4 \times 8 - 4 \times 7 = 32 - 28 = 4$

a Move the red triangle over three different numbers in the grid and do the same calculation. What do you notice?

b Repeat part **a** for three different numbers in the grid.

c The top number in the triangle is in row r. The top number is x.

   i Write expressions for the bottom left and bottom right numbers in terms of x and r. Simplify your expressions.

   ii Compare your simplified expressions to your answers to parts **a** and **b**. What do you notice? Write your findings as a rule.

Q15c hint

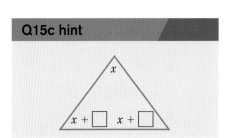

16 Reflect Think back to when you have found it difficult to answer a question in a maths test.

a Write two words that describe how you felt.

b Write two things you could do when you have difficulty answering a question in a maths test.

Q16 hint

Look back at questions in this test or previous tests as a reminder.

Reflect

4.1 Area of triangles, parallelograms and trapezia

You will learn to:
- Derive and use the formula for the area of a triangle and a parallelogram.
- Know and use the formula for the area of a trapezium.

Confidence

Why learn this?
Architects and engineers need to work out the areas of various shapes so that they can design and construct interesting buildings.

Fluency
Work out the missing numbers.
- $\frac{1}{2} \times 8 \times 7 = \square$
- $\frac{1}{2} \times 3 \times 6 = \square$
- $7 \times \square = 35$
- $\frac{1}{2}(5 + 3) \times 10 = \square$

What does perpendicular mean?

Explore
What different shapes can you make from fitting two triangles together?

Exercise 4.1

Warm up

1 Work out the area of each shape.

a 5 cm, 4 cm

b 30 mm, 70 mm

c 30 mm, 6 cm

> **Q1c hint**
> Both sides need to be in the same units.

2 Work out the missing side length for each shape.

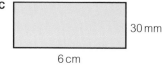

a 6 cm, Area 30 cm²

b 4 cm, Area 16 cm²

c 6 cm, Area 15 cm²

> **Q2 Literacy hint**
> Read 'cm²' as 'square centimetres'.

3 Substitute $a = 4$, $b = 5$ and $c = 2$ into these expressions.

a $\frac{1}{2}ab$ b $(c + b) \times a$ c $\frac{1}{2}(a + b)c$

4 **Reasoning**

a Copy these parallelograms on to centimetre squared paper.
Label them **A** and **B**.

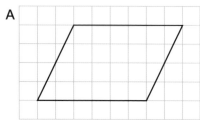

A

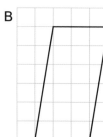

B

Topic links: Using formulae, Properties of 2D shapes

b Find the area of each parallelogram by counting squares.

c Write the measurements for each parallelogram in a table like this.

Parallelogram	Base length (cm)	Perpendicular height (cm)	Area (cm²)
A			

d What do you notice about the relationship between the base length, perpendicular height and area of a parallelogram?

e Copy and complete this formula.
Area of a parallelogram = ...

5 Work out the area of each parallelogram.

a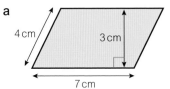

4 cm, 3 cm, 7 cm

b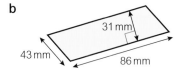

31 mm, 43 mm, 86 mm

6 Work out the missing measurement for each shape.

a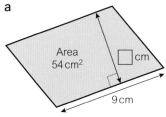

Area 54 cm², ☐ cm, 9 cm

b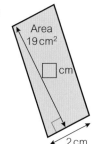

Area 19 cm², ☐ cm, 2 cm

c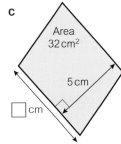

Area 32 cm², 5 cm, ☐ cm

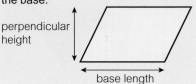

Q4c hint

The **perpendicular height** is the height measured at right angles to the base.

perpendicular height

base length

Key point

Area of a parallelogram
= base length × perpendicular height
= $b \times h$
= bh

The height measurement *must* be perpendicular (at 90°) to the base.

Investigation   Reasoning

1 Copy this parallelogram on to squared paper.
2 Calculate the area of the parallelogram.
3 Split the parallelogram in half to make two triangles.
4 What is the area of one of the triangles?
5 Complete these formulae.
  • Area of a parallelogram = ...
  • Area of a triangle = ...

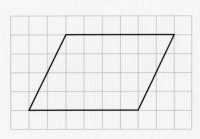

---

7 Work out the area of each triangle.

a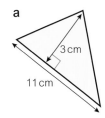

3 cm, 11 cm

b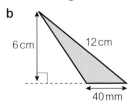

6 cm, 12 cm, 40 mm

c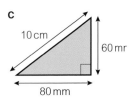

10 cm, 60 mr, 80 mm

Key point

Area of a triangle
= $\frac{1}{2}$ × base length × perpendicular height
= $\frac{1}{2} \times b \times h$
= $\frac{1}{2}bh$

8 Work out the missing measurement for each triangle.

a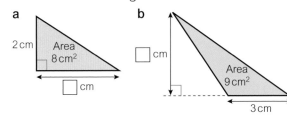

2 cm, Area 8 cm², ☐ cm

b
☐ cm, Area 9 cm², 3 cm

c
Area 7.5 cm², 3 cm, ☐ cm

Q8 hint

Substitute the values you know into the formula
Area = $\frac{1}{2}bh$
Then solve the equation.

Unit 4 2D shapes and 3D solids   70

9 **Real / Problem-solving** Meena is making some bunting.
Each flag is a triangle of height 40 cm and base 25 cm.
She wants to make 12 triangles.
Work out the total area of material that she needs.

Q9 Strategy hint

Sketch the triangle.

10 **Problem-solving** Draw as many right-angled triangles as you can
with an area of 12 cm².
Discussion How will you know when you have drawn them all?

Q10 hint

Use whole number lengths only.

11 **Reasoning** Diagram A shows a trapezium. Diagram B shows two
identical trapeziums put together.

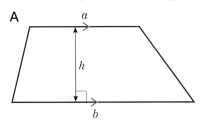

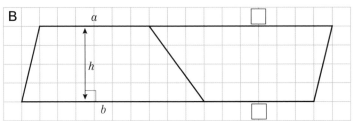

a What letters go in the two empty boxes in diagram B?
b What new shape has been made?
Copy and complete these sentences.
c The length of the base of the parallelogram is ☐ + ☐
d The area of the parallelogram is ☐ × ☐
e The area of one trapezium is ☐

12 Work out the area of each trapezium.

a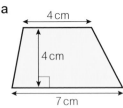

b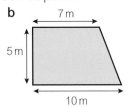

c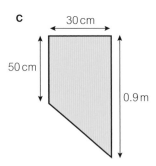

Key point

Area of a trapezium = $\frac{1}{2}(a + b)h$

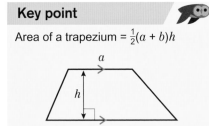

13 **Real / Finance** Car windscreen glass costs £325 per square metre.
Work out the cost of the glass for this car windscreen.

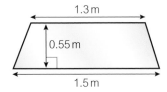

14 **Explore** What different shapes can you make from fitting two triangles together?
What have you learned in this lesson to help you to answer this question?
What other information do you need?

15 **Reflect** After this lesson, Halima says, 'Area is length × width.'
Shazia says, 'The area is the amount of space something takes up.'
Use what you have learned in this lesson to improve Shazia's definition.

*Active*Learn   Homework, Year 8, Unit 4

Explore

Reflect

4.2 Area of compound shapes

You will learn to:
- Calculate the area of compound shapes made from rectangles and triangles.

Why learn this?
Real estate agents need to calculate areas of floor plans when selling properties

Fluency
Work out
- $\frac{1}{2} \times 2 \times 3 + \frac{1}{2} \times 4 \times 3$
- $5 \times 6 - \frac{1}{2} \times 4 \times 3$
- $\frac{1}{2} \times 7 \times 4 - \frac{1}{2} \times 1 \times 8$

Explore
How much does it cost to paint the front of a house?

Exercise 4.2

1 Calculate the area of these triangles.

a
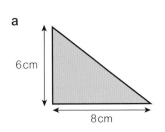
6cm
8cm

b
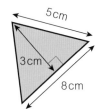
5cm
3cm
8cm

c
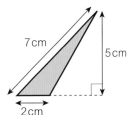
7cm
5cm
2cm

2 Find the total area of each of these compound shapes.

a
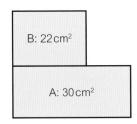
B: 22cm²
A: 30cm²

b
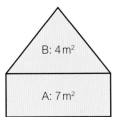
B: 4m²
A: 7m²

c
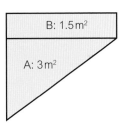
B: 1.5m²
A: 3m²

3 Copy these shapes and split them into triangles and rectangles. Write the height and width of each part.

a
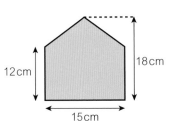
18cm
12cm
15cm

b
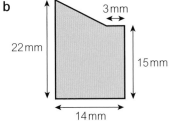
3mm
22mm
15mm
14mm

Rectangle: base = ☐ height = ☐
Triangle: base = ☐ height = ☐

Rectangle: base = ☐ height = ☐
Triangle: base = ☐ height = ☐

Warm up

4 Copy and complete to find the total area of the shape.

Triangle A: base: 32 + 8 = ☐   height: 70 − 42 = ☐

Area of triangle A = $\frac{1}{2}$ × ☐ × ☐ = ☐

Rectangle B: base: ☐ height: ☐

Area of rectangle B = ☐ × ☐ = ☐

Total area = ☐ + ☐ = ☐

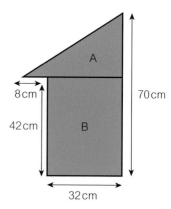

5 Find the total area of the shapes in Q3.

6 Calculate the area of each shape. Give the units with your answer.

a

b

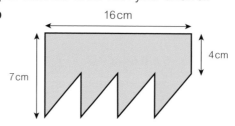

Q5 hint

Find the areas of the rectangle and the triangle first, then add the areas together.

7 Real Samir makes stained glass windows like this.

a What is the area of the window?
Give your answer in square metres.

The stained glass costs $153 per square metre.

b What is the cost of the glass for this window?

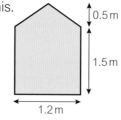

Q7a hint

Split the window into a rectangle and a triangle.

8 Real This is the floor plan of a living room. Calculate the area of the floor.

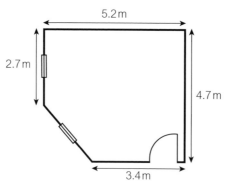

Q8 hint

Split the shape up into two rectangles and one triangle.

9 Problem-solving Find the missing sides of these shapes.

a

b

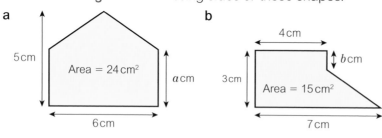

Q9 hint

Try guessing different lengths to see if they work.

10 Problem-solving Work out the shaded area of each shape.

a

b

c

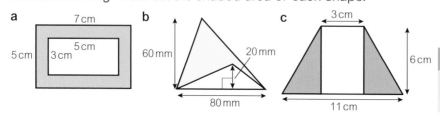

Q10 hint

Shaded area = area of whole shape − area of cut-out shape

11 Real What is the area of plastic used in this shapes stencil?

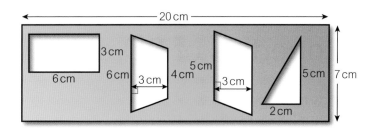

12 Problem-solving/reasoning

a Write an expression for the area of each of the shapes

i

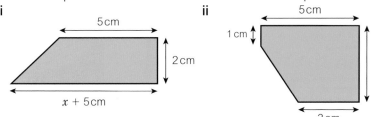

ii

b These two shapes have the same area. Find the value of x and then find the area.

13 Real Here is the front of a house. The wall is painted, but the door and windows are not. The windows are square and are all the same size.

a Calculate the area of the wall

b Paint costs $10 per litre. 1 litre of paint will cover $5\,m^2$. How much will it cost to paint

  i $1\,m^2$

  ii the front of the house?

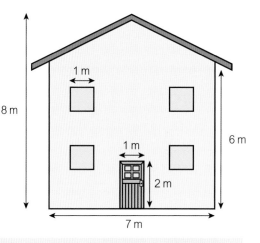

Investigation   **Reasoning**

1 A kite has diagonals of length 4 cm and 6 cm. Split the kite into triangles and find the area.

2 A rhombus has diagonals of length 5 cm each. Find the area.

3 A square has diagonals of length 12 cm each. Find the area.

4 For which quadrilaterals can you use the lengths of the diagonal to find the area? Explain why.

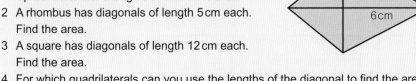

---

14 Explore How much does it cost to paint the front of a house? What have you learned in this lesson to help you to answer this question? What other information do you need to know?

15 Reflect What different strategies did you use in this lesson to find compound areas? How did you decide which strategy to use? Design a shape and ask a classmate to split it up and then work out the total area? What lengths do they need to know before they can work out the area?

Explore

Reflect

4.3 Properties of 3D solids

You will learn to:
- Identify nets of different 3D solids.
- Know the properties of 3D solids.

Why learn this?
People used to think the Earth was flat, but now we know it's a sphere.

Fluency
What are the names of these 2D shapes?

Which of these shapes have parallel sides?

Explore
How could you make a 4-sided dice?

Exercise 4.3

1 Write the names of these 3D solids.

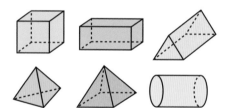

2 Problem-solving
  a Draw each **net** on squared paper and cut them out.

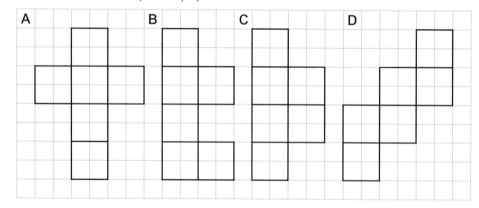

> **Key point**
>
> A **net** is a 2D shape that folds to make a 3D solid.

  b Fold them up.
    Do any of them form a cube?

  Discussion Predict which of **E** and **F** will form a cube.

  c Draw one more net that you think will form a cube.
    Cut it out and check that it works.

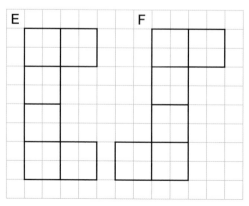

Worked example

Sketch a net of this cuboid.

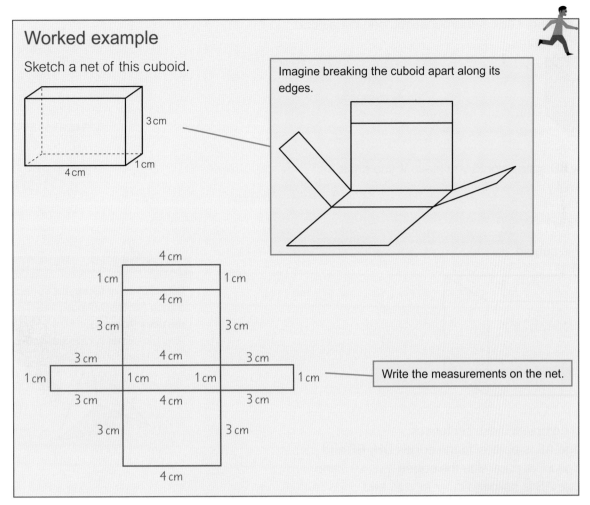

Imagine breaking the cuboid apart along its edges.

Write the measurements on the net.

3 Sketch a net for each cuboid.

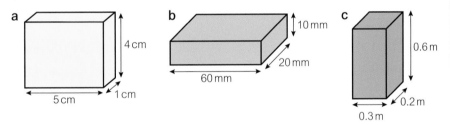

a 4 cm, 5 cm, 1 cm

b 10 mm, 60 mm, 20 mm

c 0.6 m, 0.2 m, 0.3 m

Q3 hint

For a sketch you should use a ruler and a pencil, but you don't need to measure the lengths accurately.

4 Look at these nets.

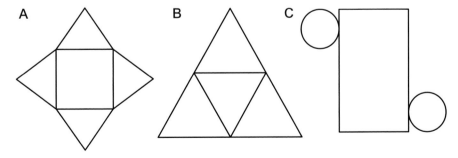

A   B   C

Which one folds to make

a a triangle-based pyramid

b a cylinder

c a square-based pyramid?

Topic links: Properties of 2D shapes, Formulae, Parallel and perpendicular lines

5 Problem-solving Look at this cube. You can cut a cube into two equal parts.

What new 3D solids would you make if you cut it
a horizontally
b vertically
c diagonally?

6 Look at this cuboid.

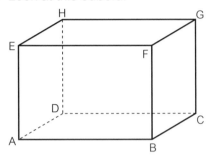

> **Q6 hint**
>
> 3D solids have **faces** (flat surfaces), **edges** (where two faces meet) and **vertices** (corners).
> A single corner is called a **vertex**.
>
>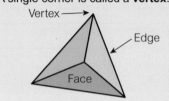

Copy and complete these sentences.
a The edge AE is parallel to the edges DH, BF and ......
b The edge EF is parallel to the edges ......, ... and ....
c The edge AB is perpendicular to .... and ....
d The faces ABCD and .... are parallel.
e The faces ABFE and BCGF meet at edge ....
f If two edges meet, they meet at a ....
g If two faces meet, they meet at an ....

7 Problem-solving This cube needs painting.

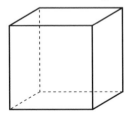

What is the smallest number of colours you must use so that no two faces that touch are the same colour?

8 Explore How could you make a 4-sided dice?
What have you learned in this lesson to help you to answer this question?
What other information do you need?

9 Reflect In Q6 you worked out which solid was being described from the shape of its faces.
Describe two other solids in terms of the shape of their faces.

4.4 Surface area

You will learn to:

- Calculate the surface area of cubes and cuboids.

Why learn this?
Upholsterers use surface area to work out how much fabric they need to cover sofa cushions.

Fluency
Work out
- $6 \times 9 = \square$
- $6 \times \square = 96$
- 5^2
- 3^2

Explore
How many posters can you fit on your bedroom walls and ceiling?

Exercise 4.4

1 Sketch a net for each shape.

a

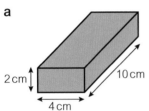

2 cm, 4 cm, 10 cm

b

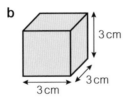

3 cm, 3 cm, 3 cm

2 Work out the area of the shaded face on each shape.

a

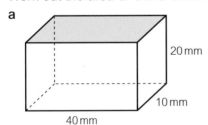

20 mm, 10 mm, 40 mm

b

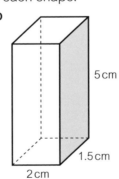

5 cm, 1.5 cm, 2 cm

3 The diagrams show a cube and its net.
Work out the **surface area** of the cube.

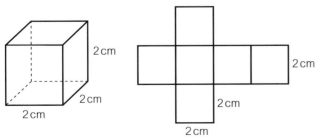

2 cm, 2 cm, 2 cm, 2 cm, 2 cm, 2 cm

Key point

The **surface area** of a 3D solid is the total area of all its faces.

Discussion You may have started by working out the area of one face of the cube. Is there a shortcut for finding the surface area of a cube?

Warm up

4 Work out the surface area of each cube.

a

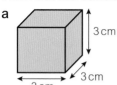

3 cm
3 cm
3 cm

b a 20 mm by 20 mm by 20 mm cube

c a cube with edge length 5 cm.

5 **Reasoning** Here is a cube with edge length n cm.

a What is the area of one face on this cube?

b Write a formula for the surface area of a cube with side n.

c Use your formula from part **b** to calculate the surface area of a cube with side 4 cm.

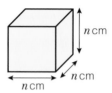

n cm
n cm
n cm

6 Work out the surface area of each cuboid.

a

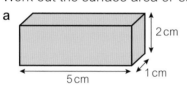

2 cm
5 cm
1 cm

b

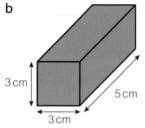

3 cm
5 cm
3 cm

Discussion Is there a shortcut for finding the surface area of a cuboid?

Q6a hint

Sketch a net. Then work out the area of each rectangle and add the areas together.

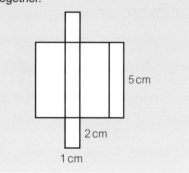

5 cm
2 cm
1 cm

Worked example

Find the surface area of this cuboid.

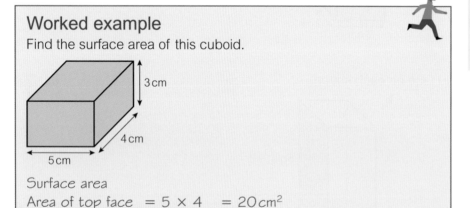

3 cm
4 cm
5 cm

Surface area

Area of top face	= 5 × 4	= 20 cm²
Area of front face	= 3 × 5	= 15 cm²
Area of side face	= 4 × 3	= 12 cm² +
Sum of 3 faces		= 47 cm²
Total surface area	= 2 × 47	= 94 cm²

Each face is part of an identical pair.

7 Work out the surface area of each cuboid.

a

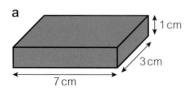

1 cm
3 cm
7 cm

b

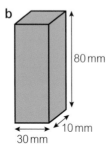

80 mm
10 mm
30 mm

c

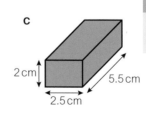

2 cm
2.5 cm
5.5 cm

Q7 hint

Use the same method as in the worked example.

8 Problem-solving A cube has a surface area of $96\,\text{cm}^2$.

  a What is the area of each face?

  b What is the length of one edge?

9 Reasoning Copy and complete using the diagram to help you.

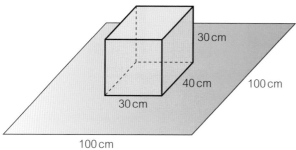

  a The area of the front face is ☐.

  b The area of the top face is ☐.

  c The area of the side face is ☐.

  d The total area of these 3 faces is ☐.

  e The total surface area (all 6 faces) is ☐.

10 Real / Problem-solving Joey wants to wrap a present for his sister.

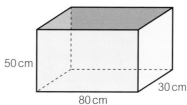

Does he have enough wrapping paper?

Discussion How does the hint help you to answer the question?

> **Q10 hint**
>
> Would a net of this box fit on the wrapping paper?

11 Real / Problem-solving Kevin wants to paint the outside of this toy box. He has enough paint to cover $15\,000\,\text{cm}^2$. Will this be enough?

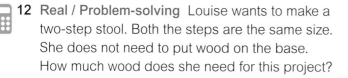

> **Q11 hint**
>
> The box only has 5 faces.

12 Real / Problem-solving Louise wants to make a two-step stool. Both the steps are the same size. She does not need to put wood on the base. How much wood does she need for this project?

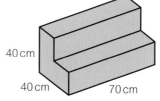

13 Explore How many posters can you fit on your bedroom walls and ceiling?

What you have learned in this lesson to help you to answer this question?

What other information do you need?

14 Reflect This lesson showed you two methods for finding the surface area of a cube or cuboid.

  • Method 1 (draw then add)

Draw a net, write the area of each face on the net and then add them together (Q6)

  • Method 2 (visualise then calculate)

Visualise pairs of opposite faces, calculate the area of each different face, add them together and then double your answer (Q7)

Which method did you prefer? Why?

> **Q14 hint**
>
> What are the advantages and disadvantages of your method?

4.5 Volume

Confidence

You will learn to:
- Calculate the volume of a cube or a cuboid.
- Convert between cm³, m*l* and litres.

Why learn this?
The number of fish that can be put in a fish tank depends on the size (volume) of the tank.

Fluency
What is the area of these shapes?

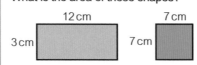

12 cm
3 cm
7 cm
7 cm

Explore
How many fish can you put in a cuboid-shaped tank that measures 50 cm by 40 cm by 80 cm?

Exercise 4.5

Warm up

1 Work out
  a $5 \times 3 \times 8$
  b $6 \times 4 \times 3$
  c $4 \times 2 \times 4$

2 How many 1 cm cubes make up each shape?

  a    **b** 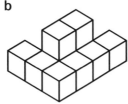   **c**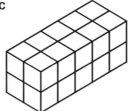

3 a How many 1 cm cubes make up each cube?

  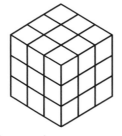

b Work out the first three cube numbers.
  $1^3 = \square$ $2^3 = \square$ $3^3 = \square$
  What do you notice?

4 A cube has a side length of 8 cm.
  What is the **volume** of the cube?

5 Problem-solving A cube has a surface area of 54 cm³.
  a What is the area of one face?
  b What is the length of one side?
  c What is the volume of the cube?

> **Key point**
> The **volume** of a solid shape is the amount of 3D space it takes up.
> The units of volume are cubic units (e.g. mm³, cm³, m³).

> **Key point**
> Volume of a cube
> = side length (*l*) cubed
> = *l*³
>

> **Q5 Strategy hint**
> Sketch a cube.

6 a Count the 1 cm cubes in each cuboid.

A 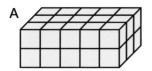   B 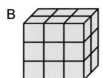   C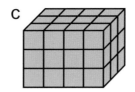

b Copy and complete this table for the cuboids.

Cuboid	Length	Width	Height	Length × width × height
A				

7 a Calculate the volume of each cuboid.

A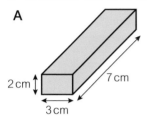
2 cm, 7 cm, 3 cm

B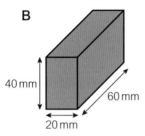
40 mm, 60 mm, 20 mm

C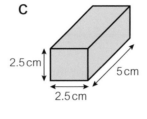
2.5 cm, 5 cm, 2.5 cm

Key point

Volume of a cuboid
= length × width × height
= $l \times w \times h = lwh$

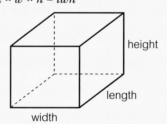
height
length
width

b Reasoning Imagine that the three cuboids are put together.
  i Will the volume of the new shape be the sum of the volumes?
  ii Will the surface area of the new shape be the sum of the surface areas?
Explain your answers.

Investigation   **Reasoning**

Look at this cuboid.

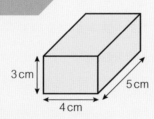
3 cm, 5 cm, 4 cm

1 What is the volume of the cuboid?
2 Write the dimensions of at least three more cuboids with the same volume.
3 Usman says that the cuboid with dimensions $\frac{1}{2}$ cm by 12 cm by 10 cm has the same volume as this cuboid.
   Is he right?
Discussion Are there more cuboids with the same volume?

---

8 Copy and complete these conversions.
   a 0.45 litres = ☐ cm³
   b 6.3 cm³ = ☐ ml
   c ☐ litres = 7346 cm³

Key point

The **capacity** of a container is how much it can hold. The units of capacity are cm³, millilitres (ml) and litres (l).
• 1 millilitre (ml) = 1 cm³
• 1 litre (l) = 1000 cm³

9 Real / Reasoning For a long-distance camping trip, students need a rucksack that has a **capacity** of at least 65 litres.
   Peter buys a rucksack measuring 34 cm by 26 cm by 75 cm.
   a Work out the capacity in cm³.
   b Work out the capacity in litres.
   c Is Peter's rucksack big enough?

---

10 Problem-solving The volume of this cuboid is 168 cm³.
Find the missing length.

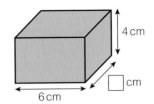

11 Problem-solving
A 3 cm by 3 cm by 3 cm cube
has a 1 cm by 1 cm square
hole cut through it.
What is the volume of the
remaining solid?

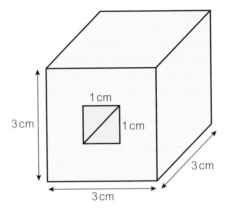

Q11 hint

What is the volume of the piece cut
out of the cube?

12 Problem-solving Here are the areas of three faces of the same cuboid.

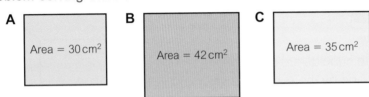

A Area = 30 cm² **B** Area = 42 cm² **C** Area = 35 cm²

   a What are the dimensions of each rectangle?
   b What is the volume of the cuboid?
   c What is the surface area of the cuboid?

13 Explore How many fish can you put in a cuboid-shaped tank that
measures 50 cm by 40 cm by 80 cm?
Is it easier to explore this question now that you have completed the
lesson?
What further information do you need to be able to answer this?

14 Reflect Maths is not the only subject where you use volume.
You use it in science too.
Describe how you have used volume in science.
In what ways is volume the same or different in science as in this
maths lesson?
Do you think volume means the same in all subjects?
Explain your answer.

4.6 STEM: Measures of area and volume

You will learn to:
• Convert between metric measures for area and volume.

Why learn this?
Ecologists use measures of area and volume when studying plants and animals in hedgerows.

Fluency
How many m² are the same as one hectare?
Multiply each number by 100
• 7
• 7.5
• 7.53

Explore
How much land is needed to support a herd of deer?

Exercise 4.6: Ecology

1 Work out
  a 2.5 × 10 × 10
  c 450 ÷ 10 ÷ 10
  b 0.04 × 100 × 100
  d 9045 ÷ 100 ÷ 100

2 Work out the missing numbers.
  a 2 × □ = 20 000   **b** 760 ÷ □ = 7.6   **c** □ ÷ 100 = 0.03

3 Which unit of area would be sensible for measuring
  a the area of a school pond
  b the area of Scotland
  c the area of an oak leaf?

> **Key point**
>
> It is important to be able to choose the most suitable metric units for measuring. Some of the metric units that you already know are
> • mm, cm, m, km (length)
> • mm², cm², m², km², hectares (area)

 4 **STEM / Modelling** A conservation trust has been given a 5.3 **hectare** piece of land. It plans to use 18 750 m² for woodland and 28 125 m² for a wildlife meadow.
  a Is the area they have been given big enough for their planned use?
  b They estimate that they will need 2.4 m × 5 m sections for every 10 oak seedlings they plant. How many seedlings can they plant?
  Discussion Is this a good model for working out the number of trees? Will they need any other space in the woodland?

> **Q4 hint**
> A **hectare** is 10 000 m². Convert km to m and then m² to hectares.

 5 **Real** A rectangular reservoir measures 1.2 km by 1.6 km. How many hectares is this?

6 Copy and complete these conversions.
  a 4 cm² = □ mm²   **b** □ cm² = 0.58 m²
  c 17 000 m² = □ km²   **d** □ m² = 3.5 km²

> **Q6a hint**
>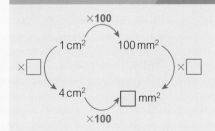

7 a i Work out the area of this rectangle in cm².
   ii Convert the area to mm².
   b Convert the lengths to mm and work out the area in mm².
   Discussion Which method was easier, the one in part **a** or part **b**?

11.2 cm

36 cm

Topic links: Powers of 10

Subject links: Science (Q3, Q4, Q8, Q11)

84

8 STEM / Problem-solving Ann is surveying the plants growing in some wasteland (unused land), measuring 7.5 m by 3.2 m. She places **quadrats** at random within the survey area. Each quadrat is a 50 cm × 50 cm square.

  a What is the maximum number of quadrats that would fit?

  b She **samples** the plants in 12 quadrats randomly.
    What proportion of the wasteland has she sampled?

9 a These cubes are the same size.
    Copy the diagrams and write in the measurements.

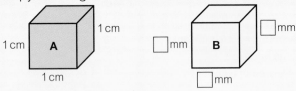

  b Find the volume of
    i A in cm³   **ii** B in mm³

  c Copy and complete these sentences.
    i To convert from cm³ to mm³ .... by ☐
    ii To convert from mm³ to cm³ .... by ☐

  d These cubes are also the same size. Copy the diagrams and write in the measurements.

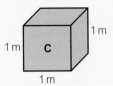 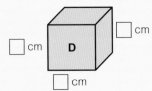

  e Find the volume of
    i C in m³   **ii** D in cm³

  f Copy and complete these sentences.
    i To convert from m³ to cm³ .... by ☐
    ii To convert from cm³ to m³ .... by ☐

10 Copy and complete these conversions.
  a 8 cm³ = ☐ mm³   **b** ☐ cm³ = 95 mm³
  c 73.4 m³ = ☐ cm³   **d** ☐ m³ = 250 000 cm³

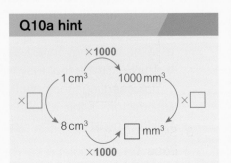
11 STEM / Problem-solving Earthworms have been called 'ecosystem engineers'. They improve soil structure and help to release important nutrients for growing plants.
Fred reads that healthy soil should have 5600 earthworms per cubic metre. He finds 40 earthworms in a 20 cm × 20 cm × 20 cm sample.
Is his sample of soil healthy? Explain your answer.

12 Explore How much land is needed to support a herd of deer?
What have you learned in this lesson to help you to answer this question?
What other information do you need?

13 Reflect Jan says, '1 cm is 10 mm so 1 cm² is 10 mm².'
Choose two questions from this lesson that will help Jan to understand her mistake.
Using your knowledge from the previous two lessons, draw a diagram or write an explanation to show Jan how many mm³ are equal to 1 litre.

4.7 Plans and elevations

You will learn to:
- Use 2D representations of 3D solids.

Why learn this?
Architects create drawings to show the side and front views of planned new buildings.

Fluency
Draw accurately
- a square with side length 3 cm
- an isosceles triangle with base length 4 cm and height 5 cm
- this circle.

5 cm

Explore
What would some famous landmarks look like if photographed from above?

Exercise 4.7

1 For each diagram, name
  i the shapes of the faces
  ii the solid.

a   **b**   **c**   **d**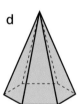

Q1a hint

4 ....

1 square

2 What 3D solid does each net make?

a 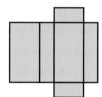 **b**   **c**

3 Sketch a net for each solid.
Label the lengths.

a
2 cm, 2 cm, 2 cm, 2 cm

b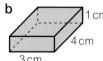
1 cm, 4 cm, 3 cm

c
6 cm, 4 cm, 4 cm

d
6 cm, 7 cm

Warm up

4 Here are two views of the same cuboid.
The second is drawn on isometric paper.

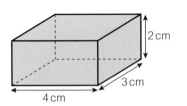 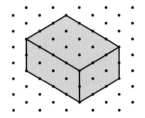

Q4 hint

Use a ruler and start with a vertical edge of the cuboid.
On isometric paper, the distance between two adjacent (neighbouring) dots represents 1 cm.

Draw these solids on isometric paper.

a 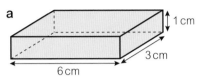 **b** 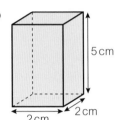 **c**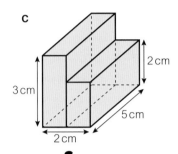

Worked example

Draw the **plan**, the **front elevation** and the **side elevation** of this cuboid on squared paper.

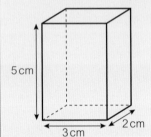

Use a ruler.
Measure accurately.
Label the lengths.

Plan	Front	Side
3 cm (2 cm)	5 cm (3 cm)	5 cm (2 cm)

Key point

The **plan** is the view from above the object.
The **front elevation** is the view of the front of the object.
The **side elevation** is the view of the side of the object.

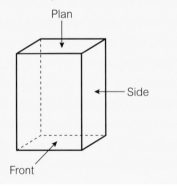

5 Draw the plan, the front elevation and the side elevation of each solid on squared paper.

a 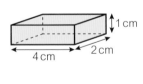 **b** 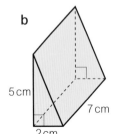 **c**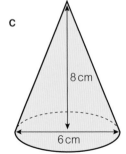

Q5c hint

Draw a circle using a pair of compasses.

6 These solids are made from centimetre cubes.
Draw the plan, front elevation and side elevation of each solid on squared paper.

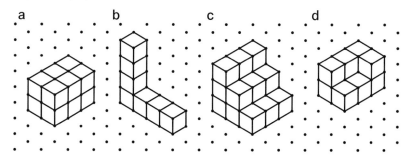

Discussion What do you notice about your answers to parts **a** and **d**?
Why does this happen?

7 Problem-solving Here are the plan, front and side elevations of an irregular 3D solid.
Use cubes to make the solid.
Then draw it on isometric paper.

Plan   Front   Side

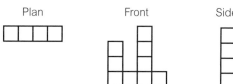

8 Here are the plan views of some solids.
What could each one be?

a   b   c   d

Discussion Is there more than one answer?

9 Problem-solving Here is the side elevation of a 3D solid.
Sketch three possible 3D solids it could belong to.

10 This cube is 'cut' in different ways along the red line.
For each cut in parts **a** and **d**, what is the name of
i the 2D shape of the new faces?
ii the new 3D solid(s) created?

a 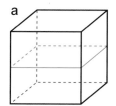   b 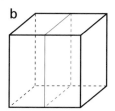   c 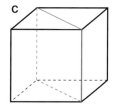   d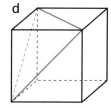

11 Explore What would some famous landmarks look like if photographed from above?
Look back at the maths you have learned in this lesson.
How can you use it to answer this question?

12 Reflect Look back at Q6.
Draw the plan, front and side elevations for a unique solid shape.
Is it possible to draw two distinct solids that look the same on isometric paper?

Q12 Literacy hint

Unique means that there can't be a different solid with the same plan, front and side elevations.
Distinct means different.

4.8 Solving problems with 3D solids and measures

You will learn to:
* Solve problems involving area, surface area and volume.
* Solve problems in everyday contexts involving measure.

Why learn this?
Builders need to calculate the amount of materials needed to create buildings.

Fluency
Write down the formula for the
* area of a parallelogram
* volume of a cube
* surface area of a cuboid.

Explore
How much wrapping paper is needed to wrap a present?

Exercise 4.8

1 Calculate the area of each shape.

a

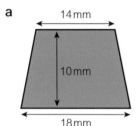

14 mm
10 mm
18 mm

b

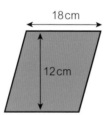

18 cm
12 cm

2 Calculate the volume of this cuboid.

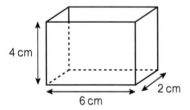

4 cm
6 cm
2 cm

3 **Problem-solving** A medicine bottle says, 'Take two 5 ml spoonfuls four times a day.'
The bottle contains 0.15 litres. Sara has to take the medicine for 4 days.
Is there enough medicine in the bottle? Explain your answer.

4 The mass of a new-born elephant is 5% of the mass of an adult female elephant.
The average mass of an adult female elephant is 3 **tonnes**.
What is the average mass in kilograms of a new-born elephant?

Key point

Mass: 1 **tonne** (t) = 1000 kg

89

5 Joe is using his calculator to solve some problems. Which value, A, B or C, should he enter for each measure?

    a 2 m 4 cm (in metres)   **A** 2.4   **B** 2.04   **C** 2.004
    b 5 kg 250 g (in kilograms)   **A** 5.25   **B** 5.025   **C** 5.0025
    c 950 m*l* (in litres)   **A** 9.5   **B** 0.95   **C** 0.095

6 An Olympic swimming pool has a length of 50 m, a width of 25 m and a depth of 2 m.
    a Write the dimensions of the pool in centimetres.
    b Work out the **capacity** of the pool in litres.

Q6b hint

$V = lwh$

7 Find the volume of this shape.

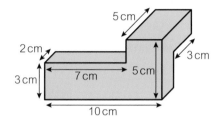

Q7 hint

Split the shape into two cuboids.

Investigation   **Problem-solving**

Each box of Akmal's Sweets contains 50 cm³ of sweets, plus about 10% air.
Here are three designs for the box.

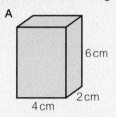 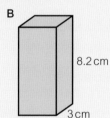 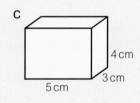

Which design is the most suitable? Why?
Work out the side length, to one decimal place, of a cube-shaped box that has the correct volume.
Work out the dimensions of two more boxes with the correct volume.

---

8 Problem-solving A cube has volume 27 cm³. What is the length of the cube?

9 Problem-solving A cuboid has a length of 3.6 m and a width of 2.5 m. Its volume is 37.8 m³. Work out the surface area of the cuboid.

Q9 hint

Use the volume to work out the height of the cuboid first.

10 Problem-solving The diagram shows the dimensions of a dice.

Q10 hint

Start by working out how many dice will fit along the length of the box.

A box has dimensions 12 cm by 10 cm by 8 cm.
How many dice will the box hold?

11 Problem-solving The diagram shows the dimensions of a water tank.

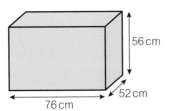

56 cm

52 cm

76 cm

Alex puts water in the tank so that it is three quarters full.
What volume of water is in the tank?
Discussion In how many different ways can you work out the volume of a water tank that is three quarters full?

12 Real A box containing a toy has height 10 cm, width 28 cm and length 38 cm.
  a Draw a net of the box.
  b Wrapping paper is 70 cm wide. What length of wrapping paper is needed if there is
    i no overlap (no extra amount)
    ii an overlap of 3 cm?

Q12b hint

Use the net to help position the box on the wrapping paper and calculate the length.

Investigation

Problem-solving

 The width of a cuboid is twice its height. Its length is three times its height. The surface area of the cuboid is 352 cm². What is its height?

13 Problem-solving Three cuboids of the same length are placed on top of each other.
Calculate the volume of the solid that is formed.

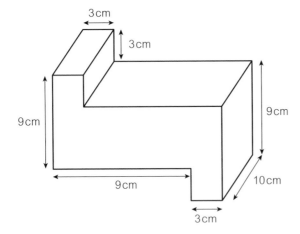

3 cm

3 cm

9 cm

9 cm

9 cm

10 cm

3 cm

14 Explore How much wrapping paper do you need to wrap a present? What have you learned in this lesson to help you to answer this question? What other information do you need to know?

15 Reflect You have learned lots of different formulae and methods for measures, area, surface area and volume. How can you remember them? Share with a friend any tips or strategies you have used to help you to remember them.

Explore

Reflect

4 Check up

Area of 2D shapes

1 Work out the area of this triangle.

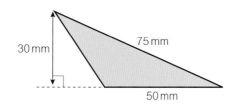

2 Work out the area of each shape.

a

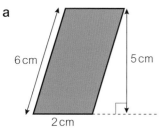

b

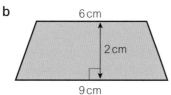

3 The diagram shows the dimensions of a badge. What is the total area of the badge?

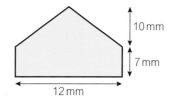

3D solids

4 Work out the surface area of this cuboid.

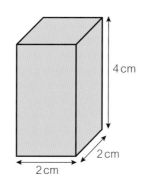

5 Sketch a net of this 3D solid.

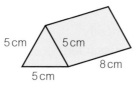

6 Calculate the volume of each of these solids.

a

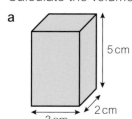

b

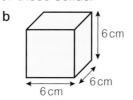

7 Calculate the volume of this solid.

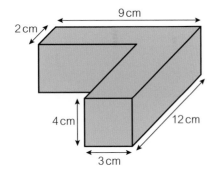

8

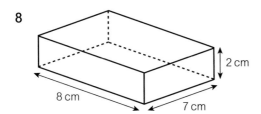

   a Draw this cuboid on isometric paper.

   b Draw the front elevation, side elevation and plan view of the cuboid.

Measures of area, volume and capacity

9 Work out the area of this rectangle in mm².

   3 cm   6 cm

10 Copy and complete these conversions.

   a $6 \, cm^2 = \square \, mm^2$ **b** $0.9 \, cm^2 = \square \, mm^2$

   c $350 \, mm^2 = \square \, cm^2$ **d** $3 \, m^2 = \square \, cm^2$

   e $5.02 \, m^2 = \square \, cm^2$ **f** $2590 \, cm^2 = \square \, m^2$

11 Copy and complete these conversions.

   a $18 \, cm^3 = \square \, mm^3$ **b** $\square \, cm^3 = 265 \, mm^3$

   c $0.7 \, m^3 = \square \, cm^3$ **d** $\square \, m^3 = 931\,000 \, cm^3$

   e $42 \, m^3 = \square \, ml$ **f** $3 \, litres = \square \, cm^3$

12 **Real** An Olympic-size swimming pool measures 50 m by 25 m and has a depth of 3 m.

   a Calculate the volume of the pool in

      i m^3 **ii** cm^3

   b How many litres of water can the pool hold?

13 **How sure are you of your answers? Were you mostly**

   😟 **Just guessing**   😐 **Feeling doubtful**   🙂 **Confident**

   What next? Use your results to decide whether to strengthen or extend your learning.

Challenge

14 A 2D shape has an area of $10 \, cm^2$.

   Sketch and label the lengths of a possible

   a triangle   **b** rectangle

   c parallelogram   **d** trapezium.

4 Strengthen

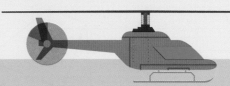

You will:
- Strengthen your understanding with practice.

Area of 2D shapes

1 For each pair of shapes, find the area of the rectangle and the area of the triangle.

a

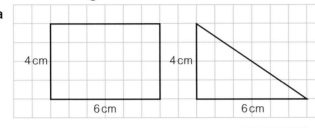

b

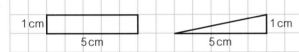

2 a For each triangle write
   i base length = ☐ cm
   ii perpendicular height = ☐ cm

A
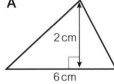

B
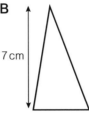

C
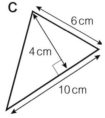

> **Q2 hint**
>
> Area of a triangle
> = $\frac{1}{2}$ × base length × perpendicular height

b Work out the area of each triangle.

3 Calculate the area of each parallelogram.

a
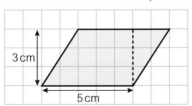

b
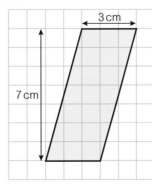

> **Q3a hint**
>
> Imagine making the parallelogram into a rectangle by moving part of the shape to the other side.
>
>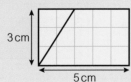

4 Sketch these trapezia.

a  b 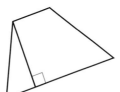 c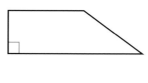

Label the parallel sides a and b and the perpendicular height h.

Q4a hint

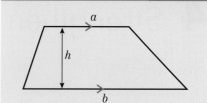

5 Copy and complete the working to find the area of this trapezium.

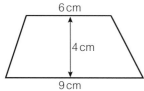

Area $= \frac{1}{2}(a + b)h$

$\quad = \frac{1}{2} \times (\square + \square) \times \square$

$\quad = \frac{1}{2} \times \square \times \square$

$\quad = \square\,cm^2$

$a = 6$
$h = 4$
$b = 9$

6 Find the area of each trapezium.

a 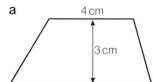 b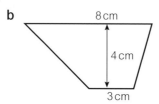

Q6 hint

Use the method in Q5.

7 Work out the area of this shape.
The working has been started for you.

area of rectangle = length × width

$\quad = 9 \times \square$

$\quad = \square\,cm^2$

area of triangle $= \frac{1}{2} \times$ base × height

$\quad = \frac{1}{2} \times 9 \times \square$

$\quad = \square\,cm^2$

total area = area of rectangle + area of triangle

$\quad = \square + \square$

$\quad = \square\,cm^2$

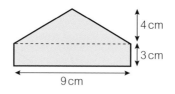

8 Work out the area of each compound shape.

a 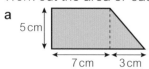 b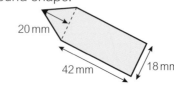

Q8a Strategy hint

Split the shape into a rectangle and a triangle.

3D solids

1 Which of these nets will fold to make a closed cube?

A   B   C

Q1 Strategy hint

Draw the shapes and cut them out.
Try to fold each one into a cube.

2 a Look at this cuboid.
Choose the correct words to make
these sentences true.

back   left-hand side   bottom

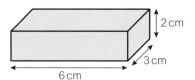

  i The area of the top face is the same
as the area of the .... face.

  ii The area of the front face is the same
as the area of the .... face.

  iii The area of the right-hand side face is the same as
the area of the .... face.

b Copy and complete the table to find the
surface area of the cuboid.

Face	Area
Top	□ × 5 = □ cm²
Bottom	
Front	3 × □ = □ cm²
Back	
Right	□ × 3 = □ cm²
Left	
Total surface area	

3 Work out the surface area of this cuboid.

Q3 hint

Use a table.

4 These cuboids are made from 1 cm cubes.

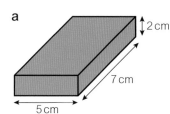 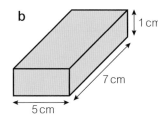 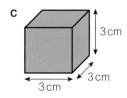

a For each cuboid write l = □ cm, w = □ cm, h = □ cm.
b Find the volume of each cuboid.
c Check your answers by counting the cubes.

Q4b hint

Volume of a cuboid
= length × width × height
= $l × w × h$ = □ cm³

5 Calculate the volume of each cuboid.

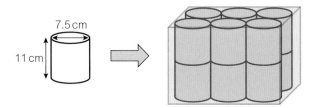

a   **b**   **c**

6 Real / Problem-solving A box holds 12 tins of baked beans
as shown.

a Work out the surface area of cardboard needed to make the box.
b What is the volume of the box?

Q6 hint

Use the dimensions of the tin to work
out the length, width and height of the
box, then work out the surface area
of the box.

Measures of area, volume and capacity

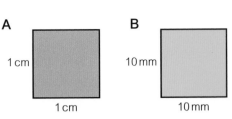
A   B

1 These squares are the same size.
   a Work out the area of each square.
   b Copy and complete this number line for converting cm² to mm².

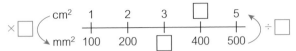

2 Work out the area of each shape in cm². Then convert it to mm².

   a
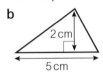
3 cm ... 4 cm

   b
2 cm, 5 cm

Q2 hint

Use your number line from Q1 to help you.

3 Work out each area in mm². Then convert it to cm².

   a 40 mm, 40 mm

   b 20 mm, 60 mm, 35 mm

4 These squares are the same size.
   a Work out the area of each square.
   b Copy and complete this number line for converting m² to cm² areas.

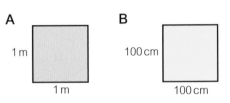
A   B

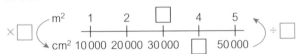

5 Copy and complete these conversions.
   a $2.05 \, \text{m}^2 = 2.05 \times \square = \square \, \text{cm}^2$ **b** $0.07 \, \text{m}^2 = \square \, \text{cm}^2$
   c $\square \, \text{m}^2 = 8600 \, \text{cm}^2$

6 Copy and complete these conversions.
   a   **i** $6 \, \text{cm}^3 = \square \, \text{mm}^3$ **ii** $0.012 \, \text{cm}^3 = \square \, \text{mm}^3$
       iii $\square \, \text{cm}^3 = 15800 \, \text{mm}^3$
   b   **i** $0.04 \, \text{m}^3 = \square \, \text{cm}^3$ **ii** $12.7 \, \text{m}^3 = \square \, \text{cm}^3$
       iii $\square \, \text{m}^3 = 1.4 \text{ million cm}^3$

Q7 hint

Use your number line from Q6 to help. Draw a similar one for converting cm³ to m³.

Enrichment

1 **Problem-solving** Jo wants to grow vegetables.
   She buys 16 raised beds measuring 1 m by 4 m by 0.5 m.
   a Calculate the volume of one raised bed.
   b Write its dimensions in centimetres.
   c Calculate the volume in cubic centimetres.
   A 40-litre bag of soil costs £2.50.
   d How many 40-litre bags of soil will Jo need for each raised bed?
   e How much will soil cost for one raised bed?
   f How much will she spend on soil in total?

Q1 hint

1 litre = 1000 cm³

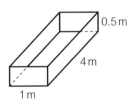

2 **Reflect** In this unit you have covered lots of different topics:
   A Area   **B** Surface area   **C** Volume   **D** Measures
   Write down something you understand from each of the topics and
   something you want to understand better. What learning strategies
   can you use to help you to understand more?

Reflect

4 Extend

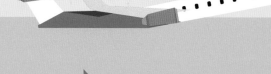

You will:
- Extend your understanding with problem-solving.

 1 A cube has a total surface area of $8.64\,\text{cm}^2$. Work out
　　a the area of one face of the cube
　　b the side length of the cube.

Q1a hint

A cube has six identical faces.

2 **Problem-solving** The diagram shows
two cubes.
The side length of the larger cube is
$4\,\text{cm}$.
The ratio of their surface areas is 1 : 4.
Work out
　　a the surface area of the smaller cube
　　b the side length of the smaller cube.

Q2a Strategy hint

Work out the surface area of the larger cube first.

3 **Problem-solving** A red cuboid has length $6\,\text{cm}$, width $3\,\text{cm}$ and
height $2\,\text{cm}$.
A blue cuboid has length $8\,\text{cm}$ and width $2\,\text{cm}$.
The red and blue cuboids have the same
surface area.
Work out the height of the blue cuboid.

Q3 Strategy hint

Draw a sketch of each cuboid and label the missing height h. Then work out the surface area of the red cuboid.

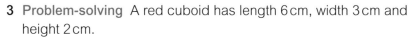

 4 **Problem-solving** The diagram shows a square
company logo.
Work out the area of blue in the logo.

Q4 hint

Work out the area of the square and the area of the trapezium.

 5 **Reasoning** The diagram shows a trapezium.
Dave says, 'If I double the height of the
trapezium, the area of the trapezium will
also double.'
Is he correct? Explain how you worked out
your answer.

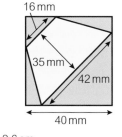

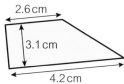

6 **Reasoning** Carmen says, 'If I double the length of one of the parallel
sides of a trapezium, but keep the other parallel side and the height
the same, the area of the trapezium will also be doubled.'
Show, using a counter example, that she is wrong.

Q6 Literacy hint

A counter example is one example that proves the statement is wrong.

Q6 Strategy hint

Draw your own trapezium to test Caroline's statement.

7 **Problem-solving** This trapezium and this parallelogram have the
same area.

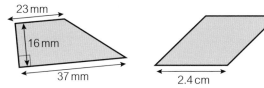

What is the perpendicular height of the parallelogram?

Q7 Strategy hint

Make sure all measurements are in the same units.

8 Write an expression for the area of each parallelogram. Write each answer in its simplest form.

a
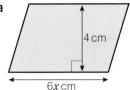
4 cm
6x cm

b
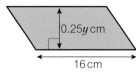
0.25y cm
16 cm

9 a Work out the area of A and B.

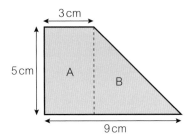
3 cm
5 cm
A
B
9 cm

b What is the total area?

c How else could you have worked out the total area?

10 Work out the shaded area of each shape.

a
7 cm
14 cm

b
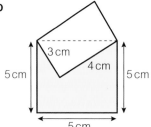
3 cm
5 cm
4 cm
5 cm
5 cm

c
4 cm
2 cm 2 cm
10 cm
8 cm

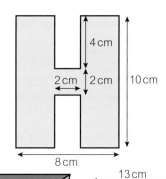
13 cm
8 cm
7 cm

Bowl   **Side**

11 **Problem-solving** The diagram shows a foldaway camping bowl. It has four sides in the shape of congruent trapezia. The bottom of the bowl is a square. Work out the total surface area of the bowl.

 12 **Problem-solving** A water container is in the shape of a cuboid. It has length 1.5 m, width 0.7 m and height 0.8 m.
a Write the dimensions of the trough in centimetres.
Water is put into the trough. The depth of the water is three quarters of the height of the trough.
b Work out the volume of the water in the trough in cm³.
c Work out the capacity of the water in the trough in litres.

 13 **Finance / Problem-solving** Ghadif has an oil tank that is approximately in the shape of a cuboid.
It has length 1.8 m, width 80 cm and height 90 cm. It contains oil to a depth of 25 cm.
a Can he fit 1000 litres more oil into his tank? Explain your answer.
Ghadif orders oil to fill his tank to 90% capacity.
b How much oil does he order to the nearest litre?
The price of oil is 69.8p per litre if you order 1000 litres or more, and 70.2p per litre if you order less than 1000 litres.
c How much does he pay for this oil?
Give your answer in pounds to the nearest penny.

Q13a Strategy hint
Draw a diagram to help you.

14 A cuboid has length 8 cm.
The width of the cuboid is three quarters of its length. The height of the cuboid is 30% of its length.
Work out the surface area of the cuboid.

15 **Problem-solving** A cuboid has length, width and height in the ratio 4 : 5 : 3. The total of the length, width and height is 96 mm.
Work out the surface area of the cuboid.

Q15 Strategy hint

Work out the length, width and height of the cuboid first, by sharing 96 mm in the ratio 4 : 5 : 3.

 16 **Problem-solving** This cube and cuboid have the same volume.
Work out the side length of the cube.
Give your answer to the nearest millimetre.

 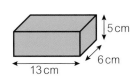

17 **Problem-solving** A gold bar is in the shape of a cuboid with length 150 mm, width 45 mm and height 45 mm.
The bar is melted and made into cubes with side length 12 mm.
How many cubes of gold can be made from the cuboid?

Q17 hint

The answer must be the largest whole number you can make.

18 **Problem-solving** A tap drips every second into a square sink 40 cm wide and 17 cm deep.
30 drips have a volume of 10 m*l*.
With the plug in, how long will it be before the sink overflows?
Give your answer in hours and minutes.

Q18 hint

Start by working out the capacity of the sink.
Use 1 cm³ = 1 m*l*.

Investigation   Real / Reasoning

These boxes have the same volume.

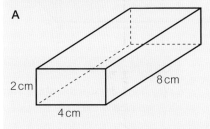 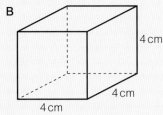 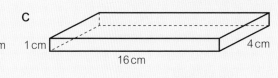

1 Do they all have the same surface area?
2 You run a packaging company. Which box would you choose and why?
3 Here are the dimensions of three more boxes with the same volume.
    2 cm by 24 cm by 3 cm   6 cm by 6 cm by 6 cm   4 cm by 9 cm by 6 cm
Which box do you think would have the smallest surface area?

19 **Reasoning** Look at this cuboid.

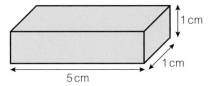

a Calculate the volume of the cuboid.
b Calculate the surface area of the cuboid.
c Jamal has six of these cuboids.
How can he put them together to make a cuboid with
    i the smallest surface area
    ii the largest surface area?

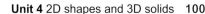

20 Calculate the volume of each solid.

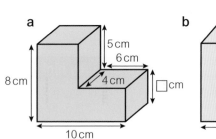

a

8 cm
5 cm
6 cm
4 cm
☐ cm
10 cm

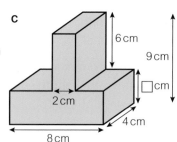

b

3 cm 3 cm
6 cm
☐ cm 2 cm
4 cm
9 cm

c

6 cm
9 cm
☐ cm
2 cm
8 cm
4 cm

Q20 hint

First calculate any missing lengths. Then divide the shape into cuboids and work out the volume of each cuboid separately.

21 The diagram shows the front, side and plan views of a shape.
Draw an isometric diagram of the shape.

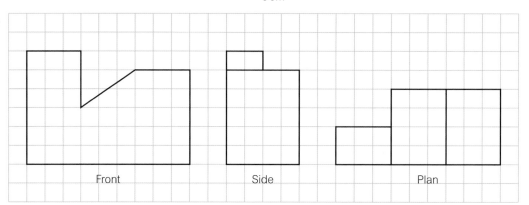

Front   Side   Plan

22 The diagram shows a shape made from cuboids.
Find the total surface area of the shape. The working has been started for you.

Base cuboid
area front and back = ☐ cm²
area right and left ends = ☐ cm²
area bottom = ☐ cm²
area top = 9 × ☐ + 3 × ☐ = ☐ cm²

Top cuboid
area front and back = ☐ cm²
area right and left ends = ☐ cm²
area top = ☐ cm²
total surface area = ☐ cm²

Discussion How else could you work out the total surface area of this shape?

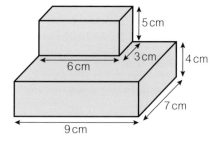

5 cm
6 cm
3 cm
4 cm
7 cm
9 cm

Q22 hint

Why don't you use the whole area of the top face in the base cuboid?

23 Calculate the surface area of each 3D solid.

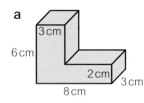

a

3 cm
6 cm
2 cm
3 cm
8 cm

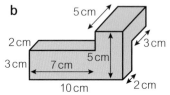

b

5 cm
2 cm
3 cm
5 cm
7 cm
3 cm
10 cm
2 cm

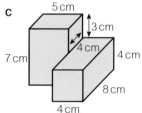

c

5 cm
3 cm
4 cm
7 cm
4 cm
8 cm
4 cm

24 **Problem-solving** The blue triangle has an area of 3.6 cm².
The area of the green triangle is 40% of the area of the blue triangle.
Work out the height of the green triangle.

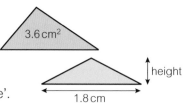

3.6 cm²

height

1.8 cm

25 **Reflect** Look back at Q6. It asked you for a 'counter example'.
What did this counter example show about Carmen's statement?
In what sort of situation might you need to prove that a statement is untrue? Could you use a counter example? Explain.

Reflect

4 Unit test

1 For this cuboid:

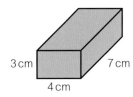

   a Work out the volume.

   b Work out the surface area.

   c Draw the cuboid on isometric paper.

   d Draw the front elevation, side elevation and plan view.

2 Work out the area of each shape.

   a

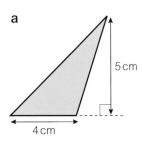

   b

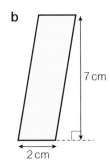

3 Work out the area of each shape.

   a A parallelogram

   b A trapezium.

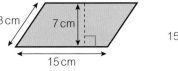
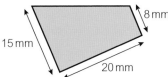

4 Work out the area of this shape.

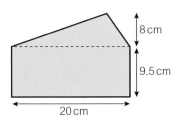

5 Calculate the shaded area of each shape.

   a

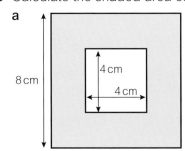

   b

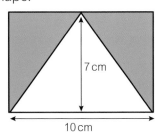

6 These two triangles have the same area.

   a Work out the area of the green triangle.

   b Work out the height of the blue triangle.

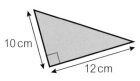
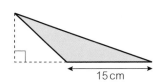

7 Work out the volume of this solid.

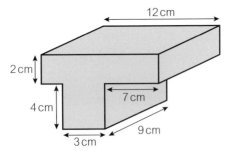

8 Copy and complete these conversions.
  a $4.3\,m^3 = \square\,cm^3$ **b** $\square\,cm^3 = 8500\,mm^3$
  c $540\,ml = \square\,cm^3$

9 An open gift box is a cuboid. It has length 18.5 cm, width 9.4 cm and height 6.2 cm.
  Work out the area of cardboard needed to make the open box.

10 Work out the area of this shape in square centimetres.

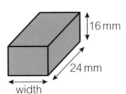

11 The diagram shows a cuboid with volume 5760 mm³.
  Work out the width of the cuboid.

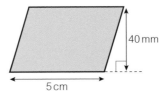

Challenge

12 The box for a wireless router measures 12 cm by 7.5 cm by 8 cm.
Boxes of wireless routers are packed into a larger box for transportation.
The larger box measures 98 cm by 32 cm by 40 cm.

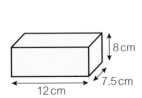

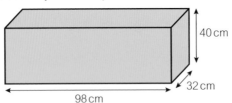

  a What is the greatest number of wireless router boxes that will fit into the larger box?
  b What volume of empty space will be left in the box?
  c Work out the dimensions of a box that will hold 60 wireless router boxes with no wasted space.

13 Reflect Write a heading, 'Five important things about area and volume'.
  Now look back at the work you have done in this unit, and list the five most important things you have learned.
  You might include
  • formulae
  • conversions
  • methods for working things out
  • mistakes to avoid (with tips on how to avoid them in future).

Reflect

5.1 Direct proportion

You will learn to:
- Recognise when values are in direct proportion.
- Plot graphs and read values to solve problems.

Why learn this?
Some bills are charged in proportion to the time spent, and some are charged as a standard fee.

Fluency
1 yard ≈ 0.9 metres.
What are the missing lengths?
- 4 yards ≈ ☐ metres
- ☐ yards ≈ 8.1 metres
- 300 yards ≈ ☐ metres

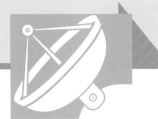

Explore
How will different exchange rates affect the amount of money you can spend on holiday?

Exercise 5.1

1 a £1 = 170 Yen. How many Yen would you get for £12?
   b Two litres of juice cost £3.50. How much does 1 litre cost?
   c 300 g of bananas cost £1.80. How much does 1 kg cost?

2 200 g of sweets cost £1.
   a How much do 100 g of sweets cost?
   b How much do 500 g of sweets cost?
   c Copy and complete this table showing the cost of sweets.

Grams of sweets	0	100	200	300	400	500
Cost in £			1			

   d Draw a graph to show this information.
      Label the x-axis 'Grams of sweets' and the y-axis 'Cost in pounds'.
      Join the points with a straight line and give your graph a title.
   Discussion Where does the line cross the y-axis?

3 Which of these graphs show two quantities in **direct proportion** to another?

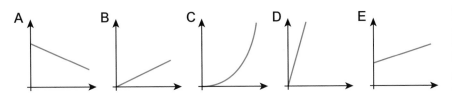

Key point

When two quantities are in **direct proportion**
- plotting them as a graph gives a straight line through the origin (0, 0)
- when one quantity is zero, the other quantity is also zero
- when one quantity doubles, so does the other.

Warm up

4 Real / Problem-solving This graph can be used to convert approximately between inches (in) and centimetres (cm).

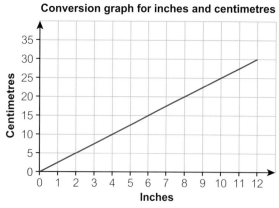

Conversion graph for inches and centimetres

a Are inches and centimetres in direct proportion?
b Copy and complete. 4 inches ≈ ☐ centimetres
c Copy and complete. 17 cm ≈ ☐ inches
d Which is longer, 6 inches or 14 centimetres?
e A car part needs to be exactly 5.3 inches long.
   How many centimetres is this?
Discussion Is a conversion graph a useful way to solve this problem?
f 15 inches ≈ ☐ cm.

Q4f hint

Convert 5 inches and multiply by 3.

5 STEM In a school science experiment, different masses are added to a spring and the extension is measured. The table shows some of the results.

Mass (g)	300	400	600
Extension (mm)	9	12	18

a Plot a line graph for these values.
b Are mass and spring extension in direct proportion?
A mass of 1000 g is added. The spring extension is 36 mm.
c When this point is added, does the graph still show direct proportion?

Q5a hint

Plot Mass up to 1000 g on the x-axis and Extension up to 40 mm on the y-axis. Use sensible scales.

6 STEM This is a conversion graph between degrees Celsius and degrees Fahrenheit.

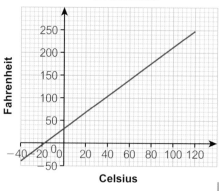

Conversion graph for Celsius and Fahrenheit

a Use the graph to estimate
   i 30°C in degrees Fahrenheit
   ii 100°F in degrees Celsius.
b What is the freezing point of water in degrees Fahrenheit?
c What is the boiling point of water in degrees Fahrenheit?
Discussion Are degrees Celsius and degrees Fahrenheit in direct proportion? Explain how you know.

Q6b, c hint

Find the freezing point and boiling point of water in degrees Celsius.

7 Keri is doing a DIY project. The cost of hiring a saw is shown on the graph.
   a How much would it cost Keri to hire the saw for 4 hours?
   b What is the cost per hour to hire the saw?
   Discussion How did you work out the cost per hour?
   c The store offers a daily fee of £59 if the customer pays in advance. After how many hours would this become the better value?

Saw hire cost per hour

8 Match the description to the graph.
   a The total cost of a phone call for x minutes at 9p per minute.
   b The total cost of a phone call for x minutes at 35p per minute.
   c The total cost of a hotel phone call with a 50p connection fee and 12p per minute.
   d The total cost of a phone call for x minutes at 20p per minute.

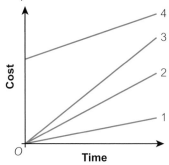

9 **Real** Which of these are in direct proportion?
   a Euros (€) and pounds (£)
   b The height of a person and their age up to 30
   c Cost and hours worked for an electrician.
   d Metres and yards

Q9 Strategy hint

Sketch or visualise a graph.

10 **Modelling** Face lotion costs £7 for 80 ml. The company plans to sell the lotion in different-sized bottles up to 200 ml.
   a Plot a line graph to show the price for up to 200 ml of lotion.
   b Are the price and volume in ml in direct proportion?
   Discussion Why don't companies usually price their goods like this?

Q10a hint

Plot the given values and two more points. Use a factor and a multiple of 80 ml.

11 **Explore** How will different exchange rates affect the amount of money you can spend on holiday?
   Is it easier to explore this question now that you have completed the lesson? What further information do you need to be able to answer this?

12 **Reflect** Shane says, 'Straight-line graphs always show direct proportion.'
   a Look back at the work you have done in this lesson and find an example to prove Shane wrong.
   b Write a sentence to describe a graph showing direct proportion.

Explore

Reflect

5.2 STEM: Interpreting graphs

Confidence

You will learn to:
- Interpret graphs from different sources.
- Understand financial graphs.

Why learn this?
A company that makes sun cream can use previous years' weather graphs to predict how much sun cream they need to make next year.

Fluency
Write down a number that is:
- at least 5
- no more than 7
- at most 18.

Explore
How do stock-market traders use graphs to help make investment decisions?

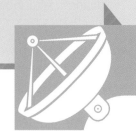

Exercise 5.2

Warm up

1 Write down the coordinates of the points marked with letters.

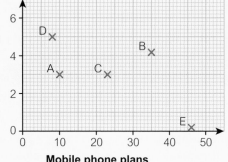

Mobile phone plans

2 **Finance / Problem-solving**
The graph shows two different phone plans.
  a How much does it cost for 100 minutes on
    i Plan A   ii Plan B?
  b What is the maximum amount you can pay on Plan B?
  c What is the minimum amount you can pay on Plan A?
  d At how many minutes is the largest difference between the cost on Plan A and B?
  e For how many minutes of calls do both plans cost the same?
  f On Plan C you pay £18 per month for unlimited calls.
    Which plan should each person choose?

	Average minutes of calls per month
Hana	30
Jeff	200
Matt	160

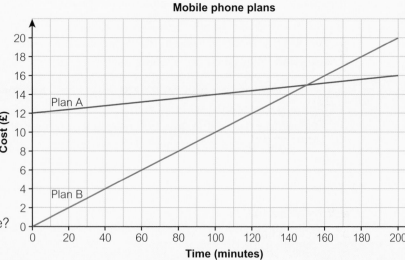

3 Finance The graph shows the share price of a company in 2013.

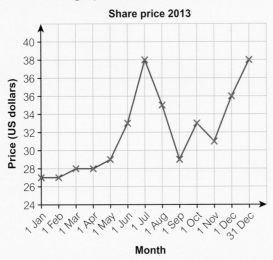

Share price 2013

a Describe the overall **trend** in the share price during 2013.
b What was the difference in price from the start of 2013 to the end?
c On what two dates did the price reach a minimum before increasing again?
d On what two dates did the price reach a maximum before decreasing again?
e Hana bought 160 shares at the beginning of March and sold them at the beginning of November. What was her **profit**?

Discussion Was the end of 2013 a good time to sell shares in this company?

Key point

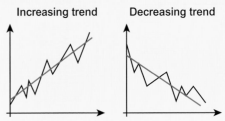

Line graphs can help you to identify **trends** in the data. The trend is the general direction of the change, ignoring the individual ups and downs.

Increasing trend   Decreasing trend

Q3 Literacy hint

The **profit** is the selling price minus the buying price.

4 Finance The graph shows the income and expenditure for a town council.

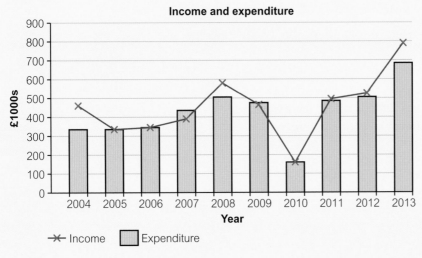

Income and expenditure

⨯ Income   ☐ Expenditure

a What does the value of 300 on the vertical axis represent?
b In 2008 what was the total expenditure of the council?
c In which years was the income over £450000?
d In which year did the council **overspend**?
e Describe the trend in the income
   i between 2008 and 2010
   ii between 2010 and 2013.
f Can you use the graph to estimate the income and expenditure in 2014?

Q4 Literacy hint

Overspending is when income is less than the amount spent.

5 Finance / Modelling The graph shows the cost of parking.

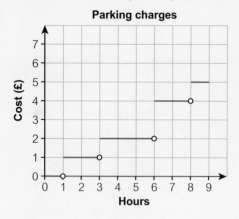

Parking charges

a How much does 4 hours' parking cost?
b How much does 6 hours' parking cost?
c Steve paid £4 for parking.
   How long did he stay?
Discussion Can you tell exactly how long Steve stayed?

6 Finance / Modelling The table shows prices for a smartphone data plan.

Data usage (MB)	Up to 100	101–300	301–500	501–800	801–1000	Over 1000
Cost (£)	Free	1	4	8	13	15

Draw a graph to show the prices.

7 Explore How do stock-market traders use graphs to help make investment decisions?
Is it easier to explore this question now that you have completed the lesson? What further information do you need to be able to answer this?

8 Reflect In this lesson you have used graphs to explore lots of real-life scenarios.
a Write down one way that graphs have helped you to answer questions.
b Write down one thing you found difficult about using graphs.
c Compare your answers with those of your classmates.

5.3 Distance–time graphs

You will learn to:
- Draw and interpret distance–time graphs
- Use distance–time graphs to solve problems.

Why learn this?
Traffic cameras measure average speed by measuring the time taken to travel a set distance.

Fluency
A car travels at a constant speed of 60 km/h.
- What does 'constant speed' mean?

How far does the car go in
- 1 hour
- 3 hours
- $\frac{1}{2}$ hour?

Explore
What story does this distance–time graph tell you?

Exercise 5.3

1 A train arrives into Cardiff Central from London Paddington at 1.25 pm. The train journey lasts 2 hours and 15 minutes. At what time did the train leave London Paddington?

2 Write each time as a decimal.
  a $\frac{1}{2}$ an hour   **b** 3 hours   **c** 2 and $\frac{1}{4}$ hours

3 Tony walks from home to the bank. On the way home he stops at the shops. The **distance–time** graph shows his journey.

> **Key point**
>
> A **distance–time graph** represents a journey. The vertical axis represents the **distance** from the starting point. The horizontal axis represents the **time** taken.

a How far away is the bank from Tony's house?

b Does his distance from home change between 10 and 25 minutes?

c How long does Tony spend at the bank?

d How long does Tony spend at the shops on the way home?

e How long does it take Tony to get from his house to the bank?

f How long does it take Tony to get from the bank to his house?

Discussion What does a horizontal line mean on a distance–time graph?

4 Liam leaves home at 1 pm and jogs 7 km to his friend's house.
It takes him $\frac{3}{4}$ of an hour.
He spends 2 hours at his friend's house. He jogs 5 km further away from home to his father's work. This takes him 30 minutes.
He waits 15 minutes for his father, and then they drive directly home.
Liam arrives home at 5 pm.
Draw a distance–time graph to show this information.

Q4 hint

Draw a horizontal axis from 1 pm to 5 pm with each square representing 15 minutes.
Draw a vertical axis from 0 km to 12 km with each square representing 1 km.

5 The distance–time graph shows the coach journey of a school trip.

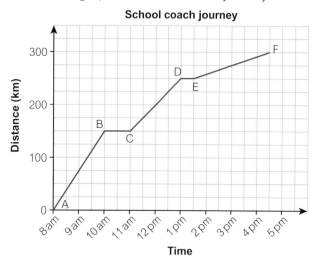

a How far is it from A to B?
b How long did it take the coach to travel from A to B?
c Calculate the average speed (km/h) from
   i B to C   **ii** C to D   **iii** E to F.
Discussion When was the coach travelling the fastest?
How can you tell this from the graph?

Key point

You can calculate **average speed** if you know the **distance** and the **time**.
Speed = $\frac{\text{Distance}}{\text{Time}}$ or $S = \frac{D}{T}$

6 Chris jogs 800 m in 15 minutes to his friend's house. He spends 1 hour at his friend's house, then walks home in 30 minutes.
a Sania and Karl sketch graphs to show Chris's journey.

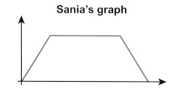
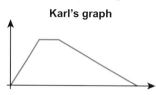

   They are both incorrect. Explain what is wrong with each graph.
b Sketch a more accurate graph for Chris's journey.

Key point

Compound measures combine measures of two different quantities. Speed is a measure of distance travelled and time taken. It can be measured in metres per second (m/s), kilometres per hour (km/h) or miles per hour (mph).

7 Michaela is travelling. She records her distance from home every hour.

Time	11 am	12 pm	1 pm	2 pm	3 pm	4 pm	5 pm
Distance from home (miles)	0	30	70	110	110	170	200

a Show this information on a graph.
b When did Michaela stop for a break?
c Michaela spent about 1 hour on a motorway.
   When do you think this was?
d Calculate Michaela's average speed between
   i 11 am and 2 pm   **ii** 1 pm and 5 pm.
Discussion Why is it an average speed?

Q7c hint

Compare the times spent in the different stages.

8 Reasoning The distance–time graph shows Arthur's progress in his swimming race.

   a Work out the speed of Arthur's swim for the first
      i 10 seconds   **ii** 50 seconds.

   b When was Arthur swimming fastest?

   c How far did Arthur swim in total?

   d What was Arthur's average speed for the swim?

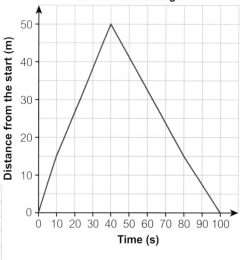

Arthur's swimming race

9 Train A travels from Bristol to Edinburgh.
  Train B travels from Edinburgh to Bristol.

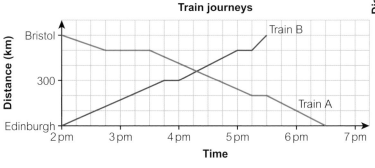

Train journeys

   a How far is Edinburgh from Bristol?

   b At what time do the trains pass each other?

   c How far is each train from Edinburgh when they pass each other?

   d What was the average speed of each train?

  Discussion How can you tell that Train B had a faster average speed
  just by looking at the graph?

10 Athletes A, B and C take part in the London Marathon.

   a How far is the race in kilometres?

   b At what time did Athlete C start the race?

   c How long did each athlete take to complete the race?

   d During the race Athlete B overtook Athlete C.

     i At what time did this happen?

     ii How far had they each run when this happened?

  Discussion According to this graph, each runner was travelling
  at a constant speed. Do you think this is true?

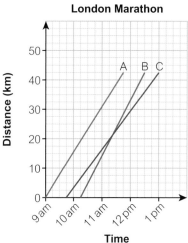

London Marathon

11 Explore What story does this distance–time graph tell you?

  Is it easier to explore this question now that you have completed
  the lesson? What further information do you need to be able to
  answer this?

12 Reflect You have seen lines like this on distance–time graphs:

   a Describe, in your own words, what each type of line tells you.

   b What would lines A and B tell you if they were steeper?

   c What would lines A and B tell you if they were less steep?

   d Would there ever be a line like this on a distance–time graph: |
     Explain.

Explore

Reflect

5.4 Rates of change

You will learn to:
- Interpret graphs that are curved.
- Interpret real-life graphs.

Confidence

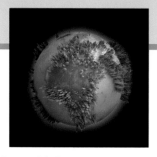

Why learn this?
Planners model the world's population by plotting graphs.

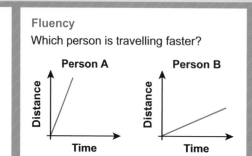

Fluency
Which person is travelling faster?

Person A

Person B

Explore
What will be the population of the world in 2050? In 2100?

Exercise 5.4

Warm up

1 Finance / Modelling Gary invests some money in a savings account with a fixed rate of interest. The graph shows how his investment will grow.

a How much money will he have after 5 years?

b After how many years will he have £3000?

c How much money did Gary invest?

d How much was Gary's investment worth after 1 year?

Gary's investment

(Graph: Money (£) on vertical axis from 0, 2000, 2200, 2400, 2600, 2800, 3000, 3200, 3400; Years on horizontal axis 0 to 10. Curve rising from 2000 at year 0 to about 3300 at year 10.)

2 Reasoning

a Match each race description to a graph.
   i Maddie starts off quickly and then runs more slowly.
   ii Sophie starts off slowly, then runs faster towards the finish.
   iii Beckie runs at a constant speed throughout the race.

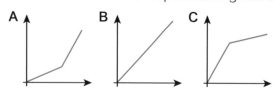

b Two other students run in this race. Here are their graphs. Write a brief description of their races.

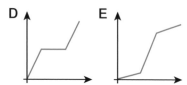

The table shows the depth of water as a pond fills up.

Time (minutes)	0	1	2
Depth (cm)	0	25	35

1 How much does the depth increase in
 a the first minute
 b the second minute?
2 Between which times is the depth increasing faster?
3 Sketch a **rate of change graph** for filling the pool.
4 Draw an accurate graph to check your prediction.
5 Complete this sentence about your graph.
 The steeper the graph, the …… the depth is increasing.
A solid object is dropped into the water.
6 What happens to the depth of water?
7 What does this look like on the graph?

Key point

A **rate of change graph** shows how a quantity changes over time.

3 The graph shows the depth of water in a bath.
 a In which three sections was water flowing into the bath?
 b At which two times was water flowing out of the bath?
 c At what time did a person get into the bath? Explain how you know.
 d How long was the person in the bath altogether?
 e Write a brief story to explain this graph.

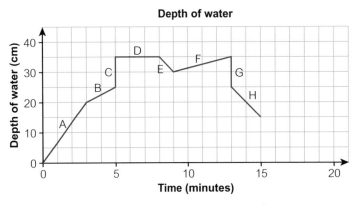

Depth of water

4 **Finance / Modelling** The graph shows the value of a car.
 a Estimate the price of the car when it is 4 years old.
 b Between which two years did the value change the most?
 c When is the car worth 50% of its original value?
 d Will the value of the car ever reach zero?
 Discussion Is this a realistic model for the value of a car?

Value of a car

5 Water is poured into these two glasses at the same constant rate.
 a Which fills faster, glass 1 or glass 2?

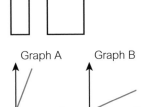

 b Which graph shows the depth of water in each glass over time?

Graph A   Graph B

Key point

For a **linear relationship** the points on a graph form a straight line. When the points are not in a straight line, the relationship is **non-linear**.

6 Water is poured into this container at a steady rate.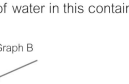
   a Which fills faster, the wide part or the narrow part?
   b Which graph shows how the depth of water in this container changes over time?

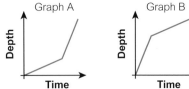

7 **Real / Modelling** Luke throws a ball straight up into the air. The table shows the ball's height above the ground on its way up.

Time (s)	0	1	2	3	4	5	6	7	8
Height (m)	1	38.1	65.4	82.9	90.6	88.6	76.6	54.9	23.4

   a Draw a graph to show this information.
   b Is the ball travelling at a constant speed? How can you tell?
   c Why does the height not start from 0?
   d Estimate the times when the height of the ball is 50 m.
   e Why are there two times when the ball is at 50 m?
   f Use the graph to estimate the time when the ball will hit the ground if Luke doesn't catch it.
   Discussion Why is the graph a curve?

Q7a hint

Put Time on the horizontal axis and Height on the vertical axis.
Plot the points and join them with a smooth curve.

8 These 4 containers are filled with water.

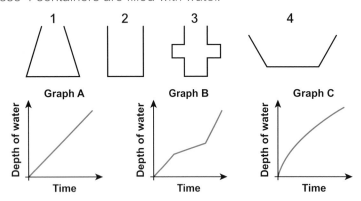

Q8 hint

When is the height of the water increasing at the fastest or slowest rate?

   a Match each container to a graph.
   b One container does not have a graph.
     Sketch a graph for that container.

9 **Explore** What will the population of the world be in 2050? In 2100? Is it easier to explore this question now that you have completed the lesson? What further information do you need to be able to answer this?

10 **Reflect** Kayo says, 'Rates of change are like ratios.
   Ratios measure how many red beads there are for every blue bead.
   Speed measures how far you travel for every hour.'
   a Look back at the questions in this lesson. Do you agree with Kayo? Explain.
   Jan says, 'Ratios compare similar things, like blue paint to yellow paint. Rates compare different things, like depth to time.'
   b Do you agree with Jan? Explain.
   c Write your own sentence, comparing ratios and rates of change.

Active Learn   Homework, Year 8, Unit 5

5.5 Misleading graphs

You will learn to:
- Understand when graphs are misleading.

Why learn this?
During an election campaign, parties present the same data in different ways to influence voters.

Fluency
What is missing from this pie chart?

Explore
How can you draw a line graph to disguise falling sales figures?

Exercise 5.5

1 Each dual bar chart shows the number of text messages Marco sent and received each day.

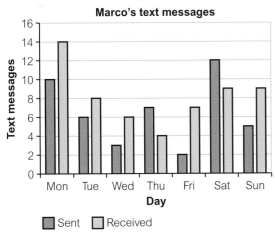

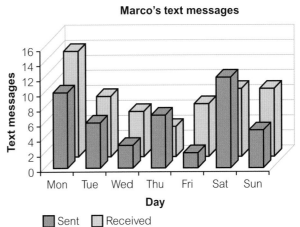

a On which day did Marco send the most text messages?

b How many more text messages did Marco receive than send on Tuesday?

c Over the whole week, did Marco send or receive more text messages?

Discussion Which chart did you use to answer each question? Was one chart easier to read than the other?

2 Students were asked to choose their favourite dessert.
The pie chart shows the results.
Write 3 ways in which this pie chart is misleading.

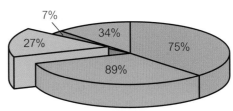

Warm up

3 **Real / STEM** The cost of 1 GB of data storage is shown on the graph.

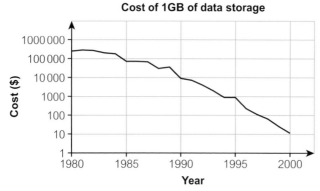

Cost of 1GB of data storage

a What is unusual about the vertical scale on the graph?
How do you get from one marked value to the next?

b Use the values in the table to draw a graph with a vertical scale of
0, 10 000, 20 000,…

Q3b hint

You could use a graph-plotting
package to plot the graph.

Year	1980	1985	1990	1995	2000
Cost ($)	213 000	71 000	34 000	950	26

c Describe the trend in the price of data storage between 1980
and 2000.
Discussion Which graph shows the trend more accurately?

4 **Finance** These two graphs show the same sales figures for Denise's
clothing store.

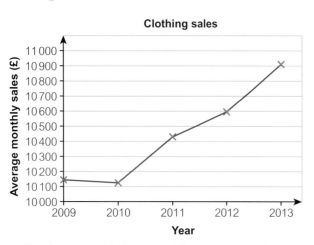

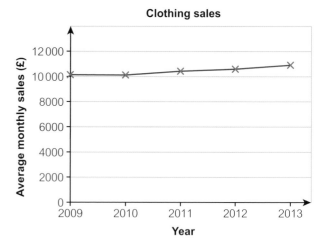

a Denise says, 'Sales are rising quickly.' Which graph is she using?
b Her bank manager says, 'Sales are almost constant.'
Which graph is she using?
c What is the actual increase in sales between 2009 and 2013?
d Work out the percentage increase in sales between 2009 and 2013.
Discussion Do the figures show a large increase in sales?

Q4d hint

Percentage increase

$$= \frac{\text{actual increase}}{\text{original amount}} \times 100$$

5 **Explore** How can you draw a line graph to disguise falling sales figures?
Is it easier to explore this question now that you have completed the
lesson? What further information do you need to be able to answer this?

6 **Reflect**
a List five ways in which graphs can mislead you.
You could begin with, 'It is misleading when the scale …'
b Why might a newspaper use misleading graphs?

Active Learn   Homework, Year 8, Unit 5

5 Check up

Direct proportion

1 a Copy and complete.
  i 10 miles ≈ ☐ km
  ii 5 km ≈ ☐ miles
  iii 1 mile ≈ ☐ km
  iv 80 km ≈ ☐ miles
b Explain how the graph shows that miles and kilometres are in direct proportion.

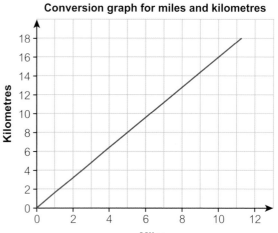

Conversion graph for miles and kilometres

2 The table shows the cost of hiring two different venues.

Hours	1	3	5
Venue A cost (£)	40	120	200
Venue B cost (£)	95	125	155

a Copy the axes and draw the graphs for the two different venues.
b Which line shows direct proportion, Venue A or Venue B?
c Which is cheaper for 4 hours' hire?
d For what number of hours' hire do both venues cost the same?
e Which venue charges a booking fee? How much is it?

Cost of venue hire

Distance–time graphs

3 Max drives from home to visit his brother.
He stops on the way to buy pizza.
  a How far does Max live from his brother?
  b How long does Max spend buying pizza?
  c How long does Max spend at his brother's house?
  d On which part of the journey was Max travelling fastest? How can you tell?

4 Jasmine leaves home at 10 am and walks $\frac{1}{2}$ km to the bus stop.
The walk takes her 15 minutes and she waits 5 minutes for the bus.
The 5 km bus journey takes 20 minutes. She spends 2 hours in town.
Her father takes her home in the car. She arrives home at 1:15 pm.
Draw a distance–time graph to show Jasmine's journey.

5 The graph shows the Langleys' journey to their holiday destination.

a How far did they travel in total?

b How many times did they stop for a break?

c What was their average speed for the whole journey?

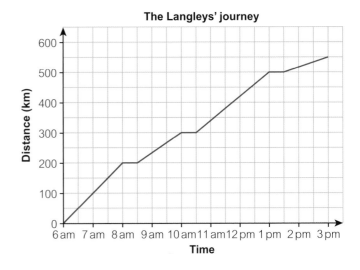

The Langleys' journey

Real-life graphs

6 The graph shows the numbers of visitors (in millions) to three different theme parks.

a Describe the trend in the numbers of visitors between 2009 and 2013 to

  i Park A

  ii Park C.

b What was the difference in the number of visitors to

  i Park B and Park C in 2012

  ii Park A and Park B in 2010?

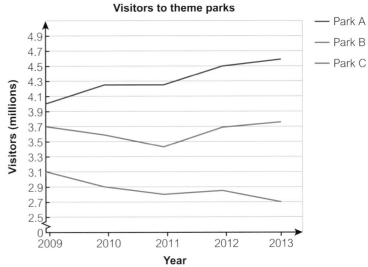

Visitors to theme parks

7 Match the vase to the correct graph showing depth of water against time when the water flows at a constant rate.

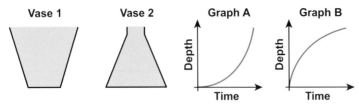

Vase 1 **Vase 2** **Graph A** **Graph B**

8 How sure are you of your answers? Were you mostly

  ☹ **Just guessing** 😐 **Feeling doubtful** ☺ **Confident**

What next? Use your results to decide whether to strengthen or extend your learning.

Challenge

9 Here are the car hire costs for two companies.

a Draw a graph for these costs.

b Unlimited Cars charges a booking fee. How much is it?

c Explain which company you should use for different numbers of days' hire.

Number of days	2	5	7
Cars Direct	£40	£100	£140
Unlimited Cars	£64	£100	£124

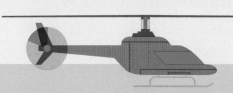

5 Strengthen

You will:
• Strengthen your understanding with practice.

Direct proportion

1 a Draw a pair of axes as shown.
  b Draw a straight-line graph through the origin.
  c Underneath your graph, copy and complete:
    When two quantities are in direct proportion, their graph
    is a s............ l............ through ....

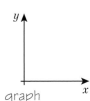

Q1b hint

The origin is (0, 0).

2 **Real** Which of these graphs show direct proportion?

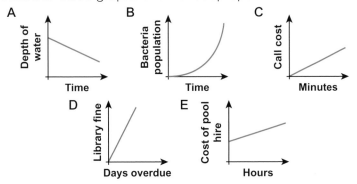

Q2 hint

Which graphs look like the graph you drew in Q1?

3 The graph shows the cost of hiring a roller-skating rink.
  a How much does it cost to hire the rink for 90 minutes?
  b How much does it cost to hire the rink for 1 hour?
  c Megan has £125. What is the maximum length of time she can hire the rink for?

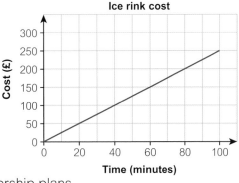

Q3a hint

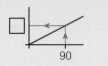

Q3c hint

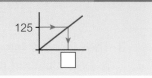

4 A gym offers two monthly membership plans.
  The table shows the costs for different numbers of visits.

Number of visits	2	5	7
Plan A	£15	£22.50	£27.50
Plan B	£8	£20	£28

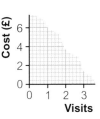

  a Draw a pair of axes as shown.
  b Plot the points for Plan A.
  c Join the points with a straight line.
  d Draw the graph for Plan B.
  e Which plan shows direct proportion?
  f Which plan charges a fixed monthly fee? How much is this fee?
  g Copy and complete, filling in the missing number:
    For more than ☐ visits, plan A is cheaper.

Q4d hint

Follow the steps in parts **b** and **c**.

Q4f hint

How much do no visits cost? This is the fixed monthly fee.

Distance–time graphs

1 Sansan drives Suki to football practice, and then home again.

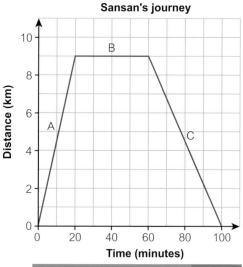

Sansan's journey

  a Match each description to the part of the graph labelled
A, B or C.
- **i** Driving home
- **ii** Driving to football practice
- **iii** At football practice.

  b How many minutes is one square on the time axis?

  c How long is Suki at football practice?

  d How many kilometres is one square on the distance axis?

  e How far away is football practice?

  f Copy and complete, filling in the missing numbers.
On the way to football practice Sansan and Suki drove
☐ km in ☐ minutes.
On the way back they drove ☐ km in ☐ minutes.

  g Did they drive faster on the way there or way back?

  h Choose 'fastest' or 'slowest' to complete this sentence.
The steepest section shows the .... speed.

> **Q1a iii hint**
>
> At football practice, the distance from home stays the same.

> **Q1g hint**
>
> Which journey took less time?

2 Dahab travelled by car to visit her mother.
She left home at 2 pm.
She drove 80 km in 1 hour 15 minutes.
She stayed at her mother's house for 1 hour 45 minutes
and then drove directly home, arriving home at 6.15 pm.

  a Copy the axes onto squared paper.

  b Draw a distance–time graph to show Dahab's
journey.

  c Give your graph a title.

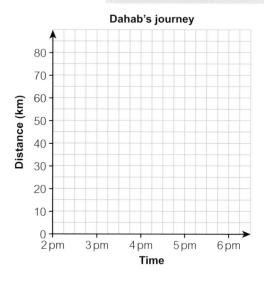

Dahab's journey

3 The Murphys' travel home after their holiday.

  a How often did they stop on the journey?

  b How many miles does one small square on the
vertical axis represent?

  c What is the total distance from holiday to home?

  d How many minutes does one small square on
the horizontal axis represent?

  e What is the total time to travel home?
Write your answer as a decimal.

  f Work out the average speed in miles per hour
using the formula

$$\text{average speed} = \frac{\text{total distance in miles}}{\text{total time in hours}}$$

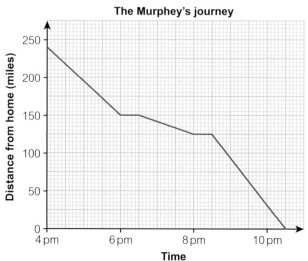

The Murphey's journey

Real-life graphs

1 The graph shows the UK average house price since 2000.

   a How many squares on the horizontal axis represent 1 year?

   b What was the average house price in

       i 2002   **ii** 2005?

   c What does one small square on the vertical axis represent?

   d In which year was the average house price £130 000?

   e In which year did the average house price reach its maximum value?

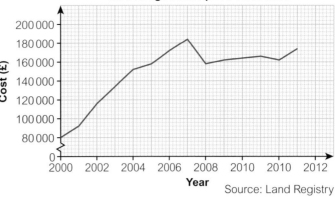

UK average house price since 2000

Source: Land Registry

2 The graph shows the value of a bike.

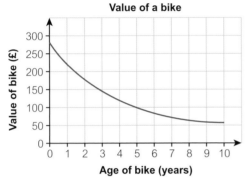

Value of a bike

   a What does one square on the vertical axis represent?

   b How much did the new bike cost?

   c Copy and complete this table.

Age of bike (years)	0	1	2	3	4	5	6	7	8	9	10
Cost (£)		220									

   d From your table, when did the value of the bike decrease the fastest?

   e How does the graph show this?

   f Will the value of the bike ever reach £0?

3 The graph shows the percentage of adults in an American town who own a car.

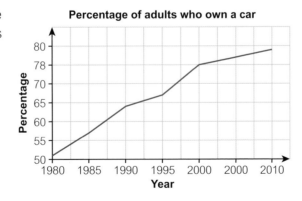

Percentage of adults who own a car

   a What percentage of adults owned a car in 1980?

   b What was the change in percentage of adults owning a car between 1990 and 1995?

   c In which 5-year period did car ownership increase the most?

   d Describe the trend in the percentage of adults who own a car.

   e Use the graph to estimate the percentage of adults who owned a car in 1992.

Q1 Strategy hint

Before you answer questions about a graph
• read the title
• read the labels on the axes
• read the key
• look at the scales on the axes.

Q2e hint

The steepest section shows the .... decrease.

Q2e hint

Imagine extending the graph. Will the line ever touch the horizontal axis?

Q3b hint

change = 1995 percentage
             − 1990 percentage

Q3c hint

Make a table, as in Q2, or look for the steepest section of the graph.

Q3e hint

Choose 'increasing' or 'decreasing' to complete this sentence.
The percentage is ....

4 The graph shows the average monthly maximum daytime and minimum night-time temperatures in Minehead.

  a Which colour graph line shows
    i maximum temperatures
    ii minimum temperatures?
  b In May, what was the average
    i maximum temperature
    ii minimum temperature?
  c Which month had the
    i highest maximum temperature
    ii lowest minimum temperature?
  d Which month had the largest difference between the maximum and minimum temperatures?

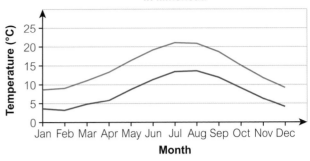

Maximum and minimum temperatures in Minehead

— Maximum daytime temperature — Minimum daytime temperature

> **Q4d hint**
> Look on the graph for the biggest gap between the maximum and minimum lines.

Enrichment

1 The graphs show the conversion rates from British pounds to Chinese yuan, and from Chinese yuan to Indian rupees.

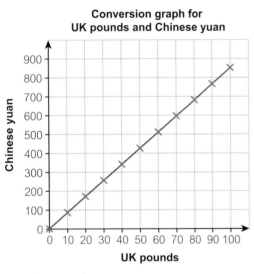

Conversion graph for UK pounds and Chinese yuan

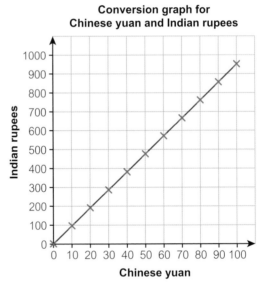

Conversion graph for Chinese yuan and Indian rupees

Use the graphs to convert
  a £40 into Chinese yuan
  b £440 in Chinese yuan
  c 50 Chinese yuan into Indian rupees
  d £20 into Indian rupees.

Salma goes on a trip. She changes £200 into Chinese yuan. She spends 700 yuan in China and then changes the remaining money into Indian rupees.
  e How many rupees does she have?
  f Salma has 800 rupees left at the end of her trip. How many pounds is this?

2 Reflect Look back at Q1 and Q2 in Distance–time graphs.
  a Which do you find harder, reading from distance–time graphs or drawing distance–time graphs?
  b What makes it more difficult?
  c Write one thing about drawing distance–time graphs and one thing about reading distance–time graphs that you think you need more practice on.

Reflect

5 Extend

You will:
- Extend your understanding with problem-solving.

1 **Modelling** The graph shows the average rainfall and maximum temperature in the Gower Peninsula, Wales.

a On average, which month is
  i the warmest   ii the driest?

Reanna is planning a trip to the Gower Peninsula. She is considering going in either April or October.

b Use the graph to work out the temperature in
  i April   ii October.

c Use the graph to work out the rainfall in
  i April   ii October.

Discussion In which month should Reanna go to the Gower Peninsula?

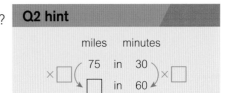

Gower Peninsula climate

Rainfall (mm) — Temperature (°C)

2 A racing car travels 75 miles in 30 minutes.
  a Calculate its average speed in miles per hour.
  b How far will it travel in 40 minutes?

Q2 hint

3 **Modelling** Remy travelled from Newcastle to Cardiff for a meeting, a distance of 300 miles. His average speed on the way there was 50 mph and on the way back it was 60 mph. Remy's meeting lasted $1\frac{1}{2}$ hours.
  a Draw a distance–time graph to show this information.
  b Calculate Remy's average speed for the whole journey.

4 Work out the average speed of each journey.
  a A plane travels 5530 km from London to New York in 6 hours.
  b A snail slides 1733 mm in 2 days.
  c A golf ball travels 293 m in 11.2 seconds.

Q5b hint

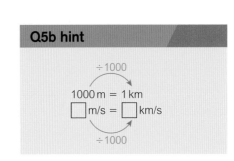

5 An athlete runs 200 m in 24 seconds.
  Work out his speed
  a in metres per second
  b in kilometres per second
  c in kilometres per minute
  d in kilometres per hour.

6 **Problem-solving / Modelling** The diagram shows a distance–altitude map for a stage in a cycling race.
  a How many km was the stage?
  b What was the lowest altitude?
  c Which of the three climbs was the steepest?
  d Sketch a possible distance–time graph for this stage.

Distance–altitude map for cycling race

Topic links: Proportion, Percentages, Averages, Measures

Subject links: Geography (Q1, 7, 10), Science (Q9, 11, 13, 16), PE (Q5, 6)

7 **Modelling** The Youngs are planning a Disney holiday and are choosing between Paris and Florida.

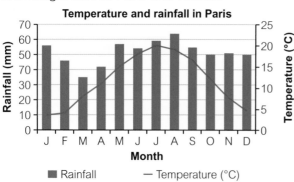

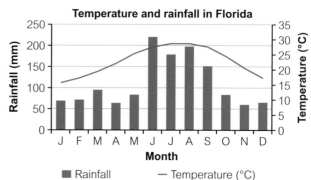

a What is the temperature in August in
  i Paris   **ii** Florida?
b What is the rainfall in January in
  i Paris   **ii** Florida?
c Explain why the scales of these graphs make it difficult to compare the weather in Paris and Florida.
d Rashid says, 'The graphs show that Florida is always warmer and wetter than Paris.' Is Rashid correct? Explain your answer.

8 a Plot two separate graphs for these tables of data.

i

Edge length of a cube (cm)	2	5	7	9
Volume of a cube (cm³)	8	125	343	729

ii

Radius of circle (cm)	1	5	7	11
Circumference of circle (cm)	$2\pi = 6.3$ (1 d.p.)	10π	14π	22π

> **Q8 hint**
>
> Work out the circumferences to 1 d.p.

b Are the two quantities in each graph in direct proportion?

9 **STEM / Modelling** The table shows the time difference between a lightning flash and the sound of thunder (seconds), and the distance to the storm (miles).

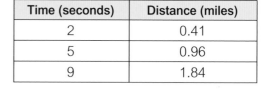

Time (seconds)	Distance (miles)
2	0.41
5	0.96
9	1.84

a Plot a graph to show the results.
b Is the distance of the thunderstorm in direct proportion to the number of seconds it takes to hear it?
Sound travels 1 mile every 5.2 seconds.
c Draw a line onto your graph to represent this.
Discussion How well can you model the distance of a storm using the speed of sound?

10 The graph shows the percentages of different age groups in the UK between 1911 and 2011.
a Approximately what percentage of the population was aged 0–14 years in
  i 1911   **ii** 2011?
b Describe the trend in the percentage of the population aged 0–14 years.
c Which age groups have seen a rise in their percentage since 1911?
d On the whole, is the UK population getting older or younger? Explain your answer.

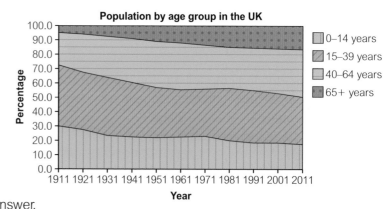

Source: ONS

11 STEM / Reasoning A scientist does an experiment to measure the different pressures created by the same force. She does this by changing the area over which the force is applied. The graph shows her results.

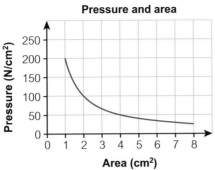

a Copy and complete: As the area increases, the pressure ....

b What is the pressure when the same force is applied over an area of $3\,cm^2$?

c Will the pressure ever reach zero?

d Explain why the graph will never meet the vertical axis.

e Use these results to explain why

    i people in high-heeled shoes should not walk on the gym floor

    ii a sharp knife will cut vegetables more easily than a blunt (not sharp) knife

    iii someone might get problems with their feet if they always walk on their toes.

12 Real Both graphs show how the numbers of websites have changed over time.

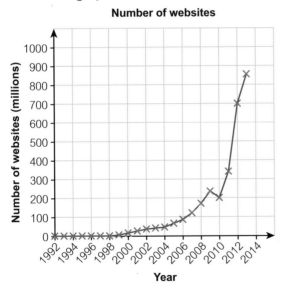

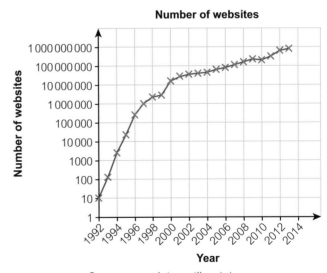

Source: www.internetlivestats.com

a In the left-hand graph, what does one square on the vertical axis represent?

b Describe how the vertical scale changes on the right-hand graph.

c When was the first website launched?

d How many websites were there in

    i 2010

    ii 2007

    iii 1996?

e Which graph was more useful for answering each question in part **d**?

f How many websites would you expect there to be in 2014?

Discussion Is this a good model for predicting the future?

13 Reasoning This table shows the speed at which some cars are travelling and their stopping distances.

Speed (km/h)	32	48	64	80	96	112
Stopping distance (m)	12	23	36	53	73	96

    a Draw a graph to show this data.

    b Are speed and stopping distance in direct proportion?

This table shows the speed of the cars and the thinking distances of their drivers.

Speed (km/h)	32	48	64	80	96	112
Thinking distance (m)	6	9	12	15	18	21

Total stopping distance = thinking distance + braking distance

    c Are speed and thinking distance in direct proportion?

    d Will speed and braking distance be in direct proportion? Explain your answer.

14 The table shows the average monthly sales for a car dealership. The owner wants a loan so that he can expand his business. He asks for a graph that shows 'Sales Rising Rapidly'. Draw a suitable graph for the owner.

Q14 hint

Use a scale on the vertical axis that will give the appearance of a big increase. You could use a graph-plotting package to plot the graph.

Year	2008	2009	2010	2011	2012	2013
Average monthly sales	£65 400	£67 300	£66 900	£68 800	£68 400	£69 300

15 Oliver takes a bath. The shape of the bath is shown in the diagram.

Oliver takes 5 minutes to fill the water to a depth of 50 cm. He then turns the taps off, gets in the bath and remains there for 10 minutes. He gets out, and then lets the water out. The bath takes 7 minutes to empty. Draw a depth–time graph to model this situation.

Q15 hint

What effect will the shape of the bath have on the shape of the graph?

16 STEM / Modelling / Reasoning A ball is dropped from a height of 5 m. The graph shows the height of the ball above the ground for the first 6 seconds.

    a How long does it take for the ball to first hit the ground?

    b During the first 2 seconds, when is the ball moving the fastest speed?

The point A is where the ball reaches its greatest height after the first bounce.

    c At point A, what is the speed of the ball?

    d If the graph continued, what would happen to the maximum height of the ball?

Discussion According to this model, would the ball ever stop bouncing?

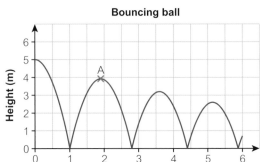

Bouncing ball

17 Reflect In these extend lessons you have used some types of graphs that you may not have used before.

    a Make a list of the questions with new types of graph.

    b For each graph, what did you do first to understand the graph?

    c Which graph did you find the most confusing?

Compare your answers with those of your classmates.

5 Unit test

1 The graph shows the number of daylight hours in London and Lerwick (Shetland Islands).
   a Use the graph to estimate the number of daylight hours in May in
      i London   ii Lerwick.
   b In which month(s) is the number of daylight hours approximately the same in both locations?
   c Which place has more hours of daylight in the summer months?
   d Which place has fewer hours of daylight in the winter months?

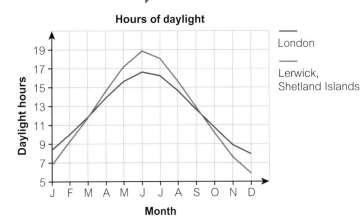

Hours of daylight

2 Pavel drives to visit a friend. On the way there, he stops to buy petrol.
   a How long did Pavel stay at his friend's house?
   b Which was the fastest part of the journey?
   c What was his average speed from his house to his friend's house?

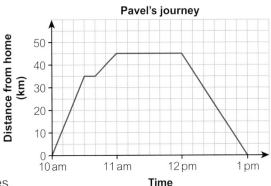

Pavel's journey

3 The graphs show the races run by 4 different athletes. Match the description to the correct graph.

i   ii   iii   iv

   A Athlete A starts off slowly and then gradually increases speed.
   B Athlete B runs at a constant speed throughout the race.
   C Athlete C runs at a slow constant speed, and then a much faster constant speed.
   D Athlete D starts off fast and the gradually slows down.

4 An electrician charges a call-out fee and then an hourly rate. Some of her charges are shown in the table.

Time (hours)	2	4	5
Cost (£)	70	100	115

   a Draw a graph to show this information. Plot Time on the horizontal axis and Cost on the vertical axis. Use suitable scales.
   b What is the electrician's callout charge?
   c What is her hourly rate?
   d Are time and cost in direct proportion? Explain

5 The number of new Year 7 students enrolling at 2 local secondary schools is shown on the graph.

a How many new students enrolled in school A in 2010?

b Which school had the higher number of new students in 2011?

c In which year was the number of new students in school A and school B the same?

d Describe the trend in the numbers of students enrolling in

  i school A   **ii** school B.

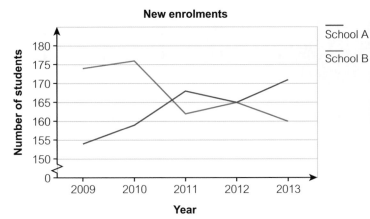

6 The graph shows two mobile phone plans.

a How much does it cost for 1 GB data on

  i Plan A   **ii** Plan B?

b For how much data do both plans cost the same?

7 Which of these graphs show direct proportion?

8 The graph shows the average weekly salary of a footballer in the top English division over the last 30 years.

a Estimate the average weekly salary

  i at the present time

  ii 10 years ago

  iii 20 years ago.

b Describe the trend in salaries over the last 30 years.

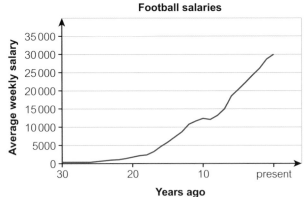

Challenge

9 A school says that its IGCSE maths grades are rising rapidly. Draw a line graph that will give the appearance of rapidly rising IGCSE grades.

Year	2010	2011	2012	2013
Percentage of students getting grade C or better	59.3%	60.2%	60.7%	60.9%

10 Reflect Working with real-life graphs uses lots of different maths topics. Make a list of the different maths skills you have used to answer the questions in this test.

Did you get stuck on any questions because you'd forgotten some of the maths skills? If so, ask your teacher for help.

Reflect

6.1 Rounding decimals

You will learn to:
- Round to decimal places.

Why learn this?
In the 2014 Sochi Olympics, the Women's Downhill race ended in a tie (an equal result), but only because the times were rounded to 2 decimal places.

Fluency
Round these numbers to the nearest 10.
- 58
- 385
- 396

Explore
Which is the most crowded city in the world?

Exercise 6.1

1 Write down the digit in the second decimal place of each number.
   a 5.64   b 37.25   c 8.0532   d 146.265

2 Round to the nearest whole number.
   a 12.3   b 2.7   c 6.5
   d 11.29   e 37.14

3 Round these numbers to 1 decimal place.
   a 5.64   b 3.89   c 0.65
   d 8.96   e 9.98

4 **Problem-solving** Toni writes an answer of 3.4 correct to 1 decimal place.
   What could her number have been correct to 2 decimal places?

5 Round these numbers to 2 decimal places.
   a 2.947   b 0.803   c 12.996   d 14.017

 6 Use a calculator to write these fractions as decimals correct to 2 d.p.
   a $\frac{5}{7}$ b $\frac{9}{11}$

7 **Reasoning** Frank says that 6.998 rounded to 2 decimal places is 7.
   a Explain why Frank is wrong.
   b What is the correct answer?
   Discussion Explain the difference between 8, 8.0 and 8.00.
   Which is the most accurate and which is the least accurate?

8 **Finance** Jilna buys a pack of four drinks for £4.39. How much does each drink cost? Round your answer to the nearest penny.

Key point
To **round** a decimal to 1 decimal place (**1 d.p.**), look at the digit in the second decimal place. If the digit is less than 5, round down. If the digit is 5 or more, round up.

Q3 hint
Write the number in the first decimal place, even if it is 0.

Key point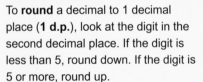
To round to two decimal places (2 d.p.), look at the digit in the third decimal place.

Q7a hint
Work out 5 ÷ 7

Warm up

9 a Copy and complete the table showing populations of different countries around the world.

Country	Population (numbers)	Population (numbers and words)
Italy	60 000 000	60 million
Canada	34 300 000	
Sri Lanka		20.4 million
Norway		5.1 million
Fiji	900 000	

b The population of Sweden is 9 658 301 and of Barbados is 285 000. Write these populations in both forms, correct to the nearest 100 000.

10 Rory works out $\sqrt{7}$. The number on his calculator is 2.645 751 311. Round this number to 3 decimal places.

Key point

To round a decimal to 3 decimal places, look at the digit in the fourth decimal place.

11 Athlete A runs the 100 m in 9.7528 seconds. Athlete B runs the same race in 9.7456 seconds.
a Which athlete has the faster time?
b The times are reported to 3 decimal places. Does the result change?
c The times are reported to 2 d.p. Does the result change?

12 Problem-solving Emily writes down an answer of 4.29 correct to 2 decimal places.
Which two of these could have been her unrounded answer?
A 4.286   **B** 4.296   **C** 4.2845   **D** 4.293

13 Problem-solving Write down a number with 3 decimal places that would round to
a 3 to the nearest whole number and 3.2 to the nearest tenth
b 3 to the nearest whole number and 2.5 to the nearest tenth
c 2 to the nearest whole number and 2.5 to the nearest tenth
d 3.2 to the nearest tenth and 3.25 to the nearest hundredth
e 3.3 to the nearest tenth and 3.25 to the nearest hundredth.

14 The numbers of a type of beetle in 4 woods are recorded. The bar chart shows the results.
a Work out the mean number of beetles in a wood.
b What is the mean to the nearest 100?

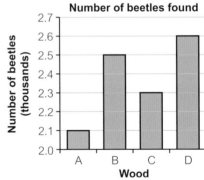

15 Explore Which is the most crowded city in the world?
What have you learned in this lesson to help you to answer this question?
What other information do you need?

16 Reflect Lee and Ethan are discussing Q12.
Lee says, 'I rounded all the numbers to 2 decimal places to see which ones rounded to 4.29'
Ethan says 'I looked at the third decimal place of all the numbers to see which ones would round up or down.'
How did you decide which numbers could have been rounded to 4.29?
Which method is most efficient?

6.2 Multiplying and dividing decimals

You will learn to:
- Multiply and divide any number by 0.1, 0.01 and 0.001.
- Multiply decimals using a written method.
- Divide by decimals.

Why learn this?
Metric measurements use decimals. You need to calculate with decimals to find lengths and areas.

Fluency
- What does the '1' represent in 0.1 and 0.01?
- How do you write 0.3 and 0.07 as fractions?

Explore
Does multiplying one number by another always make it bigger?

Exercise 6.2

1 Work out

   a   45   b   53   c   32   d   267
      × 7   × 28   × 17   × 15
      ___   ____   ____   ____

2 Estimate these by rounding one or both numbers.
   a 50 × 0.8
   b 5.3 × 7
   c 19.9 × 0.5
   d 134 × 11

3 Calculate
   a 22 × 0.01
   b 452 × 0.001
   c 36 × 0.1
   d 28 ÷ 0.1
   e 720 ÷ 0.001
   f 231 ÷ 0.01

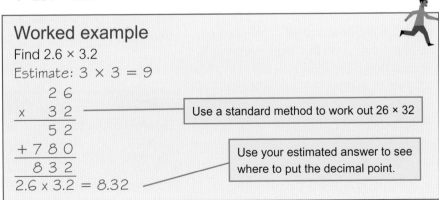

Worked example

Find 2.6 × 3.2

Estimate: 3 × 3 = 9

```
      2 6
  ×   3 2          ← Use a standard method to work out 26 × 32
      5 2
  + 7 8 0
      8 3 2
2.6 × 3.2 = 8.32   ← Use your estimated answer to see
                      where to put the decimal point.
```

4 Calculate

   a 3.7 × 2.2   **b** 2.5 × 4.2   **c** 7.22 × 3.1

   d 3.46 × 8.9   **e** 8.94 × 0.32   **f** 4.04 × 8.2

   Discussion For each part, count the number of digits after the decimal point in both numbers in the question.

   Do the same for the answer. What do you notice?

Q4 hint

Estimate first.

5 **Real** A car can travel 13.8 kilometres on 1 litre of petrol.

   How far can it travel on 8.8 litres of petrol?

6 Follow these steps to calculate 3.26 × 5.12.

   a Estimate the answer.

   b Calculate 326 × 512.

   c Decide where to position the decimal point.

7 **Problem-solving** A factory makes 3.5 silk flowers every second.

   a Each flower uses 60.3 cm of silk.

     How many metres of silk are used in one minute?

   b Each flower has a 0.325 m wire stem.

     A hotel orders 275 silk flowers.

     What length of wire is needed?

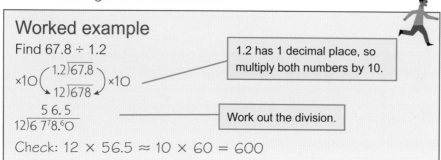

Worked example

Find 67.8 ÷ 1.2

1.2 has 1 decimal place, so multiply both numbers by 10.

Work out the division.

Check: 12 × 56.5 ≈ 10 × 60 = 600

Key point

To divide by a decimal, multiply both numbers by a power of 10 (10, 100, …) until you have a whole number to divide by.

Then work out the division.

8 Find using a written method.

   Give your answers to 1 decimal place where appropriate.

   a 43.32 ÷ 0.3

   b 348 ÷ 5.8

   c 18.9 ÷ 0.09

   d 39 ÷ 0.75

   e 131.72 ÷ 0.37

   f 82.3 ÷ 6.25

   g 367 ÷ 2.4

   h 0.556 ÷ 3.6

   i 72.5 ÷ 0.7

   Discussion 'Dividing a number by a number less than 1 gives you an answer that is larger than the first number.' Is this statement true?

Q8c hint

Multiply both numbers by 100, then work out the division.

Q8f hint

You will need to work out the second decimal place and then round, rather than just stopping at the first decimal place.

9 Find

   a 2.724 × 3.25

   b 4.59 × 2.764

   c 8.91 × 5.126

   d 7.261 × 9.28

   e 6.903 × 0.425

   f 23.241 × 7.26

Q9a hint

Set out in columns, e.g.

     2724

  ×   325

10 a Work out the volume of this cuboid.

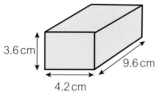

3.6 cm
9.6 cm
4.2 cm

b Another cuboid has a volume of 35.52 m³.
Its length is 4 m and its width is 2.4 m.
What is its height?

Q10b Strategy hint
Make a sketch.

Investigation

Reasoning

1 Choose a number.
Carry out these operations on your number.
×100   ×10   ×0.1   ×0.01   ÷100   ÷10   ÷0.1   ÷0.01

2 Repeat part **1** with another number.

3 Are any of these operations equivalent?
Use your answers to parts **1** and **2** to complete these rules.
×100 is equivalent to ☐
☐ is equivalent to ÷0.1
☐ is equivalent to ÷10
×0.01 is equivalent to ☐

4 What do you think the rules are for
a ×0.001   **b** ÷0.001?
Test your rules.

---

11 Explore Does multiplying one number by another always make it bigger?
Is it easier to explore this question now that you have completed the lesson?
What further information do you need to be able to answer this?

12 Reflect
    a What happens when you divide a positive number by a number between 0 and 1?
    b What happens when you multiply a positive number by a number between 0 and 1?
    c Write your own 'What happens when …?' question and answer it.

Explore

Reflect

6.3 Converting fractions to decimals

Confidence

You will learn to:
* Convert fractions to decimals by dividing the numerator by the denominator.
* Recognise recurring and terminating decimals.
* Convert recurring decimals to fractions using an algebraic method.

Why learn this?
Some fractions have simple decimal equivalents, but some have recurring digits that go on indefinitely. You need to be able to deal with these decimals when they occur.

Fluency
Round these decimals to 2 decimal places.
* 3.456
* 12.607
* 30.0067

Explore
Can you prove that 0.999 999… = 1?

Exercise 6.3

Warm up

1 Calculate
  a $20 \div 8$ **b** $4 \div 10$ **c** $12 \div 24$

2 Simplify
  a $10x - x$ **b** $100x - x$

3 Solve
  a $9x = 15$ **b** $99x = 23$ **c** $999x = 326$

4 Convert each of these fractions to a decimal.
  a $\frac{1}{8}$ **b** $\frac{3}{8}$ **c** $\frac{1}{12}$ **d** $\frac{5}{12}$
  Discussion What do you notice?

5 Write each **decimal with repeating digits** using dot notation
  a $0.666\,66\ldots$ **b** $0.171\,717\,171\ldots$
  c $0.548\,548\,548\ldots$

> **Q3 hint**
> Give your answers as fractions in their simplest form.

> **Key point**
> In a recurring decimal, a dot over the beginning and end of a sequence shows it recurs.
> For example $0.111\,111\,111$ is $0.\dot{1}$ and $4.185\,185\,185$ is $4.\dot{1}8\dot{5}$

Investigation

Problem-solving

1 Change the fraction $\frac{1}{3}$ into a decimal.
   What do you notice?
2 Change $\frac{1}{9}$ into a decimal.
   What do you notice?
3 Try changing any proper fraction with 9 as the denominator into a decimal.
   What always happens?

6 **a** Write $\frac{1}{6}$ as a decimal.
   b What would be the decimal value of $\frac{10}{6}$? Use your answer to part **a** to help you.

7 a **Reasoning** Convert $\frac{1}{11}$ and $\frac{2}{11}$ into decimals.

  b Use your answers to part **a** to write the values of

  $\frac{3}{11}, \frac{4}{11}, \frac{5}{11}, \frac{6}{11}, \frac{7}{11}, \frac{8}{11}, \frac{9}{11}, \frac{10}{11}$.

8 **Finance** On one day £11 is worth €12.
  How much is €1 worth?

9 This cake recipe is for 12 people.
  Work out how much of each
  ingredient is needed for a
  recipe for 7 people.

flour	200 g
butter	150 g
sugar	180 g
eggs	4
vanilla	50 ml

Q8 Strategy hint
Give your answer to the nearest penny.

Worked example

Write $0.\dot{7}$ as a fraction.

Call the recurring decimal n.

$$0.\dot{7} = 0.7777777\ldots = n$$

Multiply the recurring decimal by 10.

$$10n = 7.7777777\ldots$$

$$10n - n = 7.7777777\ldots - 0.7777777\ldots$$

$$= 7.000\,000\ldots$$

Subtract the value of n from the value of $10n$ so that all the decimal places become zero.

$$9n = 7$$

$$n = \frac{7}{9}$$

Solve the equation.

---

10 Write these recurring decimals as fractions.
   a $0.\dot{1}$ **b** $0.\dot{6}$

11 Write each two-figure recurring decimal as a fraction.
   a $0.\dot{1}\dot{7}$ **b** $0.8\dot{3}\dot{1}$ **c** $0.\dot{2}3\dot{4}$

12 Write these recurring decimals as fractions.
   a $0.1\dot{6}$ **b** $0.2\dot{3}$ **c** $0.4\dot{5}$

13 Change these recurring decimals into mixed numbers.
   a $3.\dot{4}$ **b** $6.\dot{1}\dot{4}$ **c** $12.3\dot{5}$

14 **Finance** On a particular day the exchange rate is
   $1 = £0.737\,373\ldots$
   Give the exchange rate as $ to £ using whole numbers of $ and £

15 **Finance** On a different day the exchange rate is $1 = £0.787\,878\ldots$
   Give the exchange rate as $ to £ using whole numbers of $ and £.

16 **Explore** Can you prove that $0.999\,999\ldots = 1$?
   Is it easier to explore this question now that you have completed
   the lesson? What further information do you need to be able to
   answer this?

17 **Reflect** In this lesson you have been doing lots of work with
   decimals.
   Imagine someone had never seen a decimal point before. How
   would you define it? How would you describe what it does? Write a
   description in your own words. Compare your description with those
   of others in your class.

Q11 Strategy hint
Multiply by 100 or 1000.

Q12 Strategy hint
Find $100n$ and $10n$, then subtract when you only have the recurring digit after the decimal point.

Q13 Strategy hint
Use the same method as for Q12 but take care with your equations.

Explore

Reflect

6.4 Multiplying fractions

Confidence

You will learn to:
- Multiply integers and fractions by a fraction.
- Use appropriate methods for multiplying fractions.

Why learn this?
Royalty fees for songwriters are split into twelfths. The publisher multiplies by twelfths to work out the fee for each person or rights holder.

Fluency
Work out
- 15×3
- 4×6
- 13×3
- $\frac{1}{2}$ of $50\,ml$
- $\frac{1}{3}$ of $12\,oz$

Explore
How many times can you halve a cake before nothing is left?

Exercise 6.4

Warm up

1 Work out

   a $\frac{3}{4}$ of $100\,kg$　　**b** $\frac{2}{5}$ of $50\,cm$　　**c** $\frac{7}{10}$ of $30\,ml$

2 Simplify these fractions.

   a $\frac{4}{12}$　　　　　**b** $\frac{15}{25}$　　　　　**c** $\frac{8}{36}$

   d $\frac{13}{10}$　　　　　**e** $\frac{25}{2}$　　　　　**f** $6\frac{3}{9}$

3 Work out

   a $\frac{1}{7} \times 56$　　**b** $\frac{3}{4} \times 24$　　**c** $60 \times \frac{1}{3}$　　**d** $27 \times \frac{2}{9}$

   e $\frac{2}{5} \times 25$　　**f** $\frac{3}{4} \times 12$　　**g** $18 \times \frac{2}{9}$　　**h** $64 \times \frac{5}{8}$

   Q3a hint

   $\frac{1}{7} \times 56$ is the same as $\frac{1}{7}$ of 56.

4 Work out these multiplications. Use the fraction wall to check your answers.

1											
$\frac{1}{3}$			$\frac{1}{3}$			$\frac{1}{3}$					
$\frac{1}{6}$		$\frac{1}{6}$		$\frac{1}{6}$		$\frac{1}{6}$		$\frac{1}{6}$		$\frac{1}{6}$	
$\frac{1}{2}$						$\frac{1}{2}$					
$\frac{1}{12}$	$\frac{1}{12}$	$\frac{1}{12}$	$\frac{1}{12}$	$\frac{1}{12}$	$\frac{1}{12}$	$\frac{1}{12}$	$\frac{1}{12}$	$\frac{1}{12}$	$\frac{1}{12}$	$\frac{1}{12}$	$\frac{1}{12}$
$\frac{1}{4}$			$\frac{1}{4}$			$\frac{1}{4}$			$\frac{1}{4}$		
$\frac{1}{8}$		$\frac{1}{8}$		$\frac{1}{8}$		$\frac{1}{8}$		$\frac{1}{8}$		$\frac{1}{8}$	$\frac{1}{8}$

   a $\frac{1}{2} \times \frac{1}{2}$　　　**b** $\frac{1}{3} \times \frac{1}{2}$　　　**c** $\frac{1}{4} \times \frac{1}{2}$

   d $\frac{3}{4} \times \frac{1}{2}$　　　**e** $-\frac{2}{3} \times \frac{1}{4}$　　　**f** $-\frac{5}{6} \times \frac{1}{2}$

   Q4e hint

   Use the rule for multiplying negtive numbers.

Topic links: Area, Perimeter, Probability, Equivalent fractions and decimals

5 **Problem-solving / Reasoning** Jane and Bhavika spin this spinner 50 times.

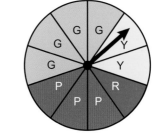

  a They want to know how many times to expect the spinner to land on red.
  Jane says, 'The probability is 0.1, so I'm going to multiply 50 by 0.1.'
  Bhavika says, 'The probability is $\frac{1}{10}$, so I'm going to multiply 50 by $\frac{1}{10}$.'
  Will they both get the same answer? Explain.

  b How many times should they expect the spinner to land on yellow?

  c Bhavika expects the spinner to land on a particular colour 15 times.
  Which colour?

Key point

To multiply two fractions, multiply their numerators and multiply their denominators.

Worked example

Work out $\frac{3}{8}$ of 12 kg.

$$\frac{3}{8} \times 12 = \frac{3 \times 12}{8} = \frac{36}{8}$$

> 12 ÷ 8 isn't a whole number, so work out 3 × 12 first.

$36 \div 8 = 4$ remainder 4

> Divide 36 by 8 and write as a whole number and a remainder.

$$\frac{3}{8} \text{ of } 12\,kg = 4\frac{4}{8}\,kg = 4\frac{1}{2}\,kg$$

> Write your answer as a mixed number in its simplest form.

6 Work out these fractions of the amounts.
  Write each answer as a mixed number in its simplest form.

  a $\frac{2}{5}$ of 18 kg   **b** $\frac{3}{4}$ of 13 m

  c $\frac{5}{6}$ of 20 mm   **d** $\frac{2}{9}$ of 21 km

7 **Real** The formula to convert a distance in kilometres to a distance in miles is

  distance in miles = $\frac{5}{8}$ of distance in kilometres

  Carlos sees this sign.
  How many miles is Carlos from Barcelona?

  Barcelona   42 km

Investigation   **Problem-solving**

Chris works out $\frac{9}{28} \times \frac{7}{12}$ like this.

$$\frac{9}{28} \times \frac{7}{12} = \frac{9 \times 7}{28 \times 12}$$
$$= \frac{63}{336}$$

Kamran works it out like this.

$$\frac{9}{28} \times \frac{7}{12} = \frac{9 \times 7}{28 \times 12}$$
$$= \frac{{}^3\cancel{9} \times \cancel{7}^1}{{}_4\cancel{12} \times \cancel{28}_4}$$
$$= \frac{3}{4} \times \frac{1}{4}$$
$$= \frac{3}{16}$$

1 Did they both get the same answer?

2 Whose method do you prefer? Why?

3 Use your preferred method to work out $\frac{8}{49} \times \frac{7}{24}$

8 Work these out, using the second method from the investigation.

a $\frac{5}{6} \times \frac{9}{10}$

b $\frac{5}{12} \times \frac{6}{15}$

c $\frac{7}{8} \times \frac{4}{7}$

d $\frac{20}{21} \times \frac{3}{10}$

e $\frac{5}{14} \times \frac{6}{15}$

f $\frac{17}{33} \times \frac{11}{34}$

Key point

When you multiply fractions you can rearrange them so they cancel.

9 **Real / Finance** A company pays a fee of £3000 to use a song in an advertisement. There are three people in the band: the writer gets $\frac{4}{12}$ of the fee, the singer gets $\frac{1}{12}$ and the guitarist gets $\frac{1}{12}$.

a What fraction of the fee does the whole band get?

b How much money does each member of the band receive?

Q9a hint

$\frac{2 \times 9}{3 \times 10} = \frac{2 \times 9}{10 \times 3}$

10 Work out

a $\frac{2}{3} \times \frac{7}{8}$

b $-\frac{3}{7} \times \frac{7}{12}$

c $\frac{4}{9} \times \frac{2}{9}$

d $-\frac{5}{6} \times \frac{2}{9}$

e $\frac{9}{11} \times \frac{2}{3} \times \frac{11}{20}$

f $\frac{9}{14} \times \frac{3}{18} \times \frac{7}{8}$

11 Work out the area of each rectangle.

a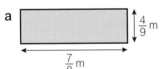

b

12 **Explore** How many times can you halve a cake before nothing is left?
Look back at the maths you have learned in this lesson. How can you use it to answer this question?

13 **Reflect** Look back at Q4.
How did you learn how to multiply fractions?
What is good and what is not so good about learning a new mathematics skill using fraction walls?
Explain your answer.
In what other ways do you like to learn new mathematics skills?

Q13 hint

Did you read the worked example?
Did your teacher explain it to you?

6.5 Dividing by fractions

You will learn to:
- Write the reciprocal of a number or a fraction.
- Divide integers by a fraction and divide fractions by a fraction.

Why learn this?
Builders of telescopes use reciprocals to work out the shapes of the lenses they need.

Fluency
- How many eighths are in 1 whole?
- Which is larger, $\frac{1}{9}$ or $\frac{1}{10}$?
- What do you multiply $\frac{1}{3}$ by to get 1 whole?

Explore
Will a sequence of reciprocals ever have a 0 term?

Exercise 6.5

1 Which of these calculations has the biggest answer?

A $4 \times \frac{1}{3}$ **B** $5 \times \frac{1}{5}$

C $5 \times \frac{5}{16}$ **D** $8 \times \frac{1}{9}$

2 Find

a $\frac{2}{5} \times \frac{2}{3}$ **b** $\frac{5}{7} \times \frac{1}{6}$

c $\frac{11}{16} \times \frac{9}{11}$ **d** $\frac{9}{20} \times \frac{5}{18}$

3 Write down the **reciprocal** of

a $\frac{2}{3}$ **b** 4

c $\frac{1}{7}$ **d** 8

e 11

4 Write down the reciprocal of

a $1\frac{1}{2}$ **b** $2\frac{2}{3}$

c $5\frac{1}{5}$ **d** $3\frac{11}{13}$

5 Use the reciprocal to work out

a $9 \div \frac{1}{3}$ **b** $6 \div \frac{2}{3}$

c $\frac{1}{5} \div \frac{2}{3}$ **d** $8 \div 1\frac{3}{5}$

e $7 \div 2\frac{2}{7}$ **f** $25 \div \frac{10}{11}$

Warm up

Key point

The **reciprocal** of a fraction is the 'upside down' or inverse of that fraction.
The reciprocal of $\frac{2}{5} = \frac{1}{\frac{2}{5}} = \frac{1 \times 5}{\frac{2}{5} \times 5} = \frac{5}{2}$

Q3b hint

$4 = \frac{4}{1}$

Q4 Strategy hint

Write mixed numbers as improper fractions first.

Q5 hint

To divide by a fraction, multiply by the reciprocal.

1 Find

    a $\frac{2}{3} \times \frac{3}{2}$ **b** $\frac{3}{4} \times \frac{4}{3}$ **c** $\frac{1}{3} \times 3$ **d** $\frac{2}{9} \times \frac{9}{2}$

2 Copy and complete.

    $\frac{a}{b} \times \square = 1$

    Discussion Is your statement from part **2** correct for $\frac{4}{5} \times 1\frac{1}{4} = 1$?

    The $\boxed{1/x}$ or $\boxed{x^{-1}}$ button on your calculator works out the reciprocal of a number.

3 a Use this button to find the reciprocal of 8.

    b Use the button again to find the reciprocal of your answer to part **a**.

4 Repeat part **3** for different numbers.
    What do you notice?

5 Copy and complete.
    If a number is greater than 1, its reciprocal is … than 1.
    If a number is less than 1, its reciprocal is … than 1.

6 Calculate

    a $\frac{2}{3} \div \frac{1}{4}$ **b** $\frac{6}{13} \div \frac{2}{3}$

    c $3\frac{1}{9} \div \frac{3}{4}$ **d** $\frac{22}{3} \div \frac{11}{4}$

7 Reasoning A length of wire is 22.5 m long.
    How many pieces of wire that are $\frac{1}{3}$ m long can be cut from the piece
    of wire?

8 Problem-solving A car travels 25 miles in $\frac{2}{5}$ hours.
    Assuming that the speed of the car remains constant, how many
    miles can the car cover in 5 hours?

9 Explore Will a sequence of reciprocals ever have a 0 term?
    Choose some sensible numbers to help you to explore this situation.
    Then use what you've learned in this lesson to help you to answer
    the question.

10 Reflect The reciprocal of a fraction is sometimes called the
    'multiplicative inverse'.
    What does 'multiplicative' mean?
    What does 'inverse' mean?
    Use what you have learned in this lesson to explain why the
    reciprocal of a fraction is its multiplicative inverse.

Strategy hint

Use examples to help your
explanation.

6.6 Adding and subtracting fractions

You will learn to:
- Add and subtract fractions with any size denominator.

Why learn this?
Fractions are used when shops have sales.

Fluency
- $\frac{2}{5} = \frac{\square}{25}$
- $\frac{4}{9} = \frac{16}{\square}$

Explore
Fractions are more accurate than decimals.

Exercise 6.6

1 a $\frac{1}{4} + \frac{2}{12} =$ **b** $\frac{5}{7} - \frac{2}{14} =$

2 Find the lowest common multiple (LCM) of 12 and 16.

> **Worked example**
>
> Work out $\frac{2}{3} + \frac{1}{4}$
>
> $\frac{2}{3} + \frac{1}{4} = \frac{8}{12} + \frac{3}{12}$ ⎯   The LCM of 3 and 4 is 12.
>
> $\quad\quad\quad = \frac{11}{12}$

3 Work out

   a $\frac{1}{2} + \frac{1}{3}$ **b** $\frac{1}{5} + \frac{2}{3}$

   c $\frac{4}{5} - \frac{1}{4}$ **d** $\frac{1}{2} - \frac{1}{5}$

4 Calculate these. Give each answer in its simplest form.

   a $\frac{1}{2} + \frac{1}{6}$ **b** $\frac{9}{10} - \frac{3}{8}$

   Discussion Can you use a common denominator that isn't the LCM?

5 Work out these. Give your answers as mixed numbers.

   a $\frac{5}{6} + \frac{2}{3}$ **b** $\frac{1}{9} + \frac{9}{10}$

   c $\frac{3}{4} + \frac{3}{5}$ **d** $\frac{1}{2} + \frac{8}{9}$

6 Evaluate

   a $\frac{8}{3} - \frac{4}{5}$ **b** $\frac{31}{6} + \frac{17}{8}$

   c $\frac{191}{9} - \frac{14}{3}$ **d** $\frac{11}{10} + \frac{17}{12}$

7 **Problem-solving** The diagram shows four fractions linked by lines.
  a Find the total of any two linked fractions.
  b Which two fractions give the greatest total?
    Work out this total and write it as a mixed number in its simplest form.
  c Find the difference between any two linked fractions.
  d Which two fractions give you the greatest difference?
    Work out this difference and write it in its simplest form.
  Discussion How did you work out your answers to parts **b** and **d**?

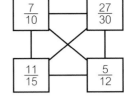

8 Calculate these. Give each answer in its simplest form and as a mixed number where necessary.

  a $\frac{1}{2} + \frac{2}{3} + \frac{3}{4}$ b $\frac{4}{5} + \frac{1}{4} + \frac{1}{2}$

  c $\frac{5}{8} + \frac{7}{12} - \frac{11}{24}$ d $\frac{24}{25} - \frac{2}{5} - \frac{13}{50}$

Q8a hint

$\frac{1}{2} + \frac{2}{3} + \frac{3}{4} = \frac{\square}{12} + \frac{\square}{12} + \frac{\square}{12}$

9 **Problem-solving** The table shows the fraction of class 7T that support three different rugby teams.

Rugby team	Scarlets	Blues	Dragons
Fraction of class	$\frac{2}{15}$	$\frac{3}{10}$	1

Q9a hint

Start by working out the total fraction of the class that support the Scarlets, Blues and Dragons.

  a What fraction of the class do not support the Scarlets, Blues or Dragons?
  b How many students do you think are in class 7T? Explain your answer.

Investigation   **Problem-solving**

Write fractions in the square so that the diagonals, rows and columns all sum to the same amount.

Create your own square for someone else to complete.

10 **Explore** Fractions are more accurate than decimals.
   Is it easier to explore this statement now that you have completed the lesson?
   What further information do you need to be able to answer this?

11 Look back at the questions in this lesson.
   a Write down the question that was the easiest to answer. What made it easy?
   b Write down the question that was the most difficult to answer. What made it difficult?
   c Look again at the question that you wrote down for part **b**. Discuss with a classmate what you could do to make this type of question easier to answer.

Explore

Reflect

6.7 Calculating with mixed numbers

You will learn to:
- Use the four operations with mixed numbers.

Why learn this?
Measurements in real life are more likely to be a mixed number than a whole number.

Fluency
Write these improper fractions as mixed numbers.
- $\frac{15}{2}$
- $\frac{10}{7}$
- $\frac{15}{9}$

Explore
Why did people use mixed numbers more in the 1950s?

Exercise 6.7

1 Work out

a $\frac{1}{2} + \frac{2}{3}$ **b** $\frac{3}{4} + \frac{1}{8}$ **c** $\frac{2}{5} - \frac{1}{4}$

d $\frac{3}{10} \times \frac{1}{3}$ **e** $\frac{1}{2} \div \frac{3}{4}$ **f** $\frac{8}{9} \div \frac{1}{3}$

2 a Work out the missing value.

  b Work out the perimeter.

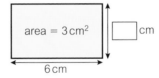

area = 3 cm²   ☐ cm

6 cm

3 Write these mixed numbers as improper fractions.

a $5\frac{1}{2}$ **b** $2\frac{3}{8}$

c $9\frac{1}{6}$ **d** $10\frac{3}{4}$

4 Work out these calculations of mixed numbers.
Write the answers in their simplest form.
The first one has been started for you.

a $3\frac{1}{4} + 2\frac{1}{2} = 5 + \frac{1}{4} + \frac{2}{4} =$ **b** $1\frac{1}{2} + 5\frac{1}{3}$ **c** $5\frac{3}{10} + 2\frac{1}{5}$

d $3\frac{2}{3} + 4\frac{4}{5}$ **e** $5\frac{3}{8} + 2\frac{7}{9}$ **f** $2\frac{3}{4} - 1\frac{1}{2}$

g $10\frac{1}{8} - 4\frac{1}{10}$

> **Q4 hint**
>
> Add the whole numbers first, then add the fraction parts by writing them with a common denominator.

5 Real / Problem-solving Paul is travelling from Pakistan to India.

a He spends $2\frac{1}{2}$ hours on the bus. He then travels for $3\frac{3}{4}$ hours by train. How long does he spend travelling?

b Paul sets off at 14 45. The time in India is 30 minutes ahead of Pakistan. What time does he arrive at his destination in India?

Topic links: Area, Measures   **Unit 6** Fractions, decimals, ratio and proportion   **144**

Warm up

Worked example

Work out $5\frac{2}{3} - 1\frac{5}{6}$

$$5\frac{2}{3} - 1\frac{5}{6} = \frac{17}{3} - \frac{11}{6}$$

Write both numbers as improper fractions.

$$= \frac{34}{6} - \frac{11}{6}$$

Write the fractions with a common denominator.

$$= \frac{23}{6}$$

$$= 3\frac{5}{6}$$

Write the answer as a mixed number.

Key point

It is usually easier to write mixed numbers as improper fractions before doing the calculation.

6 Work out these subtractions.

 a $3\frac{2}{3} - 2\frac{3}{4}$ b $2\frac{2}{5} - 2\frac{3}{10}$ c $8\frac{1}{2} - 4\frac{3}{5}$ d $2\frac{5}{6} - 5\frac{1}{3}$

 e $4\frac{3}{4} - \frac{11}{16}$ f $4\frac{3}{7} - 3\frac{1}{3}$ g $1\frac{1}{3} - 4\frac{3}{4}$ h $3\frac{2}{3} - 5\frac{8}{9}$

7 Sanjay has completed $15\frac{2}{3}$ miles of a $24\frac{5}{7}$ mile race.
 How far does he have left to run?

8 Work out

 a $2\frac{1}{2} \times 3\,\text{kg}$ b $4\frac{1}{10} \times 6\,\text{m}$ c $1\frac{3}{5} \times 10$

 d $2\frac{1}{2} \times 2\frac{1}{2}$ e $3\frac{3}{4} \times 1\frac{1}{3}$ f $5\frac{2}{3} \times 2\frac{1}{10}$

Q8a hint

Write mixed numbers as improper fractions before multiplying.

9 **Problem-solving** Mumtaz can swim $1\frac{1}{5}$ times faster than Ethan.
 Ethan can swim one length of the pool in 30 seconds.
 How long will it take Mumtaz to swim one length?

10 Work out the area of this trapezium.

$3\frac{1}{4}$ cm

$3\frac{1}{2}$ cm

$5\frac{1}{2}$ cm

Q10 hint

The formula for working out the area of a trapezium is
 area $= \frac{1}{2}(a + b)h$

11 Work out

 a $6\frac{1}{4} \div 2$ b $9\frac{2}{5} \div 3$ c $10\frac{2}{3} \div \frac{1}{2}$

 d $2\frac{3}{4} \div \frac{2}{5}$ e $15\frac{5}{8} \div \frac{3}{5}$ f $4\frac{4}{5} \div \frac{5}{6}$

12 A relay race is $1\frac{1}{4}$ miles. There are three relay runners on the team.
 Each person runs the same distance.
 How far does each person run?

13 A pancake recipe uses $1\frac{3}{4}$ pints of milk to make 20 pancakes.
 How much is needed to make 10 pancakes?

14 Find the lengths of these rectangles.

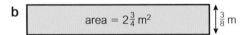

 a | area $= 6\frac{1}{3}$ m² | $\frac{3}{4}$ m
 b | area $= 2\frac{3}{4}$ m² | $\frac{3}{8}$ m

15 **Explore** Why did people use mixed numbers more in the 1950s?
 Choose some sensible numbers to help you to explore this situation. Then
 use what you have learned in this lesson to help you to answer the question.

16 **Reflect** What is the same when you calculate with fractions and
 with mixed numbers? What is different?

Explore

Reflect

6.8 Solving problems with fractions and decimals

You will learn to:
- Solve problems involving fractions and decimals.
- Use estimates to check answers.
- Solve problems involving the four operations with integers, fractions and decimals, including powers, roots and brackets.

Why learn this?
Calculations involving fractions and decimals are used in the stock markets.

Fluency
- $0.25 = \dfrac{\square}{8}$
- $0.15 = \dfrac{3}{\square}$

Explore
The population of the UK in 1900 was about $\frac{2}{3}$ of the population in 2000. What was the population in 1900?

Exercise 6.8

1 a 2.2×4.3

b $16.2 \div 0.2$

2 a $\frac{3}{8} \times \frac{2}{5}$

b $\frac{2}{7} \div \frac{1}{4}$

3 a $\frac{5}{18} \times \frac{2}{3}$

b $2\frac{7}{11} - 1\frac{3}{4}$

4 Reasoning Lynn says, '13.892 rounded to 2 decimal places is 13.9'.
 a Explain why Lynn is wrong.
 b What is the correct answer?

5 Finance Saira buys three pairs of jeans for $125.
 How much does each pair of jeans cost? Round your answer to the nearest cent.

6 A swimming pool has dimensions 10.5 m × 4.9 m × 1.2 m.
 Find the volume of the swimming pool.

7 Problem-solving A pile of paper is 2.5 cm tall. Each piece of paper is 0.1 mm thick.
 How many pieces of paper are in the pile?

Warm up

8 Finance On a particular day, £11 is worth 15 euros.
How many £ is 1 euro worth? Give your answer as a decimal using dot notation.

9 Write $2.\dot{3}\dot{4}$ as a fraction.

10 Evaluate

$$(1 + 0.5)^2 + \frac{3}{4} \div \frac{1}{5}$$

Give your answer as a fraction in its simplest form.

11 Reasoning Denil thinks that a quarter of a third is a sixth.
Is he correct? Explain your reasoning.

12 Reasoning How many twelfths are there in 2.5?

13 Problem-solving A food wholesaler buys 52.5 kg bags of rice. He puts all the rice into 250 g packets.
How many 250 g packets can he fill from five large bags?

14 Problem-solving A motorcycle can travel 20 km on $\frac{1}{3}$ of a litre of petrol.
How much petrol would be required to travel 75 km?

15 Real The US has a population of approximately 330 million people.
Given that 0.35 of the population have blue eyes, calculate the number of people in the US who do not have blue eyes.

16 Explore The population of the UK in 1900 was about $\frac{2}{3}$ of the population in 2000.
What was the population in 1900?
Is it easier to explore this question now that you have completed the lesson?
What further information do you need to be able to answer this?

17 Reflect In the last few lessons you have learned a lot about fractions and decimals.
Which topic did you find the most difficult? Why did you find it the most difficult?

Subject link: Geography (Q16)

Active Learn   Homework, Year 8, Unit 6

6 Check up

Rounding decimals

1 Round these numbers to 2 decimal places.
  a 6.8345   **b** 0.019623   **c** 12.2561

2 A pack of 6 lollies costs £2.95.
  How much does each lolly cost to the nearest penny?

3 Work out $2 \div 7$. Give your answer to 2 decimal places.

Multiplying and dividing decimals

4 Calculate
  a 3.1×1.8 **b** 2.6×4.7

5 Use a written method to evaluate
  a 2.3×12.1 **b** $0.356 \div 0.004$

> **Q5a hint**
> Estimate the answer first.

Converting fractions to decimals

6 Write each fraction as a decimal.
  a $\frac{2}{9}$ **b** $\frac{5}{6}$

7 Write the first 12 decimal digits of these decimals with repeating digits.
  a $0.\dot{1}4285\dot{7}$ **b** $0.06\dot{8}\dot{1}$

8 Write these decimals with repeating digits as fractions.
  a $0.\dot{7}$ **b** $0.72\dot{3}\dot{5}$

Multiplying fractions

9 Work these out. Write your answers in their simplest form.
  a $\frac{3}{10} \times \frac{5}{6}$ **b** $\frac{2}{3} \times \frac{3}{4}$ **c** $\frac{15}{16} \times \frac{4}{5}$ **d** $\frac{6}{11} \times \frac{1}{3}$

10 A rectangle is $\frac{9}{20}$ m long and $\frac{5}{8}$ m wide.
  a Calculate the perimeter of the rectangle.
  b Calculate the area of the rectangle.

11 Janina notices that her car petrol gauge reads half full when she leaves for work in the morning. By the time she returns home, she has used two thirds of the fuel in the tank. What does her petrol gauge read when she gets home?

Dividing by fractions

12 Work out
  a $4 \div \frac{1}{3}$ **b** $10 \div \frac{2}{5}$ **c** $7 \div \frac{5}{6}$

13 Calculate these. Give your answers as mixed numbers where needed.

    a $\frac{1}{4} \div 6$ **b** $\frac{4}{9} \div 3$ **c** $\frac{2}{3} \div \frac{1}{15}$

    d $\frac{5}{13} \div \frac{4}{25}$ **e** $\frac{1}{25} \div \frac{2}{25}$ **f** $\frac{16}{21} \div \frac{8}{3}$

14 A baker divides a 3 kg ball of dough for making bread into pieces that each weigh $\frac{1}{5}$ kg. How many pieces does she have?

Adding and subtracting fractions

15 Calculate these. Simplify your answers if possible.

    a $\frac{1}{4} + \frac{2}{5}$ **b** $\frac{1}{3} - \frac{1}{4}$ **c** $\frac{4}{9} + \frac{1}{2}$

    d $\frac{5}{6} - \frac{1}{5}$ **e** $\frac{9}{10} - \frac{5}{6}$ **f** $\frac{7}{8} - \frac{5}{12}$

    g $\frac{3}{9} + \frac{1}{6}$ **h** $\frac{7}{12} + \frac{2}{9}$

16 Theo says, ' $\frac{1}{6} + \frac{1}{4} = \frac{2}{10}$ '

Work out $\frac{1}{6} + \frac{1}{4}$ correctly to explain why Theo has made a mistake.

17 Work these out. Write your answers as mixed numbers where appropriate.

    a $\frac{4}{5} + \frac{5}{6}$ **b** $\frac{2}{3} + \frac{5}{8}$ **c** $\frac{11}{15} - \frac{1}{2}$

    d $\frac{17}{20} - \frac{3}{8}$ **e** $\frac{7}{10} - \frac{5}{24}$ **f** $\frac{6}{7} + \frac{5}{8}$

    g $\frac{7}{8} + \frac{7}{10}$ **h** $\frac{5}{8} + \frac{8}{9}$

18 $\frac{4}{9}$ of the memory on Harry's computer stores MP3 files. Video files take up another $\frac{1}{7}$.

How much memory is left on Harry's computer?

Calculating with mixed numbers

19 Evaluate

    a $1\frac{2}{7} \times 3\frac{4}{5}$ **b** $\frac{3}{8} \div 2\frac{4}{9}$

Solving problems with fractions and decimals

20 **Problem-solving** Dev cuts some pizzas into 8 equally sized pieces. How many pieces are there in 3 and a half pizzas?

21 **Problem-solving** A carpenter makes a work surface by gluing together two pieces of wood of different thicknesses. The first piece has a thickness of $\frac{3}{8}$ of an inch. The second piece has a thickness that is $\frac{1}{4}$ of the thickness of the first piece. How thick is the work surface?

22 **How sure are you of your answers? Were you mostly**
  ☹ **Just guessing**   😐 **Feeling doubtful**   ☺ **Confident**
What next? Use your results to decide whether to strengthen or extend your learning.

Challenge

23 Find two different fractions that add together to give a fraction that is a decimal with repeating digits. Write the fraction as a decimal using dot notation.

6 Strengthen

You will:
- Strengthen your understanding with practice.

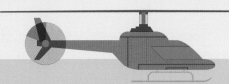

Rounding decimals

1 Which of these numbers are rounded to 2 decimal places?
2.471   12.6   9.34   0.01   102.8

2 Round each number to 2 decimal places.
   a 0.354   **b** 0.3654   **c** 0.3449

3 Poppy works out £3.96 ÷ 5 = £0.792.
Write her answer to the nearest penny.

4 Find to the nearest penny.
   a £5.80 ÷ 7   **b** £35 ÷ 3

Multiplying and dividing decimals

1 Use a written method to calculate 6.43×4.38

2 Use a written method to calculate $0.246 \div 0.06$

Converting fractions to decimals

1 Which of these decimals have repeating digits?
   a 0.582472...   **b** 0.666666...   **c** 0.382382...

2 Write the first 12 decimal digits of these decimals with repeating digits.
   a $0.\dot{7}$ **b** $0.1\dot{3}$ **c** $0.\dot{1}\dot{3}$
   d $0.12\dot{3}$ **e** $0.2\dot{3}\dot{1}$ **f** $0.\dot{3}1\dot{7}$

3 Write as decimals, using dot notation.
   a $\frac{1}{15}$ **b** $\frac{1}{7}$

4 a Write $\frac{1}{6}$ as a decimal using dot notation.

   b Write $\frac{2}{3}$ as a decimal using dot notation.

   c Write another fraction that has the same decimal equivalent as $\frac{4}{6}$

   d Do all fractions with a denominator of 6 recur? Explain your answer.

5 Copy and complete the working to convert $0.\dot{4}$ into a fraction.

$$n = 0.444...$$
$$10n = 4.444...$$
$$10n - n = \quad 4.444...$$
$$- 0.444...$$
$$9n = \square$$
$$n = \square$$

Q1 hint
Which of these numbers have 2 digits after the decimal point?

Q2a hint
Use the number line to help you.
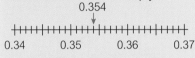
0.34   0.35   0.36   0.37
Is 0.354 closer to 0.35 or 0.36?

Q3 hint
£□.□□

Q1 hint
Estimate the answer first.

Q2 hint
Multiply both sides by 1000.

Q1 hint
Is there a repeating pattern?

Q2 hint
The digits with dots show the repeating pattern.
So $0.2\dot{4}$ means 0.242424...
   $0.2\dot{4}$ means 0.244444...
   $0.\dot{4}3\dot{6}$ means 0.436436...

Q3a hint
$15\overline{)1.000}$

Q4d hint
Try other fractions with a denominator of 6.

6 Write these decimals with repeating digits as fractions.
    a $0.\dot{6}$ **b** $0.\dot{3}$ **c** $0.\dot{5}$

Q6 hint

Use the same method as in Q5.

7 Write these decimals with repeating digits as fractions.
The first part has been started for you.
    a $0.\dot{2}\dot{3}$

$$n = 0.2323...$$
$$100n = 23.2323...$$
$$100n - n = \quad 23.2323...$$
$$- 0.2323...$$
$$99n = \square$$
$$n = \square$$

    b $0.\dot{7}\dot{4}$ **c** $0.\dot{8}\dot{1}$

8 Write these decimals with repeating digits as fractions. The first part has been started for you.
    a $0.1\dot{6}$ **b** $0.6\dot{7}$ **c** $0.4\dot{6}$

$$n = 0.1666...$$
$$10n = 1.666...$$
$$100n = 16.666...$$
$$100n - 10n = \square$$
$$90n = \square$$
$$n = \square$$

Multiplying fractions

1 Calculate

    a $5 \times \frac{1}{3} = 5$ lots of $\frac{1}{3} = \frac{1}{3} + \frac{1}{3} + \frac{1}{3} + \frac{1}{3} + \frac{1}{3} = \square\frac{\square}{3}$

    b $2 \times \frac{1}{7} = \frac{1}{7} + \frac{1}{7} = \frac{\square}{\square}$

    c $\frac{3}{5} \times 4 = 4 \times \frac{3}{5} = \frac{3}{5} + \frac{3}{5} + \frac{3}{5} + \frac{3}{5} = \frac{\square}{5} = \square\frac{\square}{5}$

    d $\frac{6}{11} \times 3$ **e** $5 \times \frac{2}{7}$ **f** $\frac{1}{4}$ of 18   **g** $\frac{9}{10}$ of 40

2 Work out these multiplications. Simplify the fractions first.

    a $\frac{5}{6} \times \frac{3}{5} = \frac{5 \times \square}{6 \times \square} = \frac{\square \times 5}{6 \times \square} = \frac{\square}{6} \times \frac{5}{\square}$

    b $\frac{12}{33} \times \frac{11}{4}$ **c** $\frac{8}{15} \times \frac{5}{24}$ **d** $\frac{14}{25} \times \frac{10}{7}$ **e** $\frac{20}{63} \times \frac{9}{10}$

Dividing by fractions

1 Write down the reciprocals of these numbers.

    a $\frac{2}{7}$ **b** $\frac{3}{4}$ **c** 5   **d** 12

    e $\frac{1}{3}$ **f** $\frac{1}{2}$ **g** $\frac{1}{8}$ **h** 6

Q1c hint

The reciprocal of a whole number,
is $\frac{1}{\text{number}}$.

2 Find

    a $\frac{3}{5} \div \frac{2}{7} = \frac{3}{5} \times \frac{\square}{2} = \frac{\square}{10}$ **b** $\frac{8}{9} \div \frac{1}{5} = \frac{8}{9} \times \frac{\square}{1} = \frac{\square}{\square}$

    c $\frac{1}{10} \div \frac{2}{3}$ **d** $\frac{3}{7} \div \frac{1}{6}$ **e** $\frac{10}{51} \div \frac{2}{5}$

Q2 Strategy hint

Multiply the first number by the reciprocal of the second.

Adding and subtracting fractions

1 Match each calculation to a diagram and find the answer.

a $\frac{2}{3} + \frac{1}{3}$ A

| $\frac{1}{2}$ | $\frac{1}{2}$ |

b $\frac{1}{3} + \frac{1}{3}$ B

| $\frac{1}{2}$ | $\frac{1}{4}$ | |

c $\frac{1}{2} + \frac{1}{2}$ C

| $\frac{1}{3}$ | $\frac{1}{3}$ | |

d $\frac{1}{3} + \frac{1}{6}$ D

| $\frac{2}{3}$ | $\frac{1}{3}$ |

e $\frac{1}{2} + \frac{1}{4}$ E

| $\frac{1}{3}$ | $\frac{1}{6}$ | |

2 Use the diagrams and your answers from Q1 to find

a $1 - \frac{1}{2}$ **b** $\frac{2}{4} - \frac{1}{4}$ **c** $1 - \frac{2}{3}$

3 **Real** The probability of rolling a 4 on a dice is $\frac{1}{6}$.
What is the probability of not rolling a 4?

4 Add together these fractions by writing them with the same denominator.

a $\frac{1}{3} + \frac{2}{9}$ **b** $\frac{3}{5} + \frac{1}{10}$ **c** $\frac{1}{8} + \frac{3}{4}$ **d** $\frac{2}{15} + \frac{2}{3} + \frac{1}{5}$

5 Work out these fraction subtractions by writing them with the same denominator.

a $\frac{3}{4} - \frac{3}{8}$ **b** $\frac{2}{5} - \frac{3}{10}$ **c** $\frac{5}{6} - \frac{1}{3}$ **d** $\frac{7}{9} - \frac{2}{3}$

6 Copy and complete. The first two have been started for you.
   a The lowest common multiple of 2 and 7 is 14.

$$\frac{3}{7} + \frac{1}{2} = \frac{6}{14} + \frac{\square}{14} = \frac{\square}{14}$$

   b The lowest common multiple of 3 and 4 is 12.

$$\frac{1}{3} + \frac{1}{4} = \frac{\square}{12} + \frac{\square}{12} = \frac{\square}{12}$$

   c The lowest common multiple of 10 and 3 is $\square$.

$$\frac{3}{10} + \frac{2}{3} =$$

7 Find

a $\frac{5}{8} + \frac{1}{6}$ **b** $\frac{2}{5} - \frac{1}{12}$ **c** $\frac{6}{11} - \frac{2}{3}$

Calculating with mixed numbers

1 Work out these mixed number calculations.

a $2\frac{2}{3} + 1\frac{1}{3}$ **b** $1\frac{2}{5} + 3\frac{1}{5}$ **c** $5\frac{1}{6} + 2\frac{5}{6}$

2 Work out

a $1\frac{1}{3} + 2\frac{3}{4}$ **b** $4\frac{3}{10} + 2\frac{1}{5}$ **c** $3\frac{9}{10} + \frac{1}{7}$
d $10\frac{2}{5} + 3\frac{5}{6}$ **e** $7\frac{1}{8} + 4\frac{15}{16}$

Q4a hint

$\frac{1}{3} = \frac{3}{9}$

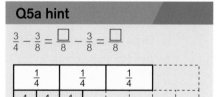

Q5a hint

$$\frac{3}{4} - \frac{3}{8} = \frac{\square}{8} - \frac{3}{8} = \frac{\square}{8}$$

Q7a hint

Use the LCM of the denominators.

Q1a hint

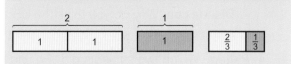

Q2a hint

How many wholes are there?

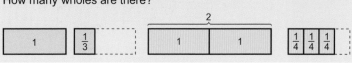

3 Work out these subtractions. Give your answers as mixed numbers.

a $5 - 3\frac{1}{2} = \frac{10}{2} - \frac{\square}{2}$ **b** $4\frac{2}{3} - 1\frac{1}{3}$ **c** $10\frac{3}{4} - 2\frac{1}{4}$

d $5\frac{4}{5} - 2\frac{1}{10}$ **e** $1\frac{1}{2} - \frac{3}{4}$ **f** $2\frac{3}{7} - 1\frac{7}{10}$

Q3a hint

Write as halves.
10 halves − ☐ halves = ☐ halves

4 Will divides his evening up like this.

Dinner: $\frac{3}{4}$ hour   Exercise: 1 hour   Homework: 1 hour 30 minutes

a How many hours and minutes has Will scheduled?

b He has 5 hours in total before bed. How much time does he have left?

Solving problems with fractions and decimals

1 Problem-solving A farmer notices that one of his grain stores is $\frac{5}{6}$ full. How much is in the grain store after he has used another $\frac{1}{3}$ of this amount?

2 Problem-solving A 3.5 m piece of rope is cut into lengths that are each 32 cm long. How much rope is left over?

Enrichment

1 Finance Jatin pays $\frac{1}{5}$ of his salary as tax.

He uses $\frac{1}{10}$ of his salary to pay back his student loan.

He pays $\frac{1}{4}$ of his salary into a pension scheme.

What fraction of his salary does he take home?

2 Real / Problem-solving Scientists recommend that babies sleep for $\frac{5}{8}$ of the day.

a How many hours should babies sleep for?

b Adults should sleep for 8 hours a day.
What fraction of the day is this?

c A mother sleeps only when her baby does.
What fraction of the day is she awake while her baby sleeps?

3 Finance / Real The US stock market used to trade in fractions. Prices were given as eighths of a dollar, instead of in cents.

Q3 Literacy hint

There are 100 cents in a dollar.

a How many cents is $\frac{1}{8}$ of a dollar?

b How many cents is $\frac{3}{8}$ of a dollar?

c Shares for one company cost $3\frac{5}{8}$ of a dollar per share.
How many shares could you get for $1125?

d Cleo's shares increased their value by $\frac{1}{2}$. They originally cost her $2\frac{1}{8}$ of a dollar. How much are they now?
Discussion Why do you think the US stock market changed to using decimals?

4 Reflect Which two subjects did you find hardest in this Unit? Explain.
Which two subjects did you find easiest in this Unit? Explain.

6 Extend

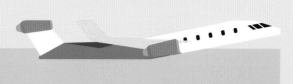

You will:
- Extend your understanding with problem-solving.

1 a Use your calculator to find these.
Then round your answer to 2 decimal places.

	Full calculator display	Rounded to 2 decimal places
$\sqrt{2}$		
$\sqrt{3}$		
$\sqrt{5}$		
$\sqrt{6}$		

b Why was $\sqrt{4}$ not included in this table?

2 Problem-solving a Find two possible original numbers.

Original number	Rounded to 1 d.p.	Rounded to nearest whole number
	6.5	6
	6.5	7

b Compare your answers with someone else in your class.
Are you both correct?

3 Problem-solving Hari gets the answer 9.7 correct to 1 decimal place.
Write down all the 2 decimal place numbers that round to 9.7.

4 A cereal box is 19.6 cm wide, 7.2 cm deep and 27.5 cm high.
a What is the volume of the cereal box?
b All three dimensions are halved. What is the ratio of the volume of
the small box to the volume of the original one?

5 Finance Sasha has $122.85 worth of shares each valued at $0.15.
How many shares does he have?

6 Find the decimal equivalent of all the fractions with denominator 14.
Discussion What is strange about this set of decimals?

7 Write these decimals with repeating digits as fractions.
a 0.22̇5̇   **b** 0.67̇4̇   **c** 0.49̇8̇   **d** 0.243̇

8 Write 0.7̇14285̇ as a fraction.

9 a Copy and complete the table.

Fraction	$\frac{1}{2}$	$\frac{1}{3}$	$\frac{1}{4}$	$\frac{1}{5}$	$\frac{1}{6}$	$\frac{1}{7}$	$\frac{1}{8}$	$\frac{1}{9}$	$\frac{1}{10}$	$\frac{1}{12}$	$\frac{1}{20}$
Decimal	0.5	0.3̇	0.25	0.2							

b Which denominators give recurring decimals?
c Which denominators give **finite** decimals?
d Write each denominator as a product of prime factors.

> **Q3 hint**
> Use the number line to help you.
>
> 9.6   9.7   9.8

> **Q6 hint**
> Look at the repeating digits in the answers.

> **Q8 Strategy hint**
> Choose which multiple of 10 to use when forming your equation.

> **Key point**
> **Finite** decimals stop after a number of decimal places.

e Dan says, 'If the denominator only has prime factors of 2 and 5, the fraction is finite'.
Is Dan correct? Test his idea on these fractions.

$$\frac{3}{5} \qquad \frac{3}{17} \qquad \frac{9}{25} \qquad \frac{12}{40} \qquad \frac{11}{100} \qquad \frac{157}{160}$$

10 Find

a $\frac{1}{8} \times \frac{2}{3}$ b $\frac{15}{43} + \frac{1}{10}$ c $\frac{3}{5} \times \frac{20}{81}$ d $\frac{19}{20} - \frac{4}{5}$

11 Real The musicians in a band share $\frac{1}{3}$ of a royalty fee for their song. There are six musicians. What fraction of the fee does each musician get?

12 Reasoning Petra has 10 cakes at her party. She wants to give all 75 guests an equal piece.
   a Explain why she won't have enough if she cuts the cakes into sevenths.
   b How many pieces should she cut the cakes into?
   c How many pieces will she have left over?

13 a Complete this square so that each row, column and diagonal adds to the same number.

$1\frac{1}{3}$		
	$1\frac{2}{3}$	
$2\frac{2}{3}$		2

   b Make your own square using fractions.

14 Reasoning The owner of a café calculates that $\frac{2}{3}$ of her customers order cake.
Half the people who order cake have cheesecake.
How many pieces of cheesecake should she have for 60 customers?

15 STEM / Real Meteorologists use these ratings to describe the level of cloud cover.

   1 Clear: $0 - \frac{1}{10}$ cloud cover

   2 Scattered: $\frac{1}{10} - \frac{5}{10}$ cloud cover

   3 Broken: $\frac{5}{10} - \frac{9}{10}$ cloud cover

   4 Overcast: fully covered

   A forecast for five days was

   Monday: $\frac{1}{4}$ covered

   Tuesday: $\frac{3}{5}$ covered

   Wednesday: $\frac{3}{4}$ covered

   Thursday: $\frac{1}{3}$ covered

   Friday: clear sky
   a What was the mean amount of cloud cover for the five days?
   b Work out the mean of the cloud cover ratings (the numbers 1–4) for the five days.

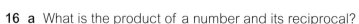

16 a What is the product of a number and its reciprocal?

b Does 0 have a reciprocal? Explain.

Q16a hint

'Finding the product' means multiplying.

17 Find the missing values.

a

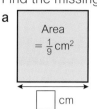

Area $= \frac{1}{9}$ cm²

☐ cm

b

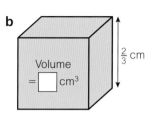

Volume $=$ ☐ cm³

$\frac{2}{3}$ cm

c

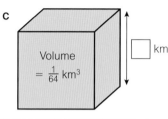

Volume $= \frac{1}{64}$ km³

☐ km

Key point

A unit fraction is a fraction that has a numerator of 1.

Investigation

Problem-solving

$\frac{1}{2} = \frac{1}{3} + \frac{1}{6}$

Zoe is trying to find out whether all unit fractions can be written as the sum of two different unit fractions.

She finds that $\frac{1}{9} = \frac{1}{10} + \frac{1}{90}$

1 Can you find a rule for writing a unit fraction as the sum of two different unit fractions? Test your rule on different fractions.

2 How many different ways can you write $\frac{1}{8}$ as the sum of two different unit fractions?

18 Johann says, 'If I add 1 to the numerator and denominator of a fraction, the fraction will be bigger than what I started with.'

a Start with $\frac{1}{3}$ and keep adding 1 to the numerator and denominator. What happens? Explain why.
Use a table like this to set out your working.

Q18a Strategy hint

Converting your fractions to decimals will make it easier to compare them.

Fraction	Decimal
$\frac{1}{3}$	0.333…
$\frac{2}{4}$	

b Try starting with $\frac{6}{5}$. What happens? Explain why.

19 Reflect The word fraction is used in lots of ways. Here are two examples:

- In everyday English, a fraction means 'a small amount'. When hanging a picture you might 'move it up a fraction' or you might ask someone to 'budge up a fraction' so that you can sit beside them.
- In chemistry, the fractionating process separates a mixture into its components.

Write a definition, in your own words, of 'fraction' in mathematics. What do you think 'fractional ownership' means? When might it be a good idea?

Reflect

6 Unit test

1 Round each of these to 2 decimal places.
   a 89.365   **b** 23.1246   **c** 0.369 24

2 Round each of these to 3 decimal places.
   a 2.456 31   **b** 0.023 57   **c** 156.234 79

3 Use a written method to calculate.
   a 2.7×3.6 **b** 15.3×14.2

4 Calculate
   a $0.2709 \div 0.003$ **b** $126.2 \div 0.020$

5 Write each decimal using the dot notation.
   a 0.166 666…
   b 0.232 323…
   c 0.136 136…

6 Calculate
   a $\frac{3}{4} \times \frac{8}{9}$ **b** $-\frac{3}{10} \times \frac{5}{6}$
   c $\frac{7}{10} \times -\frac{2}{3}$ **d** $-\frac{4}{9} \times -\frac{15}{16}$

7 Evaluate
   a $\frac{1}{3} \div \frac{1}{2}$ **b** $\frac{2}{5} \div \frac{1}{4}$
   c $-\frac{3}{4} \div \frac{7}{9}$ **d** $-\frac{5}{12} \div -\frac{2}{5}$

8 Write each fraction as a decimal.
   a $\frac{5}{9}$ **b** $\frac{5}{12}$
   c $\frac{7}{15}$ **d** $\frac{8}{11}$

9 Alex ran $2\frac{1}{2}$ miles, then swam a further $\frac{3}{4}$ of a mile, then cycled $5\frac{2}{7}$ miles.
How many miles did he travel in total?

10 Calculate
   a $3\frac{2}{5} + 4\frac{1}{3}$ **b** $10\frac{3}{4} + 1\frac{2}{3}$
   c $15\frac{5}{6} + 1\frac{7}{9}$ **d** $3\frac{7}{10} - 6\frac{3}{8}$

11 Evaluate these multiplications. Give your answers in their simplest form.
   a $\frac{5}{12} \times \frac{2}{15}$ **b** $\frac{3}{10} \times \frac{5}{18}$
   c $2\frac{1}{2} \times \frac{4}{25}$ **d** $3\frac{2}{3} \times \frac{1}{16}$

12 Calculate

   a $\frac{3}{8} \div \frac{1}{2}$ **b** $\frac{2}{5} \div \frac{8}{15}$

   c $4\frac{3}{10} \div \frac{18}{21}$ **d** $2\frac{4}{11} \div \frac{12}{33}$

13 Write each decimal with repeating digits as a fraction.

   a $0.\dot{8}$ **b** $0.\dot{2}\dot{7}$

   c $0.3\dot{9}$ **d** $0.\dot{3}4\dot{5}$

14 Find the side length of the cubes with these volumes.

   a $\frac{1}{27}\text{cm}^3$ **b** $\frac{8}{27}\text{m}^3$

15 Write these fractions as the sum of two different unit fractions.

   a $\frac{1}{3}$ **b** $\frac{1}{5}$

Challenge

16 a Fold a square of paper in half three times.
     What fraction have you split it into?

  b Find as many different ways as you can of folding the square into eight equal pieces.

  c How many sections would the paper be split into if you folded it in half seven times?

     Discussion There is a common belief that the maximum number of times you can fold a piece of paper in half is seven. Do you think it's true?

  d Is there a way of folding the paper into 10 equal pieces?

> **Q16c hint**
>
> You could draw a diagram to try different methods instead of folding the paper each time.

17 Reflect In this unit, did you work:

- slowly
- at average speed
- quickly?

Did you find the work easy, OK or hard?

How did that affect how fast you worked?

Is it always good to work quickly? Explain your answer.

Is it always bad to work slowly? Explain your answer.

Reflect

7.1 Experimental probability

You will learn to:
- Record data from a simple experiment.
- Estimate probability based on experimental data.
- Make conclusions based on the results of an experiment.

Confidence

Why learn this?
Scientists repeat experiments to make sure of the results.

Fluency
- Out of a bag of 20 balloons, three exploded as they were being blown up. What fraction exploded? What fraction did not explode?
- 95 seeds out of a packet of 100 seeds produced a flower. What percentage produced a flower? What percentage did not produce a flower?

Explore
Will it snow on 1 January in the UK?

Exercise 7.1

Warm up

1 a The tally chart shows the colours of flowers that grew from a mixed packet of seeds.
Copy and complete the table.

b What is the total frequency?

c What fraction of the flowers are red?

Colour	Tally	Frequency
Red	ЖЖ ЖЖ ЖЖ ‖	
Blue		7
White	ЖЖ ‖	

2 How would you describe each of these probabilities.
Choose from: impossible, unlikely, even chance, likely, certain.

   a 0.4   **b** $\frac{19}{20}$ **c** 0.5   **d** $\frac{1}{50}$ **e** 60%   **f** 0

Key point

You can estimate the probability of an event using the results of an **experiment**. This is called finding the **experimental probability**.

Experimental probability

$= \dfrac{\text{frequency of event}}{\text{total frequency}}$

Worked example

Andrew dropped a drawing pin lots of times.
It could fall point up or down.
He recorded the results in a frequency table.

a Work out the total frequency.

b Work out the experimental probability that the pin will fall point up.

c Work out the experimental probability that the pin will fall point down.

Position	Frequency	Experimental probability
Point up	83	$\frac{83}{100}$
Point down	17	$\frac{17}{100}$
Total frequency	100	

The total number of times Andrew dropped the drawing pin = 83 + 17 = 100

Experimental probability

$= \dfrac{\text{number of times pin pointed up}}{\text{total number of drops}}$

$= \frac{83}{100}$

$= 83\%$ or 0.83

Notice that the probabilities add up to 1 because $\frac{83}{100} + \frac{17}{100} = \frac{100}{100} = 1$

3 Real / STEM A hospital tried out a new kind of knee surgery on some patients. After two years, patients were asked how they felt. The results are shown in the frequency table.

Outcome	Frequency	Experimental probability
Symptom free	60	
Some improvement	15	
No improvement	5	
Total frequency		

a Copy the table. Work out the total frequency.

b Calculate the **experimental probabilities**.

c The hospital claims that patients undergoing the new surgery are very likely to improve. Comment on this claim.

4 Real A skateboard manufacturer gave 100 customers a set of newly designed wheels to try out. The table shows how long the wheels performed well for.

Time (months)	Frequency	Experimental probability
5	7	
6	14	
7	35	
8	25	
9	15	
10	3	
11	1	

Key point

Probability can be used to **model** what may happen in the future.

a Copy the table. Work out the experimental probabilities for the different times for which the wheels performed well. Write your answers as percentages.

b Estimate the percentage probability that the wheels will perform well for longer than 8 months.

c Reasoning Why do you think the wheels performed well for different amounts of time?

Discussion When you repeat an experiment, will you get the same results?

5 Real A manufacturer tested a new kind of mobile phone battery. They claim that there is a 95% experimental probability that the battery will last 30 hours with average use.

Key point

The more times an experiment is repeated, the more reliable is the estimated probability.

a Can you tell from the probability how many batteries they tested?

b What would make you confident that their claim was correct?

6 Real Hal counted the passengers in the first 100 cars passing his school. He found that 38 of the cars had no passengers. Estimate the probability that the next car will have

a no passengers

b some passengers.

7 Real / Modelling Records show that more than 10 cm of rain fell in Orkney during 415 of the last 1000 months.

a Estimate the probability that there will be more than 10 cm of rain next month.

b Is this a good model for predicting the rainfall in the month of July? Give a reason for your answer.

8 Problem-solving An optician's records show that 17 of the last 50 customers bought tinted lenses and 23 of them bought two pairs of glasses.

  a Estimate the probability that the next customer orders

    i tinted lenses   **ii** two pairs of glasses.

  b The optician's assistant worked out $17 + 23 = 40$ and estimated that the probability of a customer ordering tinted lenses or two pairs of glasses is $\frac{40}{50}$.
    Explain why he might be wrong.

9 Real / STEM An amateur astronomer recorded the number of shooting stars she saw each night between midnight and 1 am.

Shooting stars	0	1–2	3–5	6–10	11–20	more than 20
Frequency	3	12	20	22	15	8

  a For how many nights did she record the number of shooting stars?

  b Estimate the probability that she will see at least three shooting stars during the next night.

10 Reasoning The median number of customers visiting Lydia's café each day is 36.
  What is the probability that more than 36 customers will visit the café tomorrow?

  Discussion For which of these events can you work out the exact probability?

  A The next train is late.

  B Picking a particular colour counter from a bag.

  C A piece of toast falling on the floor butter side down.

  D Next year's price of your favourite magazine.

Investigation   **Real / Discussion**

Work in a group of five.

1 Each person draws a straight line between 1 cm and 30 cm long, secretly noting its length.

2 Take turns to show your line to the group.

3 Each person estimates the length of the line.

4 Record each estimate of the length.

5 Check whether the estimate is within 10% of the true length. (Work out 10% of the true length. Add and subtract this to the true length to give the range of estimates within 10% of the true value.)

6 Repeat until each person's line has been estimated.

7 Record all of the results in the same tally chart. Label the rows 'good estimate' and 'poor estimate'.

8 Work out the experimental probability of a person making a good estimate.

11 Explore Will it snow on 1 January in the UK?
  What have you learned in this lesson to help you to answer this question?
  What other information do you need?

12 Reflect In the Investigation in this lesson, you collected your own data and worked out the experimental probability. Other questions gave you the data.
  Which was easier? Explain.

7.2 Estimating probability

You will learn to:
* Calculate the relative frequency of a value.
* Use relative frequency to make estimates.
* Use relative frequency to estimate the probability of an event.
* Use estimated probability to calculate expected frequencies.

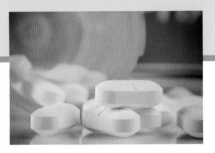

Fluency
* What is 4 as a fraction of 10?
* What is 4 as a percentage of 20?

Explore
What is the probability that a drug will stop a headache?

Why learn this?
A drug must be tested to estimate the probability that it will be effective.

Exercise 7.2

1 Work out
a $\frac{1}{4} \times 60$ **b** $\frac{3}{5} \times 200$ **c** $\frac{7}{10} \times 150$

2 Convert these fractions to percentages.
a $\frac{37}{100}$ **b** $\frac{18}{40}$ **c** $\frac{38}{250}$

> **Key point**
> For a set of data, the **relative frequency** of a value
> $= \dfrac{\text{frequency of value}}{\text{total frequency}}$
> You can calculate the expected frequency of a value in a larger set of data.

Worked example

Some Year 8 students were asked which device they use to access the internet.

a Calculate the **relative frequencies**.

Device	Frequency	Relative frequency
Smart phone	10	$\frac{10}{50}$
Tablet	18	$\frac{18}{50}$
Computer	22	$\frac{22}{50}$
Total frequency	50	

relative frequency $= \dfrac{\text{frequency}}{\text{total frequency}}$

Add all the frequencies to find the total.

b There are 200 students in Year 8 altogether.
How many would you **expect** to use a smart phone?

$\dfrac{\overset{1}{\cancel{10}}}{\underset{5}{\cancel{50}}} \times 200 = 40$

You can expect $\frac{10}{50}$ of the 200 students to use a smart phone.

I expect 40 students to use a smart phone.

3 The frequency table shows the patient outcomes in a study of a new eye treatment.

   a Copy the table.
   b Work out the total frequency.
   c Calculate the relative frequencies.
   d A further 300 people received the treatment. How many would you expect to have improved eyesight?

Discussion Is your answer to part **d** likely to be the exact number of people whose eyesight improved?

Outcome	Frequency	Relative frequency
Great improvement	75	
Slight improvement	20	
Same or worse	5	
Total frequency		

4 **a** In a survey of 200 households, 65 have high-speed broadband. There are 1000 households in the village. How many would you expect to have high-speed broadband?

   b 40 parents attended a school meeting. 27 said they preferred to have four school terms. 600 parents have children at the school. How many would you expect to prefer four school terms?

5 **Real / Reasoning** Restaurant owner Maurice recorded the number of seats reserved for each booking during a week.

Seats	Frequency	Relative frequency
2	30	
3	10	
4	25	
5	5	
6	10	
Total frequency		

   a Copy and complete the table.
   b Estimate the probability that the next booking will be for 2 seats.
   c Maurice says that it is unlikely that a booking will be for less than 4 people. Is he correct? Explain how you know.
   d The restaurant has approximately 240 bookings each month. How many of these would you expect to be for 4 seats?

> **Key point**
>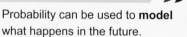
> Relative frequency can be used to estimate the probability of an event happening.

> **Q5b hint**
> Find the relative frequency of a booking for 2 seats.

6 **Modelling** An agricultural research centre counted the bananas in 1000 bunches.

Number of bananas	Frequency	Relative frequency
200–219	120	
220–239	160	
240–259	200	
260–279	230	
280–299	170	
300–319	120	

   a Copy the table and calculate the relative frequencies as percentages.
   b Estimate the probability that a bunch will contain
      i 300–319 bananas   **ii** at least 260 bananas.
   c A grower picks 5000 bunches one week. How many of these would you expect to contain at least 260 bananas?

Discussion Why might these estimated probabilities not be a good **model** for next year's crop?

> **Key point**
> Probability can be used to **model** what happens in the future.

7 Problem-solving The probability of not being connected when ringing a customer support service is 30%.
On a typical Monday, customers ring the service 400 times.
How many of these calls would you expect to be connected?

8 An optician's records show that 21 of the last 50 customers bought designer frames and 14 of them bought two pairs of glasses.
  a Estimate the probability that the next customer orders
    i designer frames
    ii two pairs of glasses.
  b Of the next 200 customers, how many would you expect to order two pairs of glasses?
Discussion Is the probability of a customer ordering designer frames or two pairs of glasses $\frac{35}{50}$?

Key point
The more data you have, the more confident you can be about any conclusions based on the data.

9 Peter tested 10 batteries and found that 80% lasted more than 30 hours. Sven tested 100 of the same batteries and found that 90% lasted more than 30 hours.
Whose results are more useful?

10 Problem-solving / Reasoning
  a Edward asked 20 people which charity they donate money to. 11 said Oxfam. Estimate the probability that a person donates money to Oxfam.
  b Odval asked 80 people which charity they donate money to. 45 said Oxfam. Use his data to estimate the probability that a person donates money to Oxfam.
  c Which estimate do you think is more reliable? Give a reason for your answer.
  d Edward and Odval shared their data.
    i Use their combined data to estimate the probability that a person donates money to Oxfam.
    ii They interview another 200 people. How many of these would they expect to donate money to Oxfam?

11 Explore What is the probability that a drug will stop a headache? Is it easier to explore this question now that you have completed the lesson? What further information do you need to be able to answer this?

12 Reflect Look back at the questions you answered in this lesson.
  a Make a list of all the different maths skills you have used.
  b Was there a question you found particularly difficult? What made it difficult?

Explore

Reflect

7 Check up

Experimental probability

1   Riikka recorded how long her new laptop battery lasted each day.

Time (hours)	Frequency	Experimental probability
7	5	
8	9	
9	16	
10	7	
11	3	
Total frequency		

a Copy and complete the table.

b Riikka said that the battery is unlikely to last more than 8 hours in a day.

   i Estimate the probability that her battery will last more than 8 hours tomorrow.

   ii Based on the data, is Riikka correct?

c Are the experimental probabilities a good model for predicting how long Riikka's battery will last

   i the day after the experiment finished

   ii 6 months later?
   Explain your answers.

2   The chart shows how a plantation's bananas were used.
   a How many bananas were grown altogether?
   b Estimate the probability that a banana
      i will go to the supermarket
      ii will be dried or processed.

3   A quality control inspection of 200 watches found that 20 were faulty.
   Estimate the probability that a watch will be faulty.

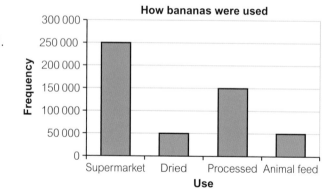

Estimating probability

Q4 hint

Count up the total number of sales made.

4   The table shows information about the number of orders for new cars received by a car dealership during certain months.

Month	May	June	July	August	September	October
Number of sales made	25	36	30	28	29	12

An order is chosen at random.
Work out the probability that the order was received in
   a July   b September or October   c Not June.

5 The table shows the visitors to a park on a Sunday.
   a Work out the relative frequencies for Adult, Girl, Boy.
   b Estimate the probability that the next visitor is a girl.
      Write your answer as a decimal.
   c The park has 300 visitors one Sunday.
      How many boys would you expect?

Visitor	Frequency	Relative frequency
Adult	70	
Girl	90	
Boy	40	
Total frequency		

6 A computer repair company keeps records of all the repairs it makes to laptops. The table shows information about all the repairs made in 2018.

Cost (£C)	Frequency
$0 < C \leqslant 100$	25
$100 < C \leqslant 200$	38
$200 < C \leqslant 300$	30
$300 < C \leqslant 400$	22
$400 < C \leqslant 500$	5

   a Amina needs to repair her laptop.
      Estimate the probability that the repair will cost
        i more than £300
       ii between £100 and £300.
   b Comment on the accuracy of your estimate.

Challenge

7 A box contains milk chocolates and dark chocolates.
There are 200 chocolates in the box. Onick takes a chocolate
at random from the box, records its type and then replaces the
chocolate.
   a Copy and complete the table of the relative frequencies for the
      number of times a milk chocolate was chosen.

Number of trials	10	25	50	100
Number of times a milk chocolate is chosen	4	8	14	30
Relative frequency	0.4			

   b What is the best estimate of the relative frequency of picking a milk
      chocolate from the box.
   c What is the best estimate of the number of milk chocolates in the
      box.

8 **How sure are you of your answers? Were you mostly**
   😟 **Just guessing**   😐 **Feeling doubtful**   😊 **Confident**
   What next? Use your results to decide whether to strengthen or
   extend your learning.

Reflect

7 Strengthen

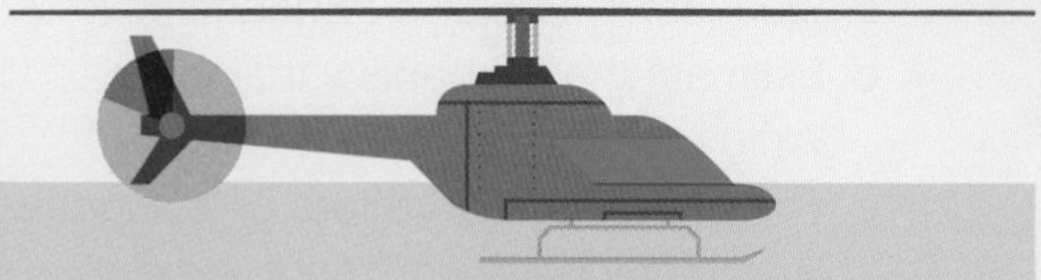

You will:
• Strengthen your understanding with practice.

Experimental probability

1 Sanchez's teacher secretly put 10 cubes in a bag. Some were blue, some yellow and some black.
Sanchez took one out and recorded its colour in the tally chart below. Then he put the cube back into the bag. He repeated this 20 times.

Colour	Tally	Frequency	Experimental probability
Blue	JHT JHT III	13	$\frac{13}{20}$
Yellow	JHT		
Black	II		
	Total frequency		

a Complete the Frequency column.

b Calculate the total frequency.

c Calculate the experimental probability of picking each colour.

d Which counter is more likely to be picked from the bag – black or yellow?

2 The tally chart shows the visits to some Post Office cashier desks on a Saturday morning.

Cashier desk	Tally	Frequency	Estimated probability
1	JHT JHT IIII	14	$\frac{14}{100} = 14\%$
2	JHT JHT JHT I		
3	JHT JHT JHT JHT JHT		
4	JHT JHT JHT JHT JHT JHT		
5	JHT JHT JHT		
	Total frequency		

a i Copy the table and complete the Frequency column.

ii Which cashier desk was visited by the most customers?

Q1b hint

The total frequency is the total number of times Sanchez took a cube from the bag.

Q1c hint

Write each frequency as a fraction with denominator 20.

b Work out the estimated probability that the next customer will visit cashier desk 3.
Write your answer as a percentage.

c **Reasoning** The Post Office manager says that the probability of a customer visiting cashier desk 1 next Monday is 14%.
Explain why this might not be true.

Q2c hint

Think of a reason why things might be different in the Post Office on Monday compared with on Saturday.

3 **Real / STEM** The bar chart shows the wildlife spotted on a Scottish boat trip in July.

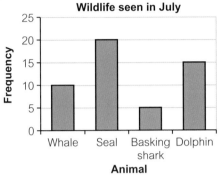

a How many animals were spotted altogether?

b Estimate the probability that the next animal spotted will be a basking shark.

c **Reasoning** Is your answer a good estimate for spotting a basking shark on a boat trip in January? Give a reason for your answer.

Q3a hint

Add up the frequencies of the bars.

Q3b hint

Probability =
$\dfrac{\text{number of basking sharks}}{\text{total number of animals}}$

Q3c hint

Think about the temperature of the water at different times of year.

4 Copy the table shown below. Roll a dice 60 times and record your results in the table. Work out the probability of rolling each number.

Score	Tally	Frequency	Probability
1			$\dfrac{\square}{60}$
2			$\dfrac{\square}{60}$
3			$\dfrac{\square}{60}$
4			$\dfrac{\square}{60}$
5			$\dfrac{\square}{60}$
6			$\dfrac{\square}{60}$
		Total	$\dfrac{\square}{60}$

Estimating probability

1 A potter made 100 plates. 10 of them cracked.
  a Estimate the probability that the next plate the potter makes cracks.
  b The potter makes 200 plates. How many would you expect to crack?

Q1a i hint

'Estimate' means 'do a calculation' not just guess.

2 Anton's aquarium has three types of fish: catfish, rainbowfish and sunfish.
He recorded the first 20 fish to swim to the surface.

Fish	Frequency	Relative frequency
Catfish	6	$\frac{6}{20}$
Rainbowfish	10	$\frac{\square}{20}$
Sunfish	4	$\frac{\square}{20}$
Total frequency	20	

a Estimate the probability that the next fish to swim to the surface is a catfish.
b Estimate the probabilities for rainbowfish and sunfish.
c Anton recorded the next 60 fish to swim to the surface.
How many would you expect to be
  i catfish
  ii rainbowfish
  iii sunfish?

Q2a hint

Use the relative frequency as the estimate of probability.

Q2c i hint

$\frac{6}{20}$ of 60 = $\frac{6}{20}$ $\square$ 60 = $\square$

3 In the last two months, Dev has taken part in the three sports shown in the table.

Sport	Frequency
Swimming	12
Cricket	8
Judo	20

a Estimate the probability that the next sport Dev plays is cricket.
b Estimate how many times Dev will take part in judo or swimming out of the next 50 times he participates in sport.

4 Kristinamarie writes each letter of her name on a card. She shuffles the cards and selects one at random. She records the letter and replaces the card. She does this 100 times. How many times would you expect her to select the letter i?

5 An ordinary 6-sided dice is rolled 250 times. How many times would you expect to get a prime number?

Enrichment

1 Find an object that has at least two different ways of landing when it is dropped.
  a Sketch the possible outcomes of dropping the object.
    Give each a short description.
  b Drop the object on the table 20 times and record the results in a tally chart.
  c i Work out the experimental probability of the object falling each way up.
    ii Write your answer as a percentage.

Q1c ii hint

Change the probability to an equivalent fraction with denominator 100 then work out the percentage.

Subject link: Sport (Estimating probability, Q3)

d i Repeat the experiment by dropping the object 25 times.
  ii Work out the experimental probabilities.
  iii Compare your experimental probabilities with those from the experiment in part **b**.

e i Combine your results into a single frequency table.
  ii Calculate the experimental probabilities for the combined data.
  iii If you dropped the object 180 times, how many times would you expect it to land each way up?

Discussion If you repeat an experiment, will you get the same experimental probabilities?

Q1d iii hint

Compare the percentage probabilities.

2 Some two-letter words begin with a vowel: in, an, of, …
Others do not: be, to, we, …

a Close your eyes, turn to a random page in this book and point to a random place on the page.
Start reading and record the first two-letter word you come to.
Repeat this 20 times.

Q2 Literacy hint

The vowels are: a, e, i, o, u.

b i Work out the experimental probability of a two-letter word in this book beginning with a vowel.
  ii Describe this probability using words.
  Discussion If you repeated the experiment with 20 more two-letter words, would the results be the same? Explain your answer.

c Make up a different experiment. For example, record 20 three-letter words.

3 **Reflect** In this Strengthen lesson you have answered probability questions involving:
  • estimating probabilities
  • experimental probability.
Make a list of the questions that you found most difficult? Why were they the most difficult?
Make a list of the questions that you found easiest? Why were they the easiest?
Write down one thing about these topics that you think you need more practice on.

Reflect

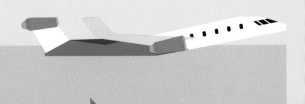

7 Extend

You will:
• Extend your understanding with problem-solving.

1 **Problem-solving** A bag contains €1 and £1 coins.
Li takes out a coin, looks at it and replaces it.
He records his results after 25, 50, 75 and 100 trials.

Number of trials	Number of €1 coins
25	13
50	21
75	33
100	45

   a What is the most accurate experimental probability
   of picking a €1 coin?
   b Li weighs the bag and works out that there are 40 coins in it.
   How many are likely to be €1 coins?

 2 Morine recorded the darts thrown by two of her favourite players.

	Tom Sharp	Sneaky Joe
Single	39	8
Double	30	5
Treble	25	7
25 ring	5	3
Bull	1	2

   a Estimate the probability of each player hitting a treble.
   b Which player is more likely to hit a treble? Explain your answer.
   c **Modelling** Whose estimated probability is a more reliable model
   for their future dart throws? Explain why.
   d If Sneaky Joe threw 200 darts tomorrow, estimate the number of
   trebles he would hit.

> **Q2b hint**
>
> Write the probabilities as
> percentages.

 3 **Finance** The number of FTSE 100 company share prices that went
up from the previous day were recorded for 50 days.

Number of share prices that went up	Frequency
1–20	7
21–40	12
41–60	18
61–80	10
81–100	3

   a Estimate the probability that on the next day
      i 21 to 40 share prices will go up
      ii more than 60 share prices will go up.
   b The London stock exchange trades for 357 days in a year. On how
   many days would you expect fewer than 21 share prices to rise?
   c Estimate the probability that fewer than 21 share prices will rise on
   each of two consecutive days.

> **Q3 Literacy hint**
>
> The largest 100 companies on the
> London stock market are called the
> **FTSE 100**. Each day, their share
> prices can go up, down or stay the
> same.

4 Real The frequency table shows the weights of organic Savoy cabbages grown without pesticide or artificial fertiliser.

Weight, w (kg)	Frequency
$0.6 \leqslant w < 0.7$	20
$0.7 \leqslant w < 0.8$	60
$0.8 \leqslant w < 0.9$	90
$0.9 \leqslant w < 1.0$	130
$1.0 \leqslant w < 1.1$	220
$1.1 \leqslant w < 1.2$	150
$1.2 \leqslant w < 1.3$	80
$1.3 \leqslant w < 1.4$	40
$1.4 \leqslant w < 1.5$	10

a Estimate the probability that an organic Savoy cabbage weighs 1.3 kg or more.

b A supermarket only buys Savoy cabbages that weigh between 0.9 kg and 1.3 kg. A farmer produces 20 000 organic Savoy cabbages each year. How many of these can the farmer expect to sell to the supermarket?

c **Reasoning** A Savoy cabbage on a market stall weighs 1450 g. The stallholder says it is organic. Do you believe him? Explain.

5 Problem-solving 400 customers were randomly telephoned in a follow-up satisfaction survey. Based on previous surveys, the probability of calling
- someone aged 20–39 is $\frac{2}{5}$
- a 'completely satisfied' customer aged over 60 is $\frac{1}{4}$
- a 'dissatisfied' customer aged 40–59 is the same as that of calling a 'mostly satisfied' customer aged 60 or over.

Copy and complete this table using the information given above.

	Completely satisfied	Mostly satisfied	Dissatisfied
20–39	80	40	
40–59	60		12
60 or over			28

6 STEM The amount of E-coli bacteria found in 200 samples of drinking water is shown in the table.

Amount of E-coli, e (cfu/100 ml)	Frequency
$0 \leqslant e < 50$	120
$50 \leqslant e < 100$	32
$100 \leqslant e < 150$	17
$150 \leqslant e < 200$	12
$200 \leqslant e < 250$	19
$250 \leqslant e < 300$	20

a Estimate the probability that a sample of drinking water contains less than 100 cfu/10 ml.

b The safe limit for E-coli in drinking water is 200 cfu/100 ml. 1000 samples of drinking water are taken. Estimate how many have unsafe levels of E-coli.

c Investigate the meaning of the unit of measurement cfu/100 ml.

7 Modelling / Problem-solving A school recorded photocopier use over the autumn term.

	Black and white	Colour	Total
A3	981	1724	2705
A4	13776	2379	16155
Total	14757	4103	18860

   a Giving your answers to 2 decimal places, estimate the probability of the next copy being

      i black and white, A4

      ii colour.

The autumn term was 16 weeks. The spring term is 12 weeks.

   b The school needs to order photocopy paper for the spring term. Paper comes in packs of 500 sheets. How many packs does the school need to order of

      i A3 paper

      ii A4 paper?

8 Real / Reasoning The table shows the earnings of a company's employees.

Earnings, e (per annum)	Number of employees
$0 < e \leqslant \$10\,000$	5
$\$10\,000 < e \leqslant \$20\,000$	21
$\$20\,000 < e \leqslant \$30\,000$	30
$\$30\,000 < e \leqslant \$40\,000$	22
$\$40\,000 < e \leqslant \$50\,000$	3

   a What is the probability that an employee picked at random earns

      i less than the median earnings

      ii more than the mean?

   b Explain why the probability you calculated in part **a ii** is an estimate.

Q8a i hint

Where is the median of a set of data?

Q8a ii hint

Calculate an estimate of the mean, to the nearest 100. Estimate how many of the employees earn more than that, using the figures in the table.

9 Three students do an experiment with a spinner coloured blue, red and green.

The table shows the results from all three experiments.

Colour	Student A	Student B	Student C
Blue	33	25	19
Red	35	46	22
Green	32	29	19

Did they all use the same spinner? Explain.

Reflect

7 Unit test

1 As part of an experiment, Luke cut off part of a rubber ball.
He predicted that the ball would be unlikely to land on the curved
surface when dropped.
Here are Luke's results.

Outcome	Tally	Frequency	Experimental probability
Curved surface	ⅢⅠ III		
Flat surface	ⅢⅠ ⅢⅠ II		
	Total frequency		

  a How many times did Luke drop the ball?
  b Work out the experimental probabilities.
  c Is Luke's prediction correct? Explain your answer.
  d How can Luke improve his estimates of the experimental
    probabilities?

2 In an honesty experiment, 60 purses were left
on the pavement.
The table shows what happened.
  a Copy and complete the table.
  b Another purse is left on the pavement.
    Estimate the probability that it will be
    handed in.

Action taken	Frequency	Experimental probability
Handed in at the nearest shop	25	
Handed in at the police station	20	
Stolen	15	
Total frequency		

3 In a video racing game, an obstacle randomly appears on the race
track five times every 40 laps.
Work out the probability that an obstacle appears on the track during
a particular lap.

4 In a survey of adults who set themselves some fitness targets,
5% achieved all of them and 15% achieved some of them.
Another fitness survey questions 400 adults. How many would you
expect to achieve all of their targets?

5 A farm produces eggs. The farmer
discards damaged eggs and sells
some for use in making food products.
He classes the rest as small, medium or
large and sells them in boxes.
The table shows how some eggs
produced on the farm were used.
  a Copy and complete the table.
  b Estimate the probability that an egg is
    not discarded.
  c The farm produces 5000 eggs in one particular week. How many
    would you expect to be large?

Use	Frequency	Relative frequency
Discarded	50	
Food products	250	
Small	200	
Medium	300	
Large	200	
Total frequency		

6 The bar chart shows the A-level mathematics grades achieved by some students one year.

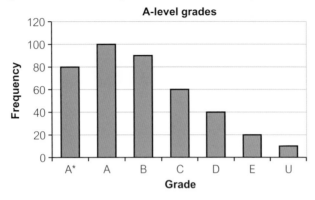

a How many students achieved grade B or C?

b How many students took A-level mathematics?

c Estimate the probability that a student will achieve grade B or C next year.

Challenge

7 a Count the letters of the first 10 words of a sentence on this page. Ignore any numbers. Record the frequencies in a table like this.

Letters	Frequency
1 or 2	
3 or 4	
5 or more	

b Estimate the probability that a randomly chosen word has 3 or 4 letters.

c If you chose 30 words at random, how many would you expect to have 3 or 4 letters?

d **i** Choose a few more sentences at random and count the letters in the first 30 words.

　ii How close was your answer to part **b**?

e Make a frequency table for all 40 word lengths (10 from part **a** and 30 from part **d**). Estimate the probability that a randomly chosen word has 3 or 4 letters. Compare your probability with a classmate.

8 Reflect Look back at the questions you answered in this test.

a Which one are you most confident that you have answered correctly?

What makes you feel confident?

b Which one are you least confident that you have answered correctly?

What makes you least confident?

c Discuss the question you feel least confident about with a classmate.

How does discussing it make you feel?

Q8 hint

Comment on your understanding of the question and your confidence.

Reflect

8.1 Equivalent fractions, decimals and percentages

You will learn to:
- Convert between fractions, decimals and percentages.
- Use the equivalence of fractions, decimals and percentages to compare proportions.

Why learn this?
Examiners convert all scores to percentages to compare results.

Fluency
Find pairs of equivalent fractions in this list.
$\frac{8}{100}$, $\frac{3}{20}$, $\frac{2}{10}$, $\frac{2}{10}$, $\frac{15}{100}$, $\frac{1}{5}$

Explore
Why do we use percentages instead of fractions to compare test results?

Exercise 8.1

1 Write these percentages as fractions and decimals.
  The first one has been done for you.

  a $55\% = \frac{55}{100} = \frac{11}{20}$ $55\% = 0.55$

  b $15\% = \frac{\square}{100} = \frac{\square}{20}$ $15\% = \square$

  c $95\% = \frac{\square}{100} = \frac{\square}{20}$ $95\% = \square$

  d $2\% = \frac{\square}{100} = \frac{\square}{50}$ $2\% = \square$

  e $24\% = \frac{\square}{100} = \frac{\square}{50} = \frac{\square}{25}$ $24\% = \square$

2 Copy and complete this table.
  Discussion Profits for a business increase by 200%. What does this mean?

Mixed number	$1\frac{1}{2}$			
Decimal		1.7		
Percentage			180%	110%

3 Write these percentages as decimals and fractions.
  The first one has been done for you.

  a $165\% = 1.65 = 1\frac{65}{100} = 1\frac{13}{20}$ **b** 235%   **c** 385%   **d** 195%

4 Copy and complete this table.

Mixed number	$1\frac{1}{20}$				
Decimal		1.35			1.45
Percentage			185%	255%	

5 Write these percentages as decimals and fractions.
The first one has been done for you.

a $172\% = 1.72 = 1\frac{72}{100} = 1\frac{18}{25}$　　**b** 216%　**c** 142%　**d** 494%

6 Write these fractions as decimals and percentages.
The first one has been done for you.

a
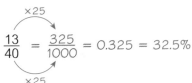
$$\frac{13}{40} = \frac{325}{1000} = 0.325 = 32.5\%$$

b $\frac{19}{40}$　　**c** $\frac{69}{200}$

d $\frac{3}{8}$　　**e** $\frac{31}{250}$　　**f** $\frac{17}{500}$　　**g** $\frac{3}{125}$

Q6d hint

8 × 125 = 1000

Strategy hint

Sometimes you might need to use
a denominator of 1000 when you
convert between fractions, decimals
and percentages.

7 Write these percentages as decimals and fractions.
The first one has been done for you.

a
$$14.5\% = 0.145 = \frac{145}{1000} = \frac{29}{200}$$
(÷5 / ÷5)

b 12.5%　　**c** 42.5%　　**d** 9.5%

Key point

A **proportion** of a whole can be
written as a fraction, a decimal or
a percentage.

8 Write these **proportions** as fractions in their simplest form.
　a 15 out of 20　**b** 9 out of 18　　**c** 40 out of 100
　d 16 out of 24　**e** 10 out of 35　**f** 20 out of 45

9 **Real** In a 25 g portion of breakfast cereal, 2 g is sugar.
　a Write the proportion of sugar in breakfast cereal as a fraction.
　b Write your fraction in part **a** as　**i** a decimal　　**ii** a percentage.

10 **Real** Here are the nutritional information panels from
two brands of crisps.
　a Write as a fraction, decimal and percentage the
　proportion of
　　i protein　　　**ii** carbohydrate　　　**iii** fibre
　in Brand A.
　b Which brand has the higher proportion of
　saturated fat?
　c Which brand has the higher proportion of total fat?

Brand A	
Per 50 g	
Protein	3.0 g
Carbohydrate	26.1 g
Saturated fat	5.2 g
Unsaturated fat	12.3 g
Fibre	3.4 g

Brand B	
percentage content	
Protein	6.5%
Carbohydrate	53.4%
Saturated fat	13.1%
Unsaturated fat	20.7%
Fibre	6.3%

11 **Real** A business is testing two different methods for delivering goods.
Method A has 24 dissatisfied customers out of 296.
1% of the Method B customers were dissatisfied.
Which method is better?

12 **Explore** Why do we use percentages instead of fractions or decimals to
compare test results?
Look back at the maths you have learned in this lesson.
How can you use it to answer this question?

13 **Reflect** After this lesson, Faiz says, 'Decimals are just another way to
write fractions.'
Do you agree with Faiz? Explain.

Explore

Reflect

8.2 Writing percentages

You will learn to:
* Express one number as a percentage of another.
* Work out a percentage increase or decrease.

Why learn this?
Some businesses give prices without VAT (Value Added Tax). You have to work out for yourself how much VAT you will have to pay.

Fluency
Find 10% and 15% of these amounts.
* £40
* 60 kg
* 120 km

Explore
How much is a car worth when it is 3 years old?

Warm up

Exercise 8.2

1 Convert these fractions to decimals to 3 d.p.

  a $\frac{2}{3}$ **b** $\frac{5}{8}$ **c** $\frac{3}{7}$

2 Give these proportions as percentages.

  a 15 out of 20   **b** 6 out of 25   **c** 3 out of 5   **d** 3 out of 4

3 Rewrite these statements giving the proportions as percentages.

  a 18 out of 60 students use a smartphone.
  b 14 out of 50 people are vegetarian.
  c 30 out of 80 residents own their home.
  d 12 out of 15 items sold cost more than £35.
  e 40 out of 300 students drink coffee.

> **Q3 hint**
>
> Write as a fraction. Change to a decimal, then to a percentage.

4 Problem-solving The bar chart shows sales figures for one weekend.

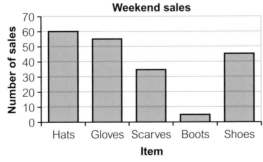

What percentage of the total sales were
  a gloves   **b** scarves   **c** boots and shoes?

> **Q4 Strategy hint**
>
> Write as a fraction of total sales first.

5 A $\frac{1}{2}$ litre bottle of mayonnaise contains 330 ml of fat.
What percentage of the mayonnaise is fat?

> **Q5 hint**
>
> Make sure the units for both quantities in the fraction are the same.

6 A 1 kg bag of mortar contains 250 g cement, 650 g sand and 100 g lime. What percentage of the bag is
  a cement   **b** lime   **c** sand and lime?

7 Sufjan buys some party lights. They cost £15 plus 20% VAT.
   a Work out 20% of £15.
   b What is the total cost of the party lights?

8 Leela gets a 2% pay rise. Her salary was £25 000.
What is her new salary?

9 **Finance** Jen buys £400 worth of financial shares.
The value of her shares increases by 35%.
What are her shares worth now?

10 A shirt costs £25. It is reduced in a sale by 10%.
   a Work out 10% of £25.   **b** Work out the sale price of the shirt.

11 **Finance** A company spends £1200 on office furniture and £1800 on computer equipment.
After 1 year the office furniture decreases in value by 15% and the computer equipment decreases by 33%.
Work out the value after 1 year of
   a the office furniture   **b** the computer equipment.

 12 **Real** A council has a housing budget of £240 000. They have to decrease their budget by 3% next year. What is their new budget?

13 **Problem-solving** Ed spends £60 in a shop. He buys shoes which normally cost £32.50, but they have a 20% discount. He spends £15.70 on a jumper. He also buys a T-shirt.
How much did the T-shirt cost?

Key point

To **increase** an amount by a percentage, you can find the percentage of the amount, then add it to the original amount.

Key point

To **decrease** an amount by a percentage, you can find the percentage of the amount, then subtract it from the original amount.

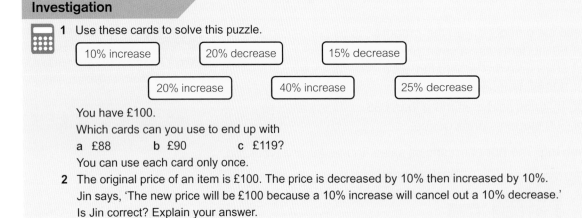

Investigation   **Reasoning**

1 Use these cards to solve this puzzle.

| 10% increase | | 20% decrease | | 15% decrease |

| 20% increase | | 40% increase | | 25% decrease |

You have £100.
Which cards can you use to end up with
  a £88   **b** £90   **c** £119?
You can use each card only once.

2 The original price of an item is £100. The price is decreased by 10% then increased by 10%.
Jin says, 'The new price will be £100 because a 10% increase will cancel out a 10% decrease.'
Is Jin correct? Explain your answer.

14 **Explore** How much is a car worth when it is 3 years old?
Is it easier to explore this question now that you have completed the lesson? What further information do you need to be able to answer this?

15 **Reflect**
Look again at part 1 of the investigation.
Ellie says, 'I began by working out each card, on its own, for £100.'
Alec says, 'I worked out the 20% cards first, so I could work with £120 and £80.'
What did you do first?
Which is the best first step, Ellie's, Alec's or yours? Why?

Explore

Reflect

8.3 Percentage of amounts

You will learn to:
- Use a multiplier to calculate percentage increase and decrease.
- Use the unitary method to solve percentage problems.

Why learn this?
When you can calculate percentages, you can check that your discount is correct.

Fluency
What percentage must be added to each of these to make 100%?
- 90%
- 60%
- 75%
- 45%

Explore
In 2030, how many people in the world will be using the internet?

Exercise 8.3

1 Work out the new amount after a 10% increase.
   a £14　　　b 240 g　　　c 20p　　　d 110 mm

2 Work out the new amount after a 15% decrease.
   a 50 ml　　b 44 kg　　c $320　　d £210

3 Use a multiplier to calculate these percentages.
   a 20% of £56　b 70% of 32 kg　c 45% of 120 ml　d 8% of 750 g

Q3a hint
20% = 0.2, so 20% = 0.2 × £56 = £☐

4 A magazine article states, 'Our number of readers has gone up by 250%.' They originally had 30 000 readers. How many do they have now?

5 Gary invests £500. He earns 5% **simple interest** per year. How much interest does he earn in one year?

Q5 hint
Work out 5% of £500.

6 Work out the amount of simple interest earned in one year for each of these investments.
   a £1000 at 5% per year　　　b £300 at 2% per year
   c £5000 at 8% per year　　　d £800 at 6% per year

Key point

Simple interest is the interest calculated only on the original amount of money invested. It is the same amount each year.

7 A jacket costs £45. In a sale, the price of the jacket is reduced by 30%.
   a Work out 30% of £45.
   b Work out the sale price of the jacket.
   c Work out 70% of £45.
   d What do you notice about your answers to parts **b** and **c**? Explain.

8 A café increases the cost of drinks by 25%.
   It originally charged £1.40 for a glass of juice.
   a Work out 25% of £1.40.
   b Work out the new price of a glass of juice.
   c Work out 125% of £1.40.
   d What do you notice? Explain.

   Discussion What multipliers would you use to find a 20% decrease and a 20% increase?

9   Work out these percentage increases and decreases.
    Use a multiplier for each one.
    a Decrease £150 by 10%.   **b** Decrease 60 ml by 25%.
    c Increase 80 kg by 15%.   **d** Increase 120 km by 30%.

Q9 hint

a 100% − 10% = ☐, so multiplier is ☐.
c 100% + 15% = ☐, so multiplier is ☐.

10 **Finance / Problem-solving** Between 2004 and 2013 the price of gold
    went up by approximately 365%.
    In 2004, 1 ounce of gold cost $425. How much did it cost in 2013?

11 **Finance** Karen invests £400 for 3 years at 2.5% simple interest per year.
    Work out
    a the amount of interest she earns in 1 year
    b the amount of interest she earns in 3 years
    c the total amount her investment is worth at the end of the 3 years.

Q11 hint

For part **a**, work out 2.5% of £400.
For part **b**, multiply your answer to part **a** by 3.
For part **c**, add your answer to part **b** onto the original £400.

12 **Finance** Mark invests £12 500 for 4 years at 6.75% simple interest.
    How much is his investment worth at the end of the 4 years?

Worked example

20% of an amount is £40.
Work out the original amount.

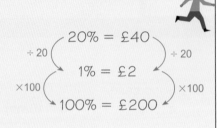

Key point

Sometimes you want to find the original amount after a percentage increase or decrease. You can use the **unitary method**.

13 Work out the original amount for each of these.
    a 30% of an amount is £180.
    b 80% of an amount is 320 kg.
    c 15% of an amount is 45 litres.
    d 120% of an amount is 720 km.
    e 165% of an amount is 82.5 cm.

Q13d hint

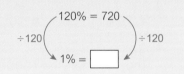

14 The cost of a DVD is reduced by 30%. It now costs £6.30.
    How much was it originally?

15 **Real** Sales of Fair trade honey products in 2012 were 95% of what
    they were in 2011. In 2012 sales were £3.6 million.
    What were they in 2011?

16 **Explore** In 2030, how many people in the world will be using the
    internet?
    Is it easier to explore this question now that you have completed the
    lesson? What further information do you need to be able to answer this?

17 **Reflect**
    a Write the steps you take to use a multiplier to calculate a percentage.
    b Write the steps you take to use a multiplier to calculate
        i a percentage increase   **ii** a percentage decrease.
    c Can you use your answers to part **b** to write one set of steps that
        work for percentage increase and percentage decrease?

Q17 hint

Describe what a multiplier is.

Explore

Reflect

8.4 Compound interest

You will learn to:
- Calculate compound interest.
- Use repeated percentage change.

Why learn this?
When you save or borrow money the interest is calculated using repeated percentage changes.

Fluency
Work out
- 5% of $150
- Increase $150 by 5%
- Decrease $150 by 5%

Explore
How much money are you likely to make if you invest $10 000 in a bank account for five years?

Warm up

Exercise 8.4

1 Work out the following
  a 10% of $550   **b** 3% of $200   **c** 1.5% of $8800

2 Write down the multiplier for a percentage increase of
  a 5%   **b** 10%   **c** 1%
  d 3.5%   **e** 0.2%   **f** 100%

3 A bank pays interest on savings at 2% per year.
Work out the amount in the account at the end of the year when you start with
  a $100   **b** $500   **c** $350

Investigation
Problem-solving

Danya starts with £750 in a bank account that pays 4% interest per year.
The interest is paid into her account.
1 How much money does Danya have in her account at the end of year 1?
  Your answer to part 1 is the starting amount for Year 2.
2 How much money does Danya have in her account at the end of year 2?
  Copy and complete this table to find how much money Danya has in her account at the end of Year 4.

	Start	Working	End
Year 1	$750	$750 × ☐	
Year 2			
Year 3			
Year 4			

4 Amir invests $3000 in a savings account.
The bank pays 5% compound interest per year.
Work out how much Amir has in his account after
  a 1 year   **b** 2 years.
Discussion Amir leaves the money in his account. What happens to the amount of interest he earns each year? Why?

Key point

In **compound interest**, the interest earned each year is added to the money in the account and earns interest the next year. Most interest rates are compound interest rates.

5 Two competing banks have very similar interest rates.
Work out the difference in the final balances if you invest
$5000 in both banks for 4 years.

Bank	Interest rate	Start balance	End of year 1 balance	End of year 2 balance	End of year 3 balance	End of year 4 balance
Bank A	1.2%	$5000				
Bank B	1.3%	$5000				

Worked example

David invests $3000 at a compound interest rate of 2.4% per year.
How much money will he have after 4 years?

After 1 year
Amount = $3000 × 1.024 ⟵ Amount after interest = 3000 × 1.024
       = $3072

After 2 years
Amount = $3072 × 1.024 ⟵ This is the same as $3000 × 1.024 × 1.024 or £3000 × 1.024²
       = 3145.73 (to the nearest penny)

After 4 years
Amount = 3000 × 1.024⁴
       = $3298.53 (to the nearest penny)

Key point

You can calculate an amount after n years' compound interest using the formula

$$\text{Amount} = \text{Initial amount} \times \left(\frac{100 + \text{Interest rate}}{100}\right)^n$$

6 Problem-solving Manoj inherits $5400. A savings account pays him 2.5% compound interest per year. How many years will it be before he has £6000?

7 Finance Nikita's salary will rise by 3.2% every year for the next 5 years. Her starting salary is $24500. What will she earn in 5 years' time?

8 Finance A credit card company charges interest at 2% per month on any outstanding balance.
A balance of $1500 is left unpaid. Work out the balance after
a 1 month   **b** 6 months   **c** 1 year.

Q8 hint

1500 × ☐ 1 month
1500 × ☐² 2 months

9 Real / Finance When people have an overdraft at a bank they are charged interest. Sonny is $45 overdrawn. His bank charges interest at a rate of 2.2% per month. Sonny doesn't pay off any of his debt for a year but he doesn't spend any more. How much will he owe at the end of the year?

10 Problem-solving There are 10 bacteria in a Petri dish at the start of the day. The number doubles every hour.
a What is the percentage increase from 10 to 20 bacteria?
b How many bacteria will there be after 24 hours?
Discussion Why is it not sensible to work out the number at the end of the first week?

11 Explore How much money are you likely to make if you invest $10000 in a bank account for five years?

12 Reflect Look back at Q10. Was your answer bigger than you expected? How did you check whether your answer was sensible?

8.5 Ratios

You will learn to:
- Simplify and use ratios involving decimals.
- Write and compare unit ratios.

Why learn this?
Most machines have gears, and gears depend on ratios.

Fluency
Simplify each ratio.
4 : 7   4 : 8   6 : 16
5 : 20   3 : 5   24 : 28
Can all the ratios be simplified?

Explore
How do mountain bikes get up steep hills?

Exercise 8.5

1 Copy and complete these equivalent ratios.
   a 18 : 12 = ☐ : 2
   b 24 : ☐ = 8 : 6
   c 72 : 24 = ☐ : 12 = 18 : ☐

2 Divide these quantities in the given ratios.
   a $435 in the ratio 2 : 3
   b 486 kg in the ratio 5 : 1
   c 4 m in the ratio 3 : 5

3 Copy and complete these equivalent ratios.
   a 4 : 8 = 1 : ☐   b 20 : 100 = 1 : ☐
   c 75 : 25 = ☐ : 1   d 42 : 7 = ☐ : 1
   e 11 : 132 = 1 : ☐   f 34 : 17 = ☐ : 1

Key point

You can compare ratios by writing them as **unit ratios**. In a unit ratio, one of the two numbers is 1.

Worked example

A new TV has aspect ratio of 16 : 9. Express this as a **unit ratio**.
Give your answer to two decimal places.

$$\div 9 \left(\begin{array}{c} 16 : 9 \\ 1.78 : 1 \end{array} \right) \div 9$$

> Divide both sides of the ratio by the smallest number, 9

4 Write each ratio as a **unit ratio**.
   Give each answer to a maximum of 2 decimal places.
   a 9 : 5   b 11 : 4   c 17 : 33   d 11 : 23

5 The ratio of teachers to children on a school trip is 17 : 136.
   Write the ratio of teachers to children in the form 1 : n

Warm up

6 Real The ratio between the width and the height of a film, TV or similar image is its **aspect ratio**.

    a Convert each aspect ratio to a unit ratio of the form $n : 1$.
        i 5 : 3 (European widescreen)   **ii** 3 : 2 (35 mm film)
       iii 8 : 5 (computer screen)   **iv** 4 : 3 (cathode ray tube TV)
        v 37 : 20 (US widescreen)   **vi** 12 : 5 (cinema widescreen)

    b If all the images have the same height, which of these ratios shows the widest picture?

7 Jasmine and Taran mix fruit juices to make drinks.
Jasmine mixes orange juice and pineapple juice in the ratio 3 : 4.
Taran mixes orange juice and grapefruit juice in the ratio 5 : 7.
    a Write both ratios in the form $n : 1$.
    b Whose drink has the greatest proportion of orange juice?

8 Simplify each ratio into a whole number ratio in its simplest form.
    a 40 : 28.5   **b** 70 : 51.2   **c** 25.5 : 17   **d** 28.6 : 5.15

Q8a hint

Simplify by multiplying by 10 or 100.
28.5 has 1 decimal place, so multiply both sides of the ratio by 10, then simplify.

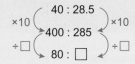

9 Real / STEM Most modern bikes have a variety of gears, with a number of different-sized cogs.
A road-racing bike has a front cog with 53 teeth and a choice of 5 cogs at the rear.

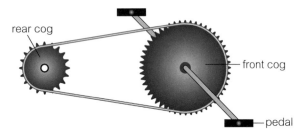

rear cog

front cog

pedal

Key point

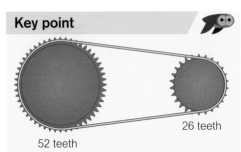

52 teeth

26 teeth

In engineering, gears are used to change speeds.
These two cogs are connected by a chain and have equal sized teeth. Each turn of the large cog makes the small cog turn twice, because 1 × 52 = 2 × 26.

One turn of the pedals turns the front cog once.
Copy and complete the table to work out, for different gears, the number of turns the rear wheel will make when the pedals are turned once.

Front cog teeth	53	53	53	53	53
Gear	1	2	3	4	5
Rear cog teeth	32	25	19	14	11
Ratio of front teeth to rear teeth	53 : 32				
Unit ratio	1.66 : 1				
Number of rear wheel turns per turn of the pedals	1.66				

10 Explore How do mountain bikes get up steep hills?
Is it easier to explore this question now that you have completed the lesson? What further information do you need to be able to answer this?

11 Reflect Why is it useful to write a ratio in the form 1 : n?
Are these ratios the same?
    2.5 : 5.5   5 : 11   1 : 2.2
Which type of ratio do you find easier to understand? Why?

Explore

Reflect

8.6 Working with ratios

You will learn to:
- Divide a quantity into three parts in a given ratio.
- Solve simple word problems using ratio and proportion.

Why learn this?
Builders often have to mix quantities in a given ratio.

Fluency
Work out these equivalences
- 4.5 cm = ☐ mm
- ☐ g = 4.05 kg
- ☐ litres = 463 ml

Explore
How much cement, sand and aggregate do you need to make 50 kg of concrete?

Exercise 8.6

1 Write each ratio in its simplest form.
  a 8 : 4   **b** 12 : 3   **c** 15 : 25
  d 4 : 18   **e** 7 : 49   **f** 40 : 60

2 **a** Share £20 in the ratio 2 : 3.
  b Share £36 in the ratio 4 : 5.
  c A piece of rope 24 m long is cut in the ratio 5 : 3.
     How long is each piece of rope?

> ### Worked example
> Share $114 between Alice, Bert and Chen in the ratio 5 : 2 : 1.
> 5 + 2 + 1 = 8 parts
> $114 ÷ 8 = $14.25 per part
> Alice: 5 × $14.25 = $71.25
> Bert: 2 × $14.25 = $28.50
> Chen: 1 × $14.25 = $14.25
>
> | First find out how many parts there are in total. |
> | Next find out how much one part is. |
> | Multiply one part by each number in the ratio. |
>
> Check: $71.25 + $28.50 + $14.25 = $114

3 Share each quantity in the ratio given.
  a $108 in the ratio 2 : 3 : 4   **b** $486 in the ratio 1 : 3 : 5
  c $510 in the ratio 1 : 2 : 3   **d** $242 in the ratio 1 : 2 : 3 : 5
  e 429 m in the ratio 2 : 3 : 6   **f** 468 kg in the ratio 3 : 6 : 7
  g 591 km in the ratio 1 : 2 : 4 : 5   **h** $1032 in the ratio 3 : 5 : 9
  Discussion How should you round when working with ratios in money? What about kg? Why?

Warm up

4 A recipe uses sugar, flour and butter in the ratio 4 : 5 : 6.
The mixture has a mass of 900 g. How much of each ingredient is used?

5 Three children inherit $24 000 in the ratio 3 : 5 : 4.
How much do they get each?

6 Write each ratio in its simplest form.
  a 250 g : 1 kg : 2.5 kg
  b 40 m*l* : 400 m*l* : 2.2 litres
  c 1500 cm : 300 m : 1.2 km
  d 4.8 cm : 12 mm: 0.12 m

7 **Real / Problem-solving** A coin is made from a mix of copper, tin and zinc in the ratio 95 : 3.5 : 1.5.
The coin has a mass of 7 g.
  a What are the masses of copper, tin and zinc in the coin?
  b What fraction of the coin is tin?

8 **Real** Turquoise paint is made by mixing blue, green and yellow in the ratio 2.5 : 1.4 : 0.1.
Copy and complete the table to show how much of each colour is needed to make the quantities of paint shown.

Quantity	Blue	Green	Yellow
1 litre			
1.5 litres			
2.5 litres			

9 **Reasoning** The triathlon is a race where competitors swim, cycle and run. Four recognised lengths of race are shown in the table below.

Race	Swim	Cycle	Run
Sprint	0.75 km	20 km	5 km
Olympic	1.5 km	40 km	10 km
Half Ironman	1.9 km	90 km	21.1 km
Ironman	3.8 km	180.2 km	42.2 km

  a What proportion of the Sprint triathlon is running?
  b Cycling is Tom's strongest sport. Which race or races would give him the best chance of winning?

10 **Explore** How much cement, sand and aggregate do you need to make 50 kg of concrete?
Look back at the maths you have learned in this lesson. How can you use it to answer this question? What further information do you need to be able to answer this?

11 **Reflect** The hint for Q4 included a diagram to help you to answer the question. Write a sentence explaining how the diagram might be helpful to some students.

Q4 hint

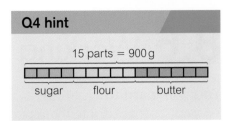

15 parts = 900 g

sugar   flour   butter

Q6 Strategy hint

Write each part of the ratio in the same units before you cancel.

Q8 hint

Simplify the ratio into whole numbers. Then share the quantity of paint in the new ratio.

Q9a hint

First find the total distance of the race. Then write the proportion for 'run' as a fraction, and simplify.

Explore

Reflect

8 Check up

Fractions, decimals and percentages

1 Copy and complete this table.

Fraction			$1\frac{2}{25}$				$4\frac{9}{20}$	
Decimal	1.04			2.05		2.36		
Percentage		156%			215%			512%

2 Write these in descending order.

$2\frac{9}{25}$ 2.9 $2\frac{7}{20}$ 209%   246%   2.6

3 Copy and complete this table. Write the fractions in their simplest form.

Fraction	Decimal	Percentage
$\frac{9}{40}$		
	0.135	
		15.5%

Using percentages

4 A $\frac{1}{2}$ kg box of cereal contains 490 g of corn.

What percentage of the contents of the box is corn?

5 A tennis racket costs $30. It is reduced in a sale by 15%.

Work out the sale price of the tennis racket.

6 Mo invests $650 for 4 years at 3% simple interest per year.
Work out
 a the amount of interest she earns in 1 year
 b the amount of interest she earns in 4 years
 c the total amount her investment is worth at the end of the 4 years.

7 A television has increased in price by 5%.
The new price is $777. What was the original price?

8 Bonita invests $450 in a building society account with a compound interest rate of 5% per annum (each year).
How much will she have at the end of 3 years?

9 Lilia invests $12 500 in a bank account and leaves the money in the account for 3 years.
The bank pays 3.5% compound interest per year.
How much does Lilia have in the account after 3 years?

Ratio

10 Write each ratio in its simplest form.

    a 10 : 2.5

    b 4.8 : 3

11 Share each quantity in the ratio given.

    a 6.5 kg in the ratio 2 : 3

    b 451 litres in the ratio 2 : 4 : 5

    c $1000 in the ratio 1 : 3 : 5

12 Write each ratio as a unit ratio.

    a 7 : 5

    b 5 : 18

Challenge

13 Nadya's grandfather wants to give her some money.
He gives Nadya 4 different options. Nadya can choose between

    i £40 per month for 5 years

  Or a once yearly payment of one of

   ii £500 increasing by 5% every year for 5 years or

  iii £550 increasing by 3% every year for 5 years or

  iv £100 doubling at the end of each year for 5 years.

Which should Nadya choose?

14 **How sure are you of your answers? Were you mostly**
🙁 **Just guessing** 😐 **Feeling doubtful** 🙂 **Confident**
**What next? Use your results to decide whether to strengthen or
extend your learning.**

8 Strengthen

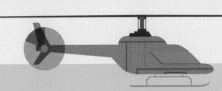

You will:
- Strengthen your understanding with practice.

Fractions, decimals and percentages

1 Copy and complete this diagram.

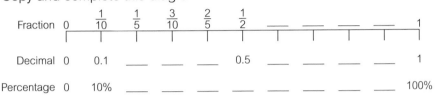

Q1 hint

Fill in the decimals and percentages first, then the fractions. Write each fraction in its simplest form.

2 Write each of these mixed numbers as a decimal and a percentage.

    a $2\frac{4}{5}$ **b** $1\frac{3}{10}$ **c** $5\frac{3}{4}$ **d** $7\frac{1}{5}$

Q2a hint

Use the number lines in Q1.
$2\frac{4}{5} = 2\square$ and $200\% + \square\% = \square\%$

3 Write an equivalent mixed number and decimal or percentage for each of these.

    a 3.7   **b** 9.5   **c** 410%   **d** 940%

Q3a hint

$3.7 = 3 + 0.7 = 3\frac{\square}{\square}$

4 Write these terminating decimals as fractions or mixed numbers in their simplest form.
    a 0.64
    b 0.82
    c 8.44
    d 0.725
    e 0.484

Q4a hint

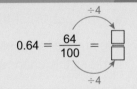

$0.64 = \dfrac{64}{100} = \dfrac{\square}{\square}$

5 Rewrite these proportions giving the numbers as percentages.
    a 12 out of 20 students like sport.
    b 13 out of 25 members of a tennis club are girls.
    c 32 out of 50 members of a football club are boys.
    d 2 out of 10 students have a cat.

Q4d hint

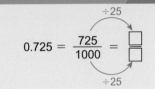

$0.725 = \dfrac{725}{1000} = \dfrac{\square}{\square}$

 6 On Saturday a coffee shop sells 250 cakes. 207 cakes were chocolate cakes.

On Sunday 80% of the cakes sold were chocolate cakes.

Which day was the biggest proportion of chocolate cakes sold?

 7 Nina got the following marks in her end of term exams:

Maths $\frac{23}{30}$ History   75%

In which subject did she do better?

8 For each of these, write the first amount as a percentage of the second amount.

   a 48 cm out of 1 m

   b 15 mm out of 5 cm

   c 300 m*l* out of 2 litres

   d 750 m out of 3 km

   e 130 g out of 0.5 kg

Using percentages

1 A shop increases the price of a mirror by 20%.

   a Work out 20% of $18.

   b What is the new price of the mirror?

2 Increase these amounts by the given percentage.

   a $46 by 20%   **b** $60 by 10%

   c $80 by 15%   **d** $56 by 25%

3 Decrease these amounts by the given percentage.

   a $85 by 5%   **b** $90 by 10%

   c $20 by 30%   **d** $72 by 15%

4 Use a multiplier to calculate these percentages. Show your working.

   a 40% of $150   **b** 65% of 550 g

   c 8% of 560 m*l*   **d** 120% of 68 litres

5 10% of an amount is $12.

   a Work out 1% of the amount.   **b** Work out 100% of the amount.

6 5% of an amount is 30 g.

   a Work out 1% of the amount.   **b** Work out the original amount.

7 The number of bees in a hive has increased from 550 to 649. Express this change as a percentage.

8 In a sale the price of jeans has been reduced by 6% to £28.20. Copy and complete the working to find the original price before the sale.

$$\begin{array}{r}\div 94 \left(\begin{array}{l}94\% = £28.20 \\ 1\% = £0.30 \\ 100\% = \square\end{array}\right)\div 94 \\ \times 100 \qquad\qquad\qquad \times 100\end{array}$$

9 In a sale, television prices have been reduced. Work out the original prices.

   a Reduced by 4% to £600

   b Reduced by 16% to £630

   c Reduced by 7.5% to £693.75

10 Marika invests £800 in the bank at 3% compound interest per year. She leaves all the money in the bank. Copy and complete to work out the amount at the end of 1 year, 2 years and 3 years.

$$800 \times 1.03 = \square \text{ end year 1}$$
$$\square \times 1.03 = \square \text{ end year 2}$$
$$\square \times 1.03 = \square \text{ end year 3}$$

Q8a hint

Convert to the same units first.

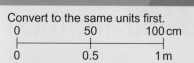

Q8c hint

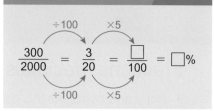

Q2a hint

Work out 10%.
Double it to find 20%.
Add it to $46.

Q2c hint

Work out 10%.
Halve it to find 5%.
10% + 5% = 15%.

Q4a hint

40% of $150 can be written as
40% × $150
40% is 0.4 ...

Q6b hint

The original amount is 100%.

Q8 hint

Q9 hint

Follow the same method as in Q8.

Q10 hint

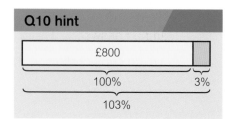

11 Idris is overdrawn by $80 and is charged 2.1% interest per month on his debt. At the end of a year he hasn't paid back any money but hasn't drawn out any more from his account. How much does he owe?

Ratio

1 A piece of rope is 8.5 m long. Josie cuts it in the ratio 3 : 2. How long will each piece be?

2 A piece of wood is 12.6 m long. Alex cuts it in the ratio 4 : 3 : 1. How long will each piece be?

3 Tips at a hotel are shared between the receptionists, porters and cleaners in the ratio 2 : 4 : 5. The total tips for two days were:
Saturday $90.75
Sunday $278.96
How much did each group receive on each day?

4 Simplify each ratio.
   a 6.5 : 3   **b** 8.5 : 3   **c** 4.8 : 2   **d** 5.4 : 6.6

5 A small dessert weighs 40 g and contains protein, carbohydrate and fat in the ratio 3.2 : 15 : 6.8.
   a What percentage of the dessert is fat?
   b A large dessert weighs 3.5 times as much as a small dessert. How many grams of protein does the large dessert contain?

Enrichment

1 Work out
   a **i** 5% of $50   **ii** 50% of $5
   b **i** 20% of 80 kg   **ii** 80% of 20 kg
   c **i** 350% of 75 m   **ii** 75% of 350 m
   What do you notice? Can you prove that this is always true?

2 Four children share a jar of sweets.
Naima takes $\frac{1}{4}$ of the sweets and leaves the rest in the jar.
Sara takes $\frac{1}{4}$ of the remaining sweets and leaves the rest.
Caris takes $\frac{1}{4}$ of the remaining sweets and leaves the rest.
Lastly Daia takes $\frac{1}{4}$ of the remaining sweets.
What percentage of the sweets are left in the jar?

3 **Reflect** Mo says, 'Working with ratio, fractions, decimals and percentages is all about multiplying and dividing.'
Look back at the questions you answered in these Strengthen lessons.
Write down two questions where you had to multiply to find an answer.
Write down two questions where you had to divide to find an answer.
Write down two questions where you had to multiply and divide to find an answer.

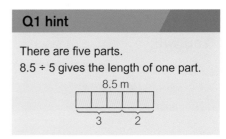

Q1 hint
There are five parts.
8.5 ÷ 5 gives the length of one part.

Q2 hint

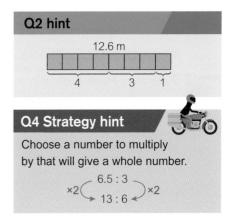

Q4 Strategy hint
Choose a number to multiply by that will give a whole number.
6.5 : 3
×2   ×2
13 : 6

Reflect

8 Extend

You will:

- Extend your understanding with problem-solving.

1 **Reasoning** Janan spends 1 hour 48 minutes doing her homework one evening.
She says, 'I have spent 1.48 hours doing homework this evening.'
Is she correct? Explain your answer.

Q1 hint

Write 48 minutes as a fraction of an hour, then use division to write it as a decimal.

2 **Finance / Real** Fatima invests $5000 for 5 years.

a Copy and complete the table showing the value of her investment at the end of each year.

Year	Value at start of year	Percentage change	Value at end of year
1st	$5000	20% increase	$6000
2nd	$6000	8% increase	
3rd		12% decrease	
4th		10% increase	
5th		3% decrease	

b Compare the value of her investment at the start of the 1st year and the end of the 5th year.
Work out

  i the actual increase in her investment

  ii the percentage increase in her investment.

Q2b ii hint

Percentage increase

$$= \frac{\text{actual increase}}{\text{original amount}} \times 100$$

3 **Reasoning** These offers are given by three supermarkets for the same packet of biscuits.

A — 12 biscuits for $1.80 plus 25% extra free!

B — 12 biscuits for $1.80 Buy 2 packets and get the 3rd half price!

C — 12 biscuits for $1.80 Now 25% off!

Which supermarket gives the best offer?
Explain how you made your decision.

4 Write these in ascending order.

$$1.4\% \quad \frac{4}{2} \quad 0.7\% \quad 1.1\% \quad \frac{1}{20} \quad \frac{3}{85} \quad 4.1\% \quad \frac{1}{68}$$

5 **Problem-solving** The pictogram shows the number of ice creams sold over a weekend.

a What fraction of the ice creams sold over the weekend were sold on Sunday?

b What percentage of the ice creams sold over the weekend were sold on Sunday?

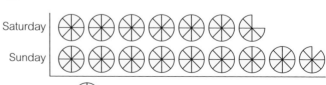

Saturday / Sunday

Key ⊗ represents 8 ice creams

6 In a large department store all workers have been given a pay rise. Find the original salary of each worker. The table shows their new salaries and the percentage increases.

Q6 Strategy hint

Remember: the inverse of multiplication is division.

Staff	Pay rise	New salary
Shop floor staff	2.4%	$18 022.40
Shop floor managers	2.8%	$24 106.60

7 A large business had to cut back its staff due to falling orders.
  a Calculate the number of staff that used to work in each department.

Department	Percentage reduction	New staff number
Telemarketing	7.1%	236
Sales	20.6%	448
Administration	12.9%	216
Accounts	9.8%	462

  b What is the overall reduction in staff as a percentage?

Investigation   Problem-solving

Original value	Percentage decrease	New value	Percentage increase	Original value
100	10%	90	11.1%	100

In the table a quantity has been reduced by a percentage, then increased by a different percentage to return it to the original value.
Investigate other percentage decreases. Is there a pattern in the increase required to return the quantity to its original value?

Hint

It might help to think of the percentage decreases and increases as fractions.

8 Real Nurses frequently carry out calculations using ratios to convert between units.
A doctor prescribes 200 mg of ibuprofen.
The medicine is in a container that has 500 mg of ibuprofen dissolved in 40 ml of water.
How much of the liquid should the nurse give to the patient so that they take the correct dose of ibuprofen?

9 A cereal box is 19.6 cm wide, 7.2 cm deep and 27.5 cm high.
  a What is the volume of the cereal box?
  b All three dimensions are halved. What is the ratio of the volume of the small box to the volume of the original one?

10 Finance Kim puts $1250 into an investment that pays 4.85% simple interest per year.
She takes the money out after 4 years and 3 months.
What is the value of her investment when she takes her money out? Give your answer to the nearest cent.

Q10 hint

In the final year she only gets 3 months' worth of the yearly amount.

11 Problem-solving Sachin invests $840 in an investment that pays simple interest for 5 years.
At the end of the 5 years his investment is worth $955.50.
What is the yearly simple interest percentage?

Q11 Strategy hint

Work backwards through the problem

12 Problem-solving The ratio of the area of the blue triangle to the area of the yellow triangle is 4 : 5.
Work out a possible base length and height of the blue triangle.

64 cm²

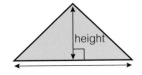

height

13 Problem-solving There are 10 members of a French club.
One member leaves and another member arrives.
The mean age of the club increases by 5% to 63 years old.
  a What is the mean age of the members before the first member
     leaves? The member who leaves is 32 years old.
  b What is the age of the member who arrives?

Q13 hint

Work out the total age of the members before the first member leaves and after the second member arrives.

14 Problem-solving Between 2017 and 2018 visitor numbers to a
museum increased by 25%.
Between 2018 and 2019 visitor numbers to the museum decreased
by 10%.
In 2019 there were 71 856 visitors.
How many visitors were there in 2017?

Q14 Strategy hint

Work out how many visitors there were in 2018 first.

15 Here is a sequence of numbers.
  200, 160, 128, 102.4, ...
Each term in the sequence is 80% of the previous term.
The term-to-term rule is 'multiply by 0.8'.
  a Write down the first four terms in each of these sequences.
    i First term is 400, then each term in the sequence is 30% of the
       previous term.
    ii First term is 80, then each term in the sequence is 120% of the
       previous term.

16 A tree surgeon reduces the height of a beech tree by 32%.
The tree is now 4.42 m tall.
How tall was it before it was reduced?

17 Arya buys a car for $7800.
The car decreases in value by 8% every year.
What is it worth after 4 years? Show your working.

18 Reasoning Between the ages of 3 and 5 years
old a tree grows at a rate of approximately 10% per year.
At 5 years old it is 2.5 m tall.
  a Work out the height of the tree when it is
    i 4 years old   **ii** 3 years old.
  Write each answer correct to the nearest cm.
  b Andy says, 'The tree has grown 10% each year for 2 years, which
     makes 20% in total. This means that if I divide 2.5 m by 1.2 I will
     find the height of the tree when it is 3 years old.'
     Is Andy correct? Explain your answer.

19 $8000 is invested in a savings account at a compound interest rate
of 3% per year.

$$\text{Amount} = \text{initial amount} \times \left(\frac{100 + \text{interest rate}}{100}\right)^n$$

  a How much is the investment worth after 5 years?
  b How many years will it be before the investment is worth more
     than £10 000?

Q19b Strategy hint

Try different numbers of years.

20 Reflect These Extend lessons had questions on percentages used by
  • supermarkets for promotions (as in Q3)
  • the cultural industries for monitoring visitor numbers (as in Q14).
List how three other types of business might use percentages.

8 Unit test

1 Write the missing fractions, decimals and percentages in this table.

Fraction		$\frac{9}{10}$				$1\frac{3}{5}$
Decimal	0.75			1.3		
Percentage			25%	275%		

2 Three groups of students were surveyed to find out if they liked a new brand of milkshake.
The table shows the results of the survey.

Group	Number of students surveyed	Number of students who liked the milkshake
A	100	72
B	50	37
C	200	142

   a For each group, write the proportion of students who liked the milkshake as a
       i fraction of those surveyed
      ii percentage of those surveyed.
   b Which group had the greatest proportion of students who liked the milkshake?
   c Which group had the greatest proportion of students who didn't like the milkshake?

3 A one-litre carton of fruit drink is made from 350 ml of mango juice, 400 ml of orange juice and some mandarin juice.
   What percentage of the fruit drink is
   a mango juice
   b orange juice
   c mandarin juice?

4 A mobile phone costs $320. It is reduced in a sale by 45%.
   Work out the sale price of the mobile phone.

5 Jatin gets a pay rise of 8%. His old salary was $22 000.
   What is his new salary?

6 a 10% of an amount is 6.2 kg. Work out the original amount.
   b 40% of an amount is 96 m. Work out the original amount.

7 Simplify each ratio.
   a 12 : 16.8
   b 1.5 : 7.5

8 Sophie mixes acid and water in the ratio 2 : 5.2
She makes 288 m*l* of the mixture.
How much acid and how much water did she mix?

9 Ben makes orange paint by mixing red, yellow and white paint in the ratio 20 : 16 : 1.5.
How much of each colour does he need to make 1.5 litres of orange paint?

10 Pink gold is made from 75% gold, 20% copper and 5% silver.
  a What fraction of pink gold is made from
    i gold
    ii copper
    iii silver?
  Write each fraction in its simplest form.
  b Write the ratio of gold : copper : silver in pink gold in its simplest form.

11 Serena invests $1800 for 5 years at 6.3% simple interest per year.
How much is her investment worth at the end of the 5 years?

12 Lyndal invests $4650 in a savings account paying compound interest of 3% each year.
How much money will she have in her account after 3 years?

Challenge

13 A surfboard in a shop has 20% off in a sale.

For one day only, the shop is advertising an extra 30% off all sale prices.
  a Choose an original price for the surfboard. Reduce it by 20%. Reduce the new price by 30%.
  b Is 20% off, then 30% off, the same as 50% off? Explain.
  c Explain how you can work out the combined discount of two discounts on the same item.

14 **Reflect** Look back at the table you completed for Q1 in this test.
Explain in general how you work out these types of conversions.
  a You have a decimal and want to find its
    i equivalent fraction
    ii equivalent percentage.
  b You have a fraction and want to find its
    i equivalent decimal
    ii equivalent percentage.
  c You have a percentage and want to find its
    i equivalent fraction
    ii equivalent decimal.

Reflect

9.1 Quadrilaterals

You will learn to:
- Identify properties of quadrilaterals.
- Use properties of quadrilaterals.

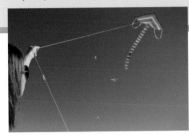

Why learn this?
Kite designers change the angles in the design of kites to make them faster or look better.

Fluency
- What do angles in a quadrilateral add up to?
- Subtract each of these from 180: 60, 45, 122
- Subtract each of these from 90: 30, 55, 61

Explore
Which quadrilaterals tessellate (fit together) with each other?

Exercise 9.1

1 Copy and complete this table showing the number of lines of symmetry and order of rotational symmetry of these quadrilaterals.

Quadrilateral	Square	Rectangle	Parallelogram	Rhombus	Kite	Trapezium	Isosceles trapezium
Number of lines of symmetry							
Order of rotational symmetry							

2 Work out the missing angles.

a

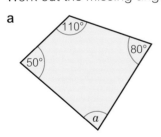

b

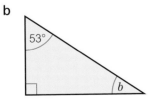

Warm up

Key point

The properties of a shape are facts about its sides, angles, diagonals and symmetry.
Here are some of the properties of the special quadrilaterals that you should know.

Square	• all sides are equal in length • opposite sides are parallel • all angles are 90° • diagonals bisect each other at 90°	Rectangle	• opposite sides are equal in length • opposite sides are parallel • all angles are 90° • diagonals bisect each other
Rhombus	• all sides are equal in length • opposite sides are parallel • opposite angles are equal • diagonals bisect each other at 90° • adjacent angles add to 180°	Parallelogram	• opposite sides are equal in length • opposite sides are parallel • opposite angles are equal • diagonals bisect each other • adjacent angles add to 180°
Kite	• 2 pairs of sides are equal in length • no parallel sides • 1 pair of equal angles • diagonals bisect each other at 90°	Trapezium	• 1 pair of parallel sides
		Isosceles trapezium	• 2 sides are equal in length • 1 pair of parallel sides • 2 pairs of equal angles

3 Name each quadrilateral being described.
  a My opposite sides are parallel and equal in length.
    None of my angles are 90°.
  b I have one pair of parallel sides, and two sides the same length.
  c I have one pair of equal angles, and no parallel sides.
  d All my angles are 90°. My **diagonals bisect** each other,
    but not at 90°.
  Discussion Is this shape a trapezium?

Q2 Literacy hint

A **diagonal** is a line that joins two opposite vertices of a shape. When diagonals **bisect** each other, they cut each other in half.

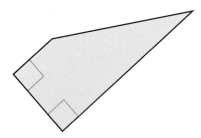

4 Write down a property that
  a a square and a rectangle have in common
  b a kite has but a rhombus does not
  c a kite and a square have in common.

5 Write down properties that make
  a a square different from a rectangle
  b a rhombus different from a parallelogram
  c a rectangle different from a parallelogram
  d a square different from a kite.
  Discussion Can a square be a rectangle? What other shapes might
  this be true for?

199

6 Problem-solving Draw a coordinate grid on squared paper with both axes going from 0 to 10. Plot these points.
A (1, 1),   B (3, 1),   C (10, 1),   D (4, 4),   E (6, 4),
F (1, 7),   G (3, 7),   H (5, 7),   I (9, 7),   J (6, 10)
Which four points can you join to make each of these quadrilaterals?
a a rectangle
b a trapezium
c a parallelogram
d a square
e a kite

7 One of the diagonals has been drawn in this rectangle.

Work out the sizes of angles a, b and c. Give a reason for each answer.

8 Lowri uses this rhombus and parallelogram in her patchwork quilt design.

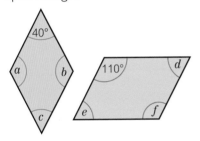

Q8 hint

Shapes tessellate if they make a repeating pattern with no gaps.

a Work out the sizes of the angles marked with letters. Give a reason for each answer.
b Draw a sketch to show how these shapes will tessellate.
Discussion Is a parallelogram a rhombus or is a rhombus a parallelogram?

9 Real Anil designs a kite on his computer. The diagram shows some of the angles.
Work out the sizes of angles a, b and c.
Give a reason for each answer.

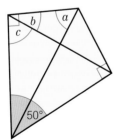

10 Problem-solving The diagram shows a chevron road sign.
A chevron is made from two congruent parallelograms.

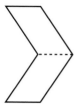

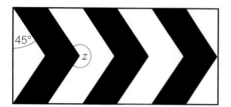

Work out the size of angle z.

Investigation

The diagram shows the pieces of a tangram puzzle.

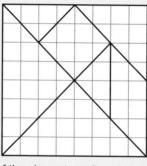

Copy the diagram on squared paper.
Cut out all the pieces.
Work out two different ways in which you can use two of the pieces to make a trapezium.
Work out two different ways in which you can use two of the pieces to make a parallelogram.
Work out how you can use all of the pieces to make each of these shapes.
a a rectangle
b a parallelogram
c a trapezium
d a triangle
e a hexagon

11 Explore Which quadrilaterals tessellate with each other?
What have you learnt in this lesson to help you to answer this?
What further information do you need to find out to answer this?

12 Reflect You have learnt about different properties of quadrilaterals
in this lesson.
Write down properties that some quadrilaterals have in common,
and properties that make them different.
How can you remember their properties?

9.2 Angles and parallel lines

You will learn to:
- Identify alternate and corresponding angles and know that they are equal.
- Solve problems using properties of angles in intersecting and parallel lines and in polygons.

Why learn this?
Snooker players use angles to plan their next shot.

Fluency
- What do the angles on a straight line add up to?
- What do the angles round a point add up to?
- What is $90 - 35$, $180 - 110$, $360 - 250$?

Explore
What different shapes can you make when you intersect pairs of parallel lines?

Exercise 9.2

1 Work out the size of each angle marked with a letter.

a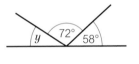

b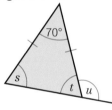

c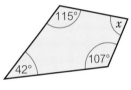

2 Work out the size of angle x in each case.

a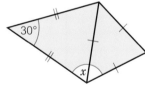

b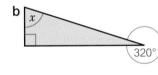

c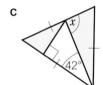

3 Work out the sizes of the angles marked with letters.

a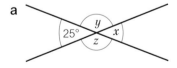

Key point

We show parallel lines using arrows.

Investigation

Reasoning

Copy this diagram on to squared paper.
Measure the acute alternate angles. What do you notice?
Find two alternate angles that are obtuse and measure them. What do you notice?
Copy and complete this rule. Alternate angles are ....
Draw another line that crosses the parallel lines at a different angle.
Check your rule works for the alternate angles.
Draw two more parallel lines.
Measure a pair of corresponding angles. What do you notice?
Copy and complete this rule. Corresponding angles are ....
Check that your rule works by measuring other pairs of corresponding angles.

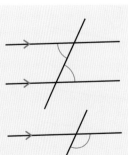

Warm up

4 The diagram shows a line crossing two parallel lines and angles labelled a, b, c and d.

a and d are **alternate angles**.
a and d are the same size.

b and c are alternate angles.
b and c are the same size.

Now look at this diagram.
Write down two pairs of alternate angles.

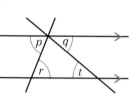

5 The diagram shows two lines crossing parallel lines.
Copy and complete these statements.
a Angle r and angle □ are alternate angles.
b Angle t and angle □ are alternate angles.
c Angle □ is the same size as angle q.
d Angle □ is the same size as angle p.

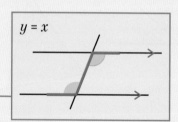

Worked example

Write down the sizes of angles x, y and z.
Give reasons for your answers.

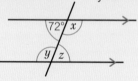

$x = 180 - 72 = 108°$ (angles on a straight line)
$y = 108°$ (alternate angle with x)
$z = 72°$ (alternate angle with 72°)

$y = x$

$z = 72°$

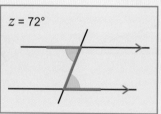

6 Write down the sizes of the angles marked with letters.
Give a reason for each answer.

a

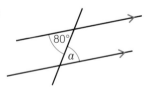

b

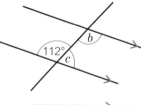

c

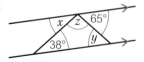

d

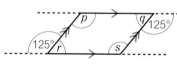

Discussion What angle facts about parallelograms have you shown in part **d**?

7 Problem-solving In this diagram, angles a and b are in the ratio 5 : 7.

Work out the size of angle c. Give a reason for your answer.

8 a Reasoning Sketch this diagram. Do not use a protractor.

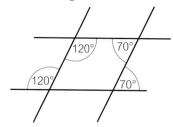

  b Work out all the unmarked angles and write them on your diagram.
  c Mark the parallel lines.

Q8c hint

Use arrows to show parallel lines.

Worked example

Write down the sizes of angles x, y and z.
Give reasons for your answers.

$x = 180 - 105 = 75°$ (angles on a straight line)
$y = 105°$ (corresponding angle with $105°$)
$z = 75°$ (corresponding angle with x)

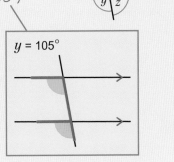

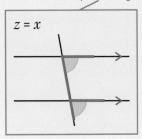

$z = x$ $y = 105°$

Key point

When a line crosses two parallel lines it creates an 'F' shape.
There are **corresponding angles** on an F shape.
Corresponding angles are equal.
Corresponding angles are on the same (corresponding) side of the diagonal line.

9 Write down the sizes of the angles marked with letters. Give a reason for each answer.

  a

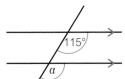

  b

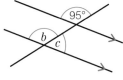

  c

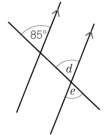

  d

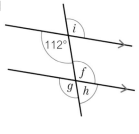

Discussion The capital letter F has corresponding angles.
What other capital letters have corresponding angles?

10 Write down the sizes of the angles marked with letters. Give a reason for each answer.

Q10 Strategy hint

Are there any corresponding angles?

a

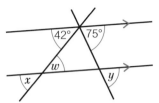

b

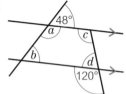

c

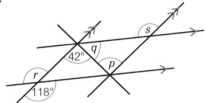

11 Reasoning Look at this diagram.

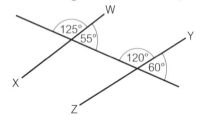

Explain why WX and YZ cannot be parallel lines.

12 Explore What different shapes can you make when you intersect pairs of parallel lines?
What have you learnt in this lesson to help you to answer the question?
What further information do you need to be able to answer this?

13 Reflect In this lesson you have learned about alternate angles and corresponding angles.
How can you help yourself remember the difference between these, and other angle properties? What do all the pairs of angles have in common?

9.3 Angles in polygons

You will learn to:
- Work out the interior and exterior angles of a polygon.

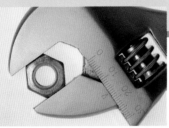

Fluency
- What is 180 − 45?
- What is 360 ÷ 6?
- What is an interior angle of a shape?

Why learn this?
Spanners are designed to fit hexagonal nuts and bolts.

Explore
After turning, a bolt appears to be in the same position. What angle could it have turned through?

Exercise 9.3

1 Work out the angles marked with letters.

a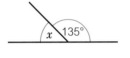

b

c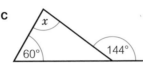

2 a i How many lines of symmetry does a regular pentagon have?
 ii What is the order of rotational symmetry for a regular pentagon?
 b Find the number of lines of symmetry and order of rotational symmetry for three different regular polygons.
 c What do you notice?
 Discussion Is a rectangle a polygon?
 Is a square a regular polygon?

Key point

A **polygon** is a closed shape with straight sides.
In a **regular polygon**, the sides and angles are all equal.

regular polygons

pentagon   hexagon   heptagon

irregular polygons

pentagon   hexagon

Investigation
Reasoning

1 Draw a pentagon and divide it into triangles using diagonals.
 The diagonals must all start from the same vertex (corner) of the pentagon.
2 Fill in the 'pentagon' row in this table.

Shape	Number of sides	Number of triangles	Sum of interior angles
Triangle	3	1	180°
Quadrilateral	4	2	360°
Pentagon	5	3	
Hexagon	6		

3 Use the triangle method above to work out the sum of the interior angles in a hexagon.
4 Copy and complete the table.
5 Write down how to work out the number of triangles from the number of sides.
6 Write down how to work out the sum of the interior angles from the number of sides.
7 Add decagon to your table.

3 Work out each unknown angle.

a

b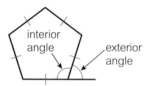

 4 **Problem-solving** The sum of the interior angles of a polygon is 2340°.
Work out how many sides it has.

> ## Worked example
>
> Work out the interior angle of a regular octagon.
>
> $S = 180° \times (n - 2)$ ⟵ Write down the formula. Substitute $n = 8$.
>
> $n = 8$
>
> $S = 180° \times (8 - 2)$
>
> $180° \times 6 = 1080°$ ⟵ A regular octagon has 8 equal angles. Divide 1080° by 8.
>
> Each interior angle $= 1080° \div 8 = 135°$

 5 Work out the interior angle of a regular
   a hexagon   **b** nonagon.

6 a Work out the interior angle of a regular pentagon.
  b Work out the exterior angle of a regular pentagon.
  c How many exterior angles are there in a regular pentagon?
  d Work out the sum of the exterior angles.

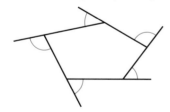

7 Repeat Q6 for a regular hexagon.
What do you notice?

8 a Draw an irregular pentagon.

  b Measure the exterior angles.
  c Work out their sum. What do you notice?
  d Copy and complete this rule.
    The exterior angles of any polygon add up to ☐°
  e Write a rule in words to work out the exterior angle of a regular polygon.
  f **Modelling** Use algebra to write an expression for the exterior angle of a regular polygon with n sides.

Q3 hint

What kind of polygon is it? What is the sum of its interior angles?

Q4 Strategy hint

First work out how many triangles it divides into: ☐ × 180° = 2340°

Key point

Sum of the interior angles of an n-sided polygon
$S = (n - 2) \times 180°$

Q6c hint

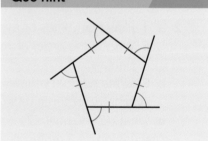

9 **Reasoning**
   a What is the sum of the exterior angles of a regular nonagon?
   b Work out the size of one of its exterior angles.
   c Work out the size of one of its interior angles.

10 **Problem-solving** The exterior angle of a regular polygon is 15°.
   a Work out the interior angle.
   b How many sides does the polygon have?

Q10b hint

$\square$ × 15° = $\square$°

11 A regular polygon has 30 sides. Work out the size of its
   a exterior angle
   b interior angle.
   Discussion Is it easier to work out the exterior or interior angle of a regular polygon first?

12 **Real / Problem-solving** The diagram shows parts of some floor tiling using regular polygons.
   Work out the angles marked with letters. Give reasons.

Q12 hint

Work out the interior angle of each polygon.

a

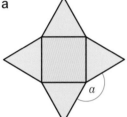

b

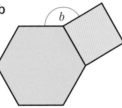

c

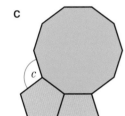

d

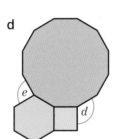

13 **Problem-solving** The diagram shows the face of a gem stone.

   The face has two lines of symmetry. Work out the angle marked x.
   Give reasons for your working.

14 **Explore** After turning, a bolt appears to be in the same position. What angle could it have turned through?
   Is it easier to explore this question now that you have completed the lesson? What further information do you need to be able to answer this?

15 **Reflect** Look back at the investigation. You used lots of different maths topics to work on it. Write a list of all the different maths you used in the investigation.
   Compare your list with a friend's.

Explore

Reflect

9 Check up

Quadrilaterals

1 Name each quadrilateral being described.
 a All my angles are 90°. My diagonals bisect each other at 90°.
 b My diagonals bisect each other at 90°, all my sides are equal, but my angles are not 90°.
 c I have one pair of parallel sides and two sides of equal length

2 One of the diagonals has been drawn in this parallelogram.

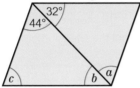

 Work out the size of angles a, b and c.
 Give a reason for each answer.

3 Here is an isosceles trapezium.
 a Work the size of angles a and b.
  Give a reason for each answer
 b Write down the length of c.
  Give a reason for your answer.

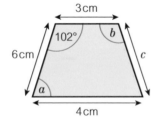

Angles and parallel lines

4 Work out the size of angle x in each diagram. Give reasons.

 a

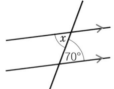

 b

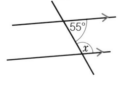

 c

 d

5 Work out the sizes of the angles marked with letters in these diagrams.
Give reasons for your answers.

a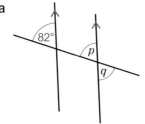

b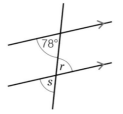

c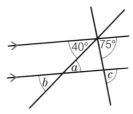

d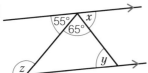

e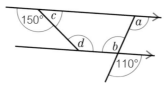

Angles in polygons

6 Work out the sum of the interior angles of this polygon.

7 The diagram shows an irregular hexagon.
a What is the sum of the interior angles of a hexagon?
b Work out the size of angle *z*.

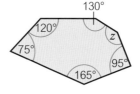

8 a Work out the exterior angle of a regular decagon (10-sided polygon). Show your working.
b Work out the interior angle of a regular decagon.

9 The diagram shows the exterior angle of a regular polygon.
Work out how many sides the polygon has.

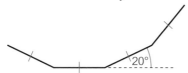

10 How sure are you of your answers? Were you mostly
🙁 Just guessing   😐 Feeling doubtful   🙂 Confident
What next? Use your results to decide whether to strengthen or extend your learning.

Challenge

11 The diagram shows two sets of parallel lines.
Write down
a two pairs of alternate angles
b two pairs of corresponding angles
c two pairs of angles that sum to 180°
d two sets of three angles that sum to 180°
e two sets of four angles that sum to 360°
f two sets of six angles that sum to 360°.

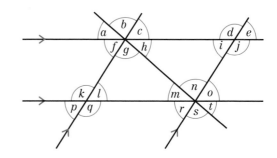

Reflect

9 Strengthen

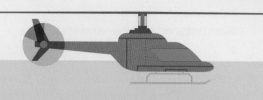

You will:
- Strengthen your understanding with practice.

Quadrilaterals

1 Write down the quadrilateral being described.
 a All the sides are equal in length and the diagonals intersect at 90°, but the angles are not necessarily 90°.
 b Two sets of parallel sides and all angles are 90°, but the sides are not necessarily equal in length.
 c One pair of parallel sides and two sides are equal in length.

Q1 Strategy hint

Look at what is different about properties of quadrilaterals to help you decide.

2 Write down all the properties of a square.

3 a Copy and complete this statement.
 The sum of the angles in any quadrilateral is ☐°.
 b Work out the sizes of the angles marked with letters in these quadrilaterals.

Q3b Strategy hint

1 Look for symmetry.
2 Look for equal angles.

 i trapezium

 ii parallelogram

 iii rhombus

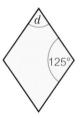

 iv kite

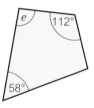

4 The diagram shows a parallelogram and an isosceles triangle.
 a What is the size of angle a?
 b Work out the size of angle b.
 c What is the size of angle c?
 d Work out the size of angle d.

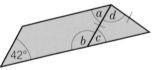

Q4d hint

$d = 180 - c - c$

5 The diagram shows a right-angled triangle and a rhombus.
 a Work out the size of angle x.
 b Work out the size of angle y.
 c Work out the size of angle z.

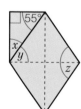

6 In this rectangle, work out the size of angle CED. Show your steps for solving this problem and explain your reasoning.

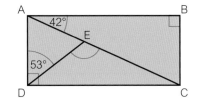

Q6 Strategy hint

Copy the diagram. Work out any angles you can and mark them on the diagram.

Angles and parallel lines

1 The diagram shows a set of parallel lines.

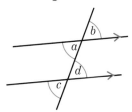

Copy and complete these statements using words from the box.

a a and b are .... angles.

b a and d are .... angles.

c a and c are .... angles.

d b and d are .... angles.

e c and d are .... angles.

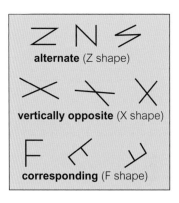

alternate (Z shape)

vertically opposite (X shape)

corresponding (F shape)

2 Copy the diagrams. Look for the Z-shape.
Write the size of each marked **alternate angle**.
Give a reason for each answer.

a

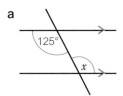

b

c

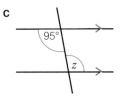

Q2 hint

When a line crosses two parallel lines it creates a 'Z' shape.
Inside the Z shape are **alternate angles**. Alternate angles are equal.

Alternate angles are on different (alternate) sides of the diagonal line.

3 Copy the diagrams. Look for the F-shape.
Write the size of each marked **corresponding angle**.
Give a reason for each answer.

a

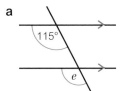

b

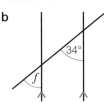

c

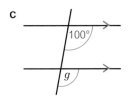

Q3 hint

When a line crosses two parallel lines it creates an F shape.
There are **corresponding angles** on an F shape. Corresponding angles are equal.

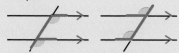

Corresponding angles are on the same (corresponding) side of the diagonal line.

4 Work out the angles marked with letters.
Copy and complete the sentences.

a

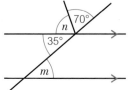

b

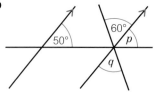

m = ... (alternate angles)

n = ... (angles on a straight line)

p = ... (corresponding angles)

q = ... (vertically opposite angles)

Q4 hint

Look for ⅄ℤ⧅ and ⅂⅄.

5 Work out the angles marked with letters.

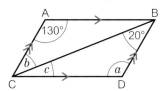

a = ☐° (opposite angles of a parallelogram)
b = ☐° (alternate angles)
c = ☐° (angle sum of a triangle)

Angles in polygons

1 a Name these polygons.

A   B   C

  b Write down the number of sides of each polygon.
  c Write down the number of interior and exterior angles of each polygon.
  d What do you notice about your answers to parts **b** and **c**?

2 Follow these steps to find the angle sum of a polygon.
  1 Sketch the polygon.
  2 Hold your pencil on one vertex.
  3 Draw lines to the other vertices.
  4 Write 180° in each triangle.
  5 Work out the total, e.g. 3 × 180° = ☐°.
  Use this method to find the angle sums of these polygons and fill in the table.

Polygon	Angle sum
Pentagon	
Hexagon	
Heptagon	
Octagon	

3 Work out the sizes of the angles marked with letters.

a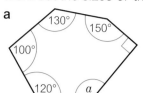

b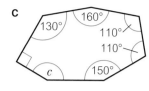

c

Q3a hint

Use the angle sums you found in Q2.
$a = \text{sum} - \Box° - \Box° - \Box° - \Box° - \Box°$

4 Jess measured the exterior angles of this pentagon and added them together.

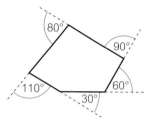

Explain how you know that her measurements are wrong.

Q4 hint

What should the exterior angles add up to?

5 **Problem-solving** The exterior angle of a regular polygon is 30°.

a How many exterior angles does the polygon have?
b How many sides does the polygon have?

Q5a hint

The exterior angles add up to 360°.
$\Box × 30° = 360°$

Enrichment

1 a Draw two parallel lines on squared paper.
Cross the lines with a third line.

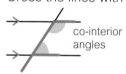

co-interior angles

b Measure the two marked angles.
c Repeat part **b** with two more diagrams.
d Add the marked angles together. What do you notice?

2 These Strengthen lessons cover topics on:
   • quadrilaterals
   • angles and parallel lines
   • angles in polygons.
Write down one thing about each topic that you fully understand and one thing you are still unsure about.
What strategies can you use to help you to understand the things you are still unsure about?

Reflect

9 Extend

You will:
• Extend your understanding with problem-solving.

1 **Problem-solving** The diagram shows quadrilateral ABCD. Work out the size of ∠CDE.

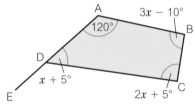

2 **Problem-solving** The diagram shows a star made from four kites.

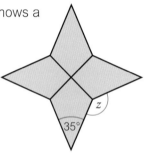

Work out the size of angle z.

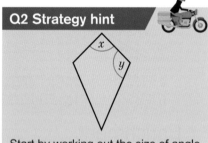
3 **Real / Problem-solving** Marcin makes metal wall art by overlapping shapes around a point. He starts with one rhombus, then overlaps the next one by dividing the angle at the base in the ratio 2 : 1.

a Work out the sizes of angles a and b.
b Show that angle c is 30°.
Marcin continues the pattern, overlapping each rhombus by the same amount each time.

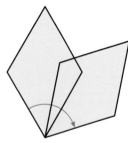
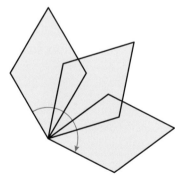

The table shows the total angle used around the centre point each time an extra rhombus is added.

Number of rhombuses	1	2	3	4	5
Total angle	45°	75°			

c Copy and complete the table.

d What is the term-to-term rule for the 'Total angle' sequence of numbers?

e The pattern is complete when the final rhombus overlaps behind the first rhombus.
How many rhombuses will Marcin need to complete the pattern?

4 a What is the sum of the angles in a pentagon?
Explain how you worked out your answer.
The diagram shows a pentagon.

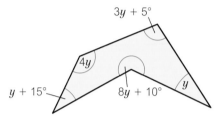

b Work out the value of y.

c Work out the sizes of all the angles in the pentagon.

d Show how to check that your answers to part **c** are correct.

5 **Real** The diagram shows a ship S and a lighthouse L on a map.
The arrows both point to north.
They are parallel.
Work out the size of the angle marked x.

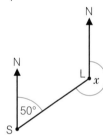

Q4d hint

The sum of the angles in part **c** should equal your answer to part **a**.

Q5 hint

Extend the line SL.

6 **Reasoning** Show that the sum of the interior angles of a dodecagon (12-sided shape) is 1800°.

Q6 Strategy hint

'Show that' means work out the answer and show that it is the same as the one given.

7 Work out the angles marked with letters.
Give reasons for your working.

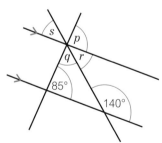

8 Copy and complete this proof that angles a and b sum to 180°.
$a = \Box$ (................. angles)
$b = \Box - \Box$ (angles on a straight line)
$a + b = ... + ...$
$\quad = ...$

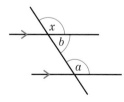

Q8 hint

You must prove that $a + b = 180°$.
Find the expressions for a and b and then add them together.

9 Work out angles a, b and c.

a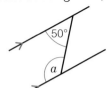

b

c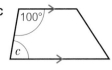

Q9 hint

Look at Q8.

10 Real / Problem-solving / Reasoning The diagram shows a leaning building being supported by two parallel wooden beams.

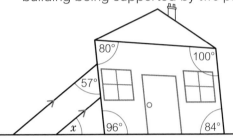

a Work out the angle x that the beams make with the ground.

b Are the floor and ceiling parallel? Give a reason for your answer.

11 Problem-solving / Reasoning The diagram shows an adjustable ladder on a horizontal surface.

a The ladder has two equal legs held together by DE. DE is horizontal.
What does this tell you about lines AC and DE?

b What shape is ADEC?

c Work out

  i the angle that leg BC makes with the ground

  ii the angle ABC between the two legs.

12 Reasoning Here are some regular polygons.

a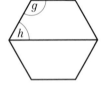

b

c

Q12 hint

Use line symmetry.

  i Work out the sizes of the angles marked with letters.

  ii Give a reason for each answer.

13 A hectogon (not 'hexagon') is a polygon with 100 sides.
For a regular hectogon, work out the

a exterior angle

b interior angle.

Investigation   Reasoning

The centre of this regular pentagon has been joined to its vertices.
The lines from the centre are all equal. Explain why.

a How many angles at the centre are there?

b Work out the size of each angle at the centre.

c Work out the angle marked x.

d How can you use x to work out the interior angle?

Repeat step 2 for a regular hexagon.

Write a rule to work out the interior angle from the angle at the centre.

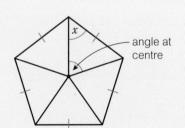

angle at centre

14 Reasoning These red shapes are made from regular polygons.

The centre of each polygon is marked using a dot.
Work out the angles marked with letters.

15 Reasoning The diagram shows a polygon in the shape of a star.

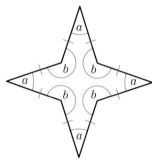

Q15 hint

Work out the sum of the interior angles.

Angle a is 40°. Work out angle b.

16 Problem-solving The diagram shows four identical kites that fit exactly around a point.

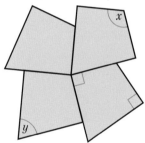

Angle x is double the size of angle y.
Work out the sizes of angles x and y.
Explain your reasoning.

17 Reasoning Callie says it is not possible to draw a polygon that has interior angles that sum to 1500°.
Is she correct? Explain your reasoning.

18 Reflect Look back at the questions you answered in these Extend lessons.
Find a question that you could not answer straight away, or that you really had to think about.
While you worked on this question:
• What were you thinking about?
• How did you feel?
• Did you keep trying until you had an answer? Did you give up before reaching an answer, and move on to the next question?
• Did you think you would get the answer correct or incorrect?
Write down any strategies you could use to help you stay calm when answering tricky maths questions. Compare your strategies with those of your classmates.

9 Unit test

1 Here is a rhombus.
   a Copy the diagram and mark any equal angles, equal sides and parallel lines.
   b Draw on the diagonals and mark any equal sides, equal angles or other properties.

2 Write down all the quadrilaterals that have these properties.
   a All sides are equal in length.
   b The diagonals intersect at 90°.
   c Two pairs of parallel sides.

3 A quadrilateral has two pairs of equal sides and one pair of equal angles.
   What is its name?

4 Work out the sizes of the angles marked with letters.

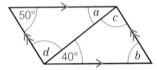

   Give a reason for each answer.

5 The diagram shows a kite and a right-angled triangle.
   Work out the size of angle w.

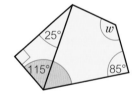

6 a Copy and complete these statements.
       i The angles in a triangle add up to ☐°.
       ii The angles in a quadrilateral add up to ☐°.
       iii The angles in a pentagon add up to ☐°.
       iv The angles in a hexagon add up to ☐°.
   b The diagram shows an irregular hexagon.
      Work out the size of angle m.

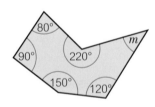

7 Work out the sizes of the angles marked with letters.
   Give a reason for each answer.

a
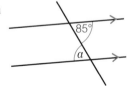

b
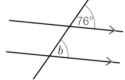

c
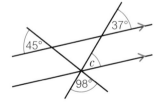

8 The diagram shows the exterior angles of a polygon.
  a Work out angle x.
  b Work out the sum of the interior angles.

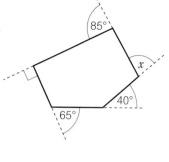

9 Copy the diagram.

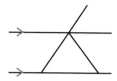

  a Mark a pair of alternate angles with the letter a.
  b Mark a pair of corresponding angles with the letter c.

10 a Work out the exterior angle of a regular 15-sided polygon.
  b Work out the interior angle of a regular 15-sided polygon.

11 A regular polygon has an exterior angle of 12°.
  How many sides does the polygon have?

12 The diagram shows part of a regular polygon.
  The point marked A is the centre of the polygon.
  a Work out the number of sides the polygon has.
  b Work out angle x.
  c Work out the interior angle of the polygon.

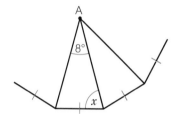

Challenge

13 A tessellation is a pattern of repeated shapes with no gaps
  in between.
  These diagrams show some different tessellations.

Q13 Strategy hint
Draw a diagram to help you explain
each answer.

  a Do all quadrilaterals tessellate?
  b Do all triangles tessellate?
  c Which regular polygons will tessellate?
  d Some regular polygons will not tessellate.
    Do they tessellate with other shapes?

14 Reflect Which of these statements best describes your work on
  shapes and angles in this unit?
  • I did the best I could.
  • I could have tried harder.
  Why did you choose that statement?
  Was it true for every lesson?
  Write down one thing you will do differently to make sure you do the
  best you can in the next unit.

Reflect

10 Charts and diagrams

| Master | Check P236 | Strengthen P238 | Extend P242 | Test P246 |

10.1 Using tables

You will learn to:
- Calculate the mean from a frequency table.
- Design and use two-way tables.
- Design and use tables for grouped data.

Confidence

Why learn this?
Sorting data into tables can help you to see patterns.

Fluency
Find the mean, median, mode and range of
0, 4, 7, 4, 3, 4, 2, 1

Explore
How many cheesecakes should a chef make for 100 diners, at lunchtime and at dinnertime?

Exercise 10.1

Warm up

1 The table shows the numbers of books borrowed from a library over one hour last Tuesday.

Number of books	Frequency
1	7
2	10
3	8
4	6
5	1

a How many people borrowed books during that hour?

b How many people borrowed fewer than four books?

c What was the modal number of books borrowed?

d What was the range?

Worked example

Jack asked students in his class how many pets they had.
Here are his results. Work out the mean.

Number of pets	Frequency	Total number of pets
0	7	$0 \times 7 = 0$
1	8	$1 \times 8 = 8$
2	6	$2 \times 6 = 12$
3	3	$3 \times 3 = 9$
4	1	$4 \times 1 = 4$
Total	25	33

Add a column to the table to work out the total numbers of pets.

Work out the total frequency (number of people in the survey) and the total number of pets.

mean = 33 ÷ 25 = 1.32

mean = total number of pets ÷ number of people

221

2 The table shows the numbers of goals scored in netball matches in one season.
Work out the mean.

Goals scored	Frequency
0	3
1	8
2	5
3	3
4	1

3 **Real / STEM** In science, a primary school class grew pea plants and then counted the numbers of peas in a pod.
   a What is the modal number of peas in a pod?
   b What is the range?
   c Work out the mean number of peas in a pod.

Number of peas	Frequency
0	2
1	2
2	9
3	7
4	6
5	11
6	3

4 **Problem-solving** The label on a matchbox says, 'Average contents 32'.
The quality control department counted the contents of some matchboxes one day.
Is the label on the matchbox correct?
Discussion Which average should you use for 'Average contents'? Does it matter?

Number of matches	Frequency
29	5
30	21
31	21
32	22
33	14
34	12
35	2

5 This **two-way table** shows the numbers of tickets sold at a cinema.

	Standard seats	Luxury seats	Total
Adult	39	33	72
Child	15	9	
Total	54		

   a Work out the total number of luxury seat tickets sold.
   b How many child tickets were sold?
   c How many tickets were sold altogether?
   d What fraction of the tickets sold were for children?

Q5 hint

A **two-way table** divides data into groups in rows across the table and in columns down the table. You can calculate the totals across and down.

Q5a hint

Use the 'Luxury seats' column.

Q5b hint

Use the 'Child' row.

6 The table shows the numbers of members of a photography club.

	Beginners	Intermediate	Advanced	Total
Men	33	36		90
Women			38	110
Total	65			

   a Copy and complete the table.
   b How many men are in the advanced group?
   c How many men are above beginner level?
   d Which level has the greatest difference in numbers of men and women?
   e What percentage of the total membership is women at advanced level?

7 **Reasoning / Finance** Tim records the food sold in his café one weekend.

a Which food is most popular on
   i Friday   ii Saturday?

b Tim makes a profit of
   • 35p on each sandwich
   • 50p on each salad
   • £1.30 on each portion of fish and chips
   • 40p on each cake.
   Which is his most profitable item over this weekend?

	Friday	Saturday	Total
Sandwiches	25	21	
Salads	12	9	
Fish and chips	7	6	
Cakes	13	27	
Total			

c Tim wants to remove a menu item on Saturdays. Which should he remove? Explain why.

Discussion How could a spreadsheet help you with this question?

Q7c hint

Look at the profit for each item on Saturday.

8 **STEM** In science, tutor group 8B measured the lengths of pea pods they had grown.
   Daisy started this table for the results.

a The first class includes all lengths up to, but not including, 2.0 cm.
   Which class contains the length 2.0 cm?

Length, l (cm)	Tally	Frequency
$0 \leqslant l < 2$		
$2 \leqslant l < 4$		
$4 \leqslant l < 6$		
$6 \leqslant l < 8$		

b i Copy the table and tally these lengths in cm.
     5.7, 2.0, 3.7, 6.1, 5.0, 2.4, 6.8, 4.5, 6.8, 3.7, 4.0, 5.6, 6.3, 4.9, 6.0, 4.1
   ii Fill in the frequency column.

c Which is the modal class?

Discussion Can you use the frequency table to work out the exact range of the pod lengths?

9 These are the times taken, in seconds, to pile and unpile a set of 10 plastic cups.
   8.2, 10.9, 13.5, 14.6, 12.7, 8.1, 9.5, 11.3, 20.0, 12.7,
   9.9, 10.6, 15.4, 18.2, 14.7, 9.5, 10.8, 12.5, 19.4, 16.7

a Record this data in a grouped frequency table with no more than five classes.

b Which is the modal class?

c Estimate the range.

Q9a hint

Make sure your classes are of equal size.

10 **Explore** How many cheesecakes should a chef make for 100 diners, at lunchtime and dinnertime?
   Look back at the maths you have learned in this lesson. How can you use it to answer this question?

11 **Reflect** Freddie and Claudia are talking about tables.
   Freddie says, 'Tables show information in columns and rows.'
   What do you think of Freddie's definition of a table? Is it true for all the tables in this lesson?
   Claudia says, 'Tables are everywhere. Click "Menu" on our TV remote control. It shows you a table.'
   Where else do you see tables displaying information in everyday life?

10.2 Stem and leaf diagrams

You will learn to:
- Draw stem and leaf diagrams for data.
- Interpret stem and leaf diagrams.

Fluency
- Work out the median of
  1, 2, 2, 2, 2, 3, 4, 4, 4, 5
- Find the mode and range.

Explore
How rich is the average billionaire?

Why learn this?
A stem and leaf diagram gives a quick, detailed overview of a set of data.

Exercise 10.2

1 Priya has written 10 data values in order.
  1, 1, 2, 3, 5, 7, 8, 8, 8, 9
  She says, 'For ten data values in order, the median is the fifth one.'
  Is she correct? Explain your answer.

2 These sets of data are written in order.
  i 3, 5, 7, 7, 8, 9, 9, 10, 11
  ii −5, −3, 0, 1, 2, 4, 7, 8, 10, 11, 13, 14, 15, 17, 20, 22, 25, 27
  For each set
  a count the number of values, n
  b work out $\frac{n+1}{2}$ to find the middle value(s)
  c write down the median.

Key point

In a set of 9 data values, the median is the $\frac{9+1}{2}$ = 5th value.
In a set of 10 data values, the median is the $\frac{10+1}{2} = \frac{11}{2}$ = 5.5th.
In a set of n data values, the median is the $\frac{n+1}{2}$th.

Key point

A **stem and leaf diagram** shows numerical data split into a 'stem' and 'leaves'.
The key shows you how to read the values.

Worked example

Here are the heights of some tomato seedlings (in cm).
  2.8, 3.4, 4.5, 4.1, 4.3, 2.7, 1.6, 3.2, 1.9, 2.5
Construct a stem and leaf diagram for this data.

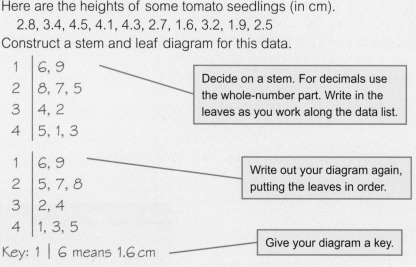

```
1 | 6, 9
2 | 8, 7, 5
3 | 4, 2
4 | 5, 1, 3
```
Decide on a stem. For decimals use the whole-number part. Write in the leaves as you work along the data list.

```
1 | 6, 9
2 | 5, 7, 8
3 | 2, 4
4 | 1, 3, 5
```
Write out your diagram again, putting the leaves in order.

Key: 1 | 6 means 1.6 cm
Give your diagram a key.

Topic links: Percentages, Bar charts

Warm up

3 The numbers of visitors each day to a stately home were
61, 52, 65, 77, 79, 84, 86, 91, 85, 70, 64,
53, 77, 56, 68, 73, 92, 85, 87, 78, 90

  a Construct a **stem and leaf diagram** for this data.

  b **Problem-solving** Use your diagram to answer these questions.

    i On how many days was the stately home open?

    ii On how many days were there more than 70 visitors?

The manager calculates that the house needs at least 65 visitors each day to make a profit.

    iii On what percentage of days did it make a profit?

Discussion What assumption did you make to answer part **b i**? Was this assumption reasonable?

Q3a hint

Use the 'tens' digit as the stem.
Remember the key.

4 The stem and leaf diagram shows the heights of Year 8 students, measured to the nearest centimetre.

$$
\begin{array}{c|l}
14 & 6, 9 \\
15 & 1, 1, 2, 3, 5, 5, 5, 6 \\
16 & 2, 3, 4, 5, 5, 5, 7, 9, 9 \\
17 & 0, 2, 4 \\
\end{array}
$$

Key: 14 | 6 means 146 cm

Find

a the mode   **b** the range   **c** the median.

Discussion Why didn't you need to write the data in order before finding the middle one?

Discussion Which average can you find most easily from a stem and leaf diagram?

Q4c hint

The median is the $\frac{n+1}{2}$ th value.

5 **Finance / Problem-solving** Jay owns a newsagent's. He recorded the amounts his customers spent one morning.

$$
\begin{array}{c|l}
0 & 65, 87 \\
1 & 08, 12, 36, 88, 97 \\
2 & 40, 52, 56, 68, 87, 95 \\
3 & 05, 15, 20, 35, 38, 40, 46, 62, 77, 99 \\
4 & 39, 68 \\
\end{array}
$$

Key: 1 | 08 means £1.08

Jay wants to increase the 'average' spend by £1 per customer.
He puts a special offer of 'Chocolate bars, 3 for a £1' by the till.
He recorded the amounts spent the next morning.

$$
\begin{array}{c|l}
0 & 92 \\
1 & 12, 18, 36, 52 \\
2 & 36, 40, 75, 99 \\
3 & 15, 19, 24, 36, 42, 49, \\
  & 51, 60, 66, 85, 90 \\
4 & 04, 39, 78, 82 \\
\end{array}
$$

Key: 1 | 36 means £1.36

Has the special offer increased the average spend by £1?

Q5 Strategy hint

Which average will you choose?
Compare for the two diagrams.

6 Real At the end of a secretarial course, students were tested on their typing speeds for
  • number of words per minute typing their own text (Composition)
  • number of words per minute when typing words spoken to them (Transcription).
This back-to-back stem and leaf diagram shows their results.

Transcription		Composition
9, 6, 5	2	1, 3, 4, 5, 7
9, 7, 6, 3	3	0, 2, 2, 3, 3, 4, 4, 5, 7, 8, 8, 9
8, 8, 7, 7, 7, 6, 5, 5, 4, 3, 0	4	1, 6, 7
4, 2	5	

Key: 5 | 2 means
25 words per min

Key: 2 | 1 means
21 words per min

Q6 hint

The circled value is 52.

a The course leader says, 'Most of the transcription scores are between 40 and 49.'
Write a sentence like this for the composition scores.

b Work out the median and range for
  i composition
  ii transcription.

c Write two sentences comparing the median and the range for composition and transcription.

Q6c hint

You could begin with, 'The median score for transcription is ☐'.

Investigation

Problem-solving

1 Put the visitor data from Q3 into a grouped frequency table.

2 Draw a bar chart for the data. Remember to label your axes and give your chart a title.

Part 1 hint

Use classes 50–59, 60–69 etc.

3 Which of the parts in Q3 can you answer from your bar chart?
If there are any you cannot answer, explain why not.

4 Can you work out a median from a bar chart?

5 a Which is better, a stem and leaf diagram or a bar chart? Write your reasons in a table.

Stem and leaf is better for	Bar chart is better for
	Colourful diagrams

b Is there anything they are equally good for?

7 Explore How rich is the average billionaire?
Is it easier to explore this question now that you have completed the lesson? What further information do you need to be able to answer this? Who is 'the average billionaire'?

8 Reflect Hana, Sam and Tilly discuss how they use worked examples.
Sam says, 'I read the question, then the answer, then all the note boxes telling me what to do.'
Hana says, 'I only read the note boxes and bits of the answer when I get stuck.'
Tilly says, 'I read the question, then the first part of the answer and its notes. Then I read the next bit of the answer and its notes, and so on.'
Describe how you read the worked example for this lesson.
Try reading it again in different ways (like Sam, Hana and Tilly).
Which way do you think is best? Why?

Explore

Reflect

10.3 Pie charts

You will learn to:
- Draw and interpret pie charts.

Why learn this?
Pie charts can show who receives portions of income.

Fluency
- How many degrees are there in a circle?

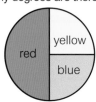

- What fraction is blue?

Explore
How much do bands get paid?

Confidence

Exercise 10.3

Warm up

1 Work out the fraction of each amount.

  a $\frac{1}{2}$ of 60   **b** $\frac{1}{4}$ of 32   **c** $\frac{1}{8}$ of 16

  d $\frac{1}{3}$ of 120   **e** $\frac{1}{4}$ of 360   **f** $\frac{1}{8}$ of 260

2 Use a ruler and protractor to draw these angles.

  a 60°   **b** 135°

3 The **pie chart** shows the favourite musical instruments of some Year 7 students.

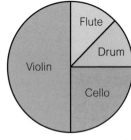

> **Key point**
>
> A **pie chart** is a circle divided into slices called **sectors**.
> The whole circle represents a set of data.
> Each sector represents a fraction of the data.

  a Which is the most popular instrument? How do you know?

  b What fraction of students prefer the
     i cello
    ii flute?

  c There are 32 students altogether.
    Copy and complete this frequency table.

Instrument	Frequency
Violin	
Flute	
Cello	
Drum	

> **Q3c hint**
>
> Work out a fraction of 32 for each instrument.

Topic Links: Fractions, Drawing angles

Worked example

Draw a pie chart to show this data about the tracks on a classical CD.

Track	Frequency
Opera	6
Orchestra	4
Piano	2

Total number of tracks = 6 + 4 + 2 = 12

> The total number of tracks is the total frequency.

÷ 12 (12 tracks is 360°) ÷ 12
(1 track is 30°)

> Work out the angle for one track.

Opera × 6 (1 track is 30°) × 6
(6 tracks are 180°)

> Work out the angle for each type of music.

Orchestra 4 × 30° = 120°

Piano   2 × 30° = 60°

Check: 180° + 120° + 60° = 360°

> Check that the angles add up to 360°.

> Draw the pie chart. Label each sector or make a key (you do not have to label the angles). Give your pie chart a title.

Tracks on CD

4 The table shows the numbers of woodwind, string and percussion instruments in a school orchestra.

Instrument	Frequency	Angle
Woodwind	12	
String	9	
Percussion	3	

a Work out the total number of musicians.

b Copy and complete: one musician is 360° ÷ □ = □°

c Work out the angles for woodwind, string and percussion instruments. Check that the angles add up to 360°.

d Draw a pie chart.

Q4d hint

Draw a circle. Draw in a radius. Then use a protractor to draw the angles. Label the sectors.

5 The table shows the percentages of sales in a bakery in one month.

Item	Percentage
Bread	40%
Cakes	10%
Pies	30%
Pastries	20%

a What angle in a whole circle represents

  i 40%

  ii 30%

  iii 10%?

b Draw a pie chart of the data.

6 A travel company asked 180 people where they went for their holidays. The table shows their answers.

Holiday	Frequency
England	90
Scotland	30
Ireland	15
Wales	45
Total	180

  a When you divide a circle into equal sectors to show 180 people, how many degrees represent one person?

  b Work out the angles for 15, 30, 45 and 90 people.

  c Draw a pie chart to show the holiday data.

7 **Problem-solving** The pie charts show a band's income in 2004 and 2014.

  a In 2004, $\frac{1}{3}$ of income was from concerts. How much did the band earn from concerts in 2004?

  b How much did the band earn from CDs in 2014?

  c Hedda says, 'The pie charts show that the band earned more from CDs in 2004 than in 2014.' Explain why she is wrong.

  d Copy and complete the two-way table to show the income.

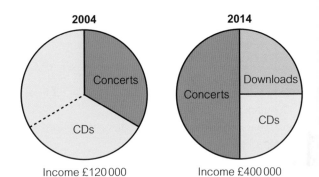

Income £120 000   Income £400 000

	Concerts	CDs	Downloads
2004			
2014			

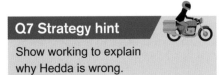

Q7 Strategy hint

Show working to explain why Hedda is wrong.

Investigation   Problem-solving

  1 Use a spreadsheet to draw a pie chart for this data on the top popular music.
  Pop 27%, Rock 20%, RnB 15%, Classical 8%, Dance 5% Country 4%, Other 21%
  a Input the data.
  b Select the cells containing the data.
  c Click the **Insert** tab on the top menu and select **Pie**.
  d Try 2D and 3D charts.
  e Give your pie chart a title.
  2 Save your pie chart, then move the Classical, Dance and Country to the 'Other' section.
  Create and save a new pie chart. Which pie chart is easier to read?
  Discussion What do you think is the maximum number of sectors for a pie chart to be able to read it clearly? Why?
  3 Create and save a new pie chart showing 'Pop' and 'Other'.
  Discussion Is two sectors enough for a pie chart? Explain your answer.

---

8 **Explore** How much do bands get paid?
  Is it easier to explore this question now that you have completed the lesson? What further information do you need to be able to answer this?

9 **Reflect** Tomar says that fractions help you to interpret pie charts (as in Q3).
  What other areas of mathematics help you to interpret pie charts?
  What maths skills do you need to draw pie charts?

10.4 Comparing data

You will learn to:
- Compare two sets of data using statistics or the shape of the graph.
- Construct line graphs.
- Choose the most appropriate average to use.

Why learn this?
Companies compare their performance with other companies to see if they are doing better than the competition.

Fluency
- What does it tell you when one set of data has a larger range than the other?
- What percentage of the data is less than the median?

Explore
Why does the UK government use the median salary to describe average income, instead of the mean?

Exercise 10.4

1 Here are the quarterly profit figures for two small businesses.

	1st quarter	**2nd quarter**	**3rd quarter**	**4th quarter**
Business A	£5324	£9637	£14 658	£5017
Business B	£8471	£9365	£8852	£10 345

a For each business, work out
   i the mean quarterly profit
   ii the range.

b Write two sentences comparing the profits of the two businesses.

c **Problem-solving** One of the businesses makes ice cream. Which one do you think it is?

Q1 Literacy hint

The quarterly profits are the profits for a quarter of the year (3 months). The 1st quarter is January–March, and so on.

Q1b hint

Write one sentence comparing the means and one comparing the ranges.

2 **Real / Reasoning** The graphs show the scores of the winning and losing teams each week in the TV quiz University Challenge.

a One line shows the winning team's scores. Which one?

b In which week(s) was the difference between the winning and losing scores
   i the greatest
   ii the smallest?

c Min says, 'The winning teams' scores are all higher than the losing teams' scores.'
Is she correct? Explain your answer.

Discussion Did you need to read exact values from the graph to answer these questions?

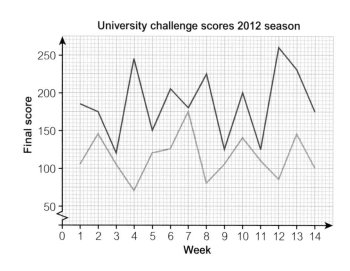

University challenge scores 2012 season

Warm up

3 The manager of a shoe shop keeps a spreadsheet record of all the women's shoes sold over a month.

	A	B	C	D	E	F	G	H	I	J	K	L
1	Smarter shoes - March sales, women's shoes											
2	Size	3 1/2	4	4 1/2	5	5 1/2	6	6 1/2	7	7 1/2	8	8 1/2
3	Pairs sold	0	12	9	11	21	24	38	22	12	5	0
4												

a Which shoe size was the mode?

b What was the median shoe size?
The spreadsheet calculates that 6.1 is the mean shoe size sold.
The manager uses the averages to help her to decide which size shoes to order.

c Which size should she order most of? Which average should she use?

Discussion How useful is the mean shoe size? How could she use the range to help her to decide what sizes to order?

4 The table shows two boys' results in an under-15 long jump competition.

	1st jump	2nd jump	3rd jump	4th jump
Alex	5.27 m	5.19 m	2.78 m	5.40 m
Dan	5.01 m	5.12 m	5.15 m	5.08 m

a From the results in the table, which boy do you think can jump the longest distance?

b Calculate the mean distance for each boy.

c Work out the median distance for each boy.

d Which average, mean or median, best represents each boy's performance?

e Reasoning Which value affected Alex's mean distance? Why didn't it affect the median?

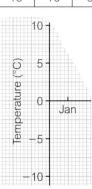

Q4e Literacy hint

A data value that doesn't fit the pattern of the other values is called an outlier.

5 Real The table gives the mean monthly temperatures (°C) in Moscow and Barbados over one year.

	Jan	Feb	Mar	Apr	May	Jun	Jul	Aug	Sept	Oct	Nov	Dec
Barbados	25	25.3	25	26.3	27	27	26.7	27	27	26.7	26.3	25
Moscow	−8	−7	−2	5	12	15	17	15	10	3	−2	−6

a Draw a line graph to show both sets of temperatures.
Start your axes like this.

b Write two sentences about your graph, comparing the temperatures in Barbados and Moscow.
You could use some of these words: warmer, colder, maximum, minimum, range, extreme, temperate.

Subject links: PE (Q4), Geography (Q5)

6 The pie charts show the ages of patients at two different dental surgeries.

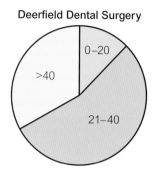

Deerfield Dental Surgery

0–20

>40

21–40

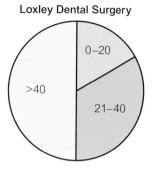

Loxley Dental Surgery

0–20

>40

21–40

a Which surgery has
  i the greatest proportion of patients over 40
  ii the lowest proportion of patients under 20?

Loxley Dental Surgery has 1500 patients. Deerfield Dental Surgery has 2400 patients.

b Which surgery has
  i the greatest number of patients over 40
  ii the lowest number of patients under 20?

Discussion What do you need to know to compare the numbers of patients in each pie chart sector?

7 Finance Here are the annual salaries of eight people working in a small company.
£27 000, £15 500, £23 750, £16 000, £18 950, £31 000, £18 200, £75 000
a Which salary do you think is the managing director's?
b Work out
  i the mean salary
  ii the median salary.
c How many people in the company earn less than the mean?
d How many people earn less than the median?
e Which best represents the average salary for this company – the median or the mean?
f Which average would best suit the needs of
  i the managing director, who wants to attract more staff to the company
  ii the staff, who want a pay rise?

8 Explore Why does the UK government use the median salary to describe average income, instead of the mean?
What have you learned in this lesson to help you to answer this question?
What other information do you need?

9 Reflect In this lesson, there were three discussion questions.
Look at each one again. Did the discussion help you with your mathematics learning? Explain your answer.

Explore

Reflect

10.5 STEM: Scatter graphs and correlation

You will learn to:
- Interpret and draw scatter graphs.
- Describe the correlation between two measures.
- Draw a line of best fit and use it to estimate values.

Why learn this?
Biologists and ecologists collect data about plants and animals. This helps us understand how habitats are changing and the impact we have on the natural world.

Fluency
Look at these coordinate axes. What does one small square represent
- on the horizontal axis
- on the vertical axis?

Explore
How can a biologist work out whether water pollution in a river has any effect on the growth of plants and wildlife?

Exercise 10.5

1 What are the coordinates of points A, B, C and D?

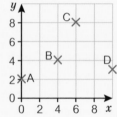

2 Copy the coordinate grid from Q1.
Plot these points. A (8, 4) B (5, 0) C (3, 10) D (7, 1)

Key point

A **scatter graph** shows a data set using two measures on the same graph.
The shape of a scatter graph shows if there is a relationship or **correlation** between two measures.

Positive correlation

Negative correlation

No correlation

3 STEM / Reasoning This **scatter graph** shows the heights of 20 trees in a conservation area, and the diameter of their trunks 1 m above the ground.
  a Describe the **correlation** shown by this scatter graph.
  b Write down the height of the tree that had a trunk diameter of 6 cm.
  c Write down the trunk diameter of the trees that had a height of 26 m.
  d Nisha believes that one of the points has been plotted incorrectly. Which point do you think this is?
  Give a reason for your answer.
  Discussion Can you suggest another reason why one of the data points might not be in line with the others?

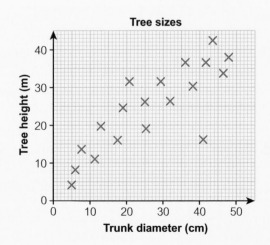

Tree sizes

233

4 STEM / Reasoning This table shows the gestation period and litter size for 12 mammals.

Mammal	Baboon	Dog	Goat	Hamster	Hedgehog	Raccoon	Squirrel	Tiger
Gestation period (days)	180	62	150	16	34	64	38	104
Average litter size	1	4	2	6.3	4.6	3.5	3	3

a Copy these axes onto graph paper.
Draw a scatter graph to show this information.

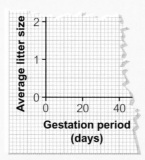

Q4a hint

Remember to give your scatter graph a **title**.

Q4 Literacy hint

The gestation period for a mammal is the length of time it takes a foetus to grow from fertilisation to birth.

b Describe the correlation between gestation period and litter size.

c Choose two words from the cloud to complete this sentence:
Mammals with .... gestation periods tend to have .... offspring (babies) in each litter.

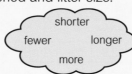

shorter
fewer   longer
more

Worked example

The scatter graph shows the body length and wingspan of 10 peregrine falcons.

a Draw a line of best fit on the scatter graph.

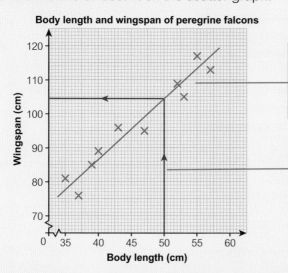

Body length and wingspan of peregrine falcons

Use a transparent ruler to draw your **line of best fit**. Try it in different positions until you have approximately the same number of points on each side of the line. The line can pass through some of the points.

Draw a line from 50 cm body length to the line of best fit. Draw a line across and read off the wingspan.

b Use your line of best fit to estimate the wingspan of a peregrine falcon with a body length of 50 cm.

104 cm

Key point

A **line of best fit** shows the relationship between two sets of data. There should be the same number of crosses on each side of the line. There may also be crosses on the line.

5 STEM / Real This table shows the age and shell size of 8 Dungeness crabs.

Shell size (mm)	152	150	140	133	156	138	142	155
Age (years)	3.3	3.0	2.4	2.3	3.3	2.5	2.7	3.4

a Draw a scatter graph for this data.
Use axes like these.

b Describe the correlation between shell size and age.

c Draw a line of best fit on your scatter graph. In California, fishermen are not allowed to catch Dungeness crabs with a shell size smaller than 146 mm.

d Use your line of best fit to estimate the minimum age of a Dungeness crab which can be legally caught in California.

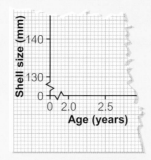

Q5a hint

Read the scales carefully and work out what each small subdivision represents.

6 STEM / Reasoning This table shows the number of plaice recorded at 12 different points in the Barents Sea, and the sea temperature at each point.

Temperature (°C)	1.6	2.4	2.9	0.4	1.2	0.2	1.0	0.6	2.2	2.9	1.7	2.6
Number of fish	135	70	30	225	145	290	160	250	130	45	100	75

a Draw a scatter graph for this data.

b Describe the correlation between number of fish and sea temperature.

c Draw a line of best fit on your scatter graph.

d Use your line of best fit to estimate the number of fish where the sea temperature is 2.1 °C.

e Climate scientists estimate that average sea temperatures have increased by approximately 0.2 °C. Use your graph to discuss how this could affect the population of plaice in the Barents sea.

Q6a Strategy hint

Use one centimetre square to represent 50 fish.

7 Explore How can a biologist work out whether water pollution in a river has any effect on the growth of plants and wildlife?
Is it easier to explore this question now that you have completed the lesson?
What further information do you need to be able to answer this?

8 Reflect What are the limitations of the data given in Q6?
Think about your answer to Q6e.
How confident are you in your statement?
What additional data would you need to improve your confidence?

10 Check up

Using tables

1 The frequency table shows the numbers of merit points Hetty earned each week.
   a Find the mode.
   b Work out the range.
   c Work out the mean number of merit points for a week.

Number of points	Frequency
0	5
1	7
2	9
3	6
4	3

2 This table shows ages and genders of members of a tennis club.
   a How many members are males over 40?
   b How many members are females under 18?
   c Copy and complete the table.
   d How many members are over 40?
   e What percentage of members are under 18?

	Under 18	18–40	Over 40	Total
Male	10		55	95
Female		38		
Total	40			200

3 The table shows the masses, in grams, of some newly-born chicks.
   a How many chicks were weighed in total?
   b Which is the modal class?
   c Estimate the range.
   d These three masses were missed out of the table
      36 g, 42 g, 40 g
      When they are put in the table, will the modal class change? Explain your answer.

Mass, m (g)	Frequency
$0 \leqslant m < 30$	8
$30 \leqslant m < 40$	13
$40 \leqslant m < 50$	14
$50 \leqslant m < 60$	6

4 The table shows the distances (in kilometres) that some students travel to school.

| Alpha Academy | 1.2 | 0.8 | 2.2 | 1.1 | 1.5 | 2.6 | 0.9 | 3.0 | 2.1 | 1.6 |
| Catling College | 3.0 | 0.5 | 6.1 | 1.5 | 1.1 | 5.2 | 9.9 | 2.8 | 8.5 | 1.4 |

   a Calculate the mean travel distance for each school.
   b Which school's students travel the shortest distance?
   c Calculate the range for each school.
   d Which school has the largest range?
   e One of the schools is in a city. Which one? Give a reason for your answer.

Presenting and comparing data

5 This stem and leaf diagram shows students' marks in a maths test.
   a What is the lowest mark?
   b Work out the range.
   c What is the modal mark?
   d Find the median mark.
   e Students who scored less than 35 had to re-sit the test. How many students had to do this?

```
2 | 6, 7, 9
3 | 0, 5, 7, 8, 8, 9
4 | 1, 3, 6, 6, 9
5 | 2, 4, 6, 8, 9, 9, 9
6 | 0, 2, 4, 8, 8
7 | 1, 5, 8, 8
```
Key: 3 | 2 means 32 marks

6 The pie charts show how Dana and Karen spent their money one day.

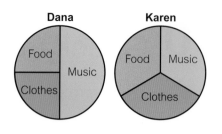

a Who spent the bigger proportion of money on clothes?

b What fraction of her money did Dana spend on music?

c Dana had $40. How much did she spend on music?

d What fraction of her money did Karen spend on food?

e Karen had $30. How much did she spend on food?

f Copy and complete the table to show the amounts Dana and Karen spent on music, clothes and food.

	Music	Clothes	Food
Dana			
Karen			

Q6a hint

Which colour shows clothes? Who has the bigger sector for clothes?

Scatter graphs

7 **STEM / Reasoning** The table shows the size of engine and top speed of some cars.

Engine size (litres)	1.2	1.4	2	1.6	1.4	1	2.4	1.2	2
Top speed (km/h)	182	202	226	211	219	158	240	178	214

a Copy these axes onto graph paper and draw a scatter graph to show the information.

b Copy and complete:
The larger the engine size, the .... the top speed.
The graph shows .... correlation.

c Add a line of best fit to your graph.

d Estimate the top speed of a car with an engine size of 1.8 litres.

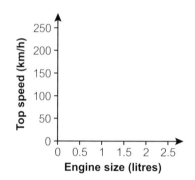

Key point

An **outlier** is a value that doesn't follow the trend or pattern of the rest of the data.

8 **How sure are you of your answers? Were you mostly**
☹ **Just guessing** ☺ **Feeling doubtful** ☺ **Confident**
What next? Use your results to decide whether to strengthen or extend your learning.

Challenge

9 a Design a two-way table to record any information you choose.

b In pencil, write numbers in all the cells so that the totals all add up correctly.

c Rub out some of your numbers so that you can still work out the missing values from the ones that are left.

d What is the smallest number of values you can keep so that someone else could work out the rest?

e Give your table to a partner to see if they can fill in the gaps.

Q9a hint

You could could choose one of the designs from the beginning of this exercise, or you could design your own.

Q9d hint

Try rubbing out another value. Can you still work out the missing ones?

Reflect

10 Strengthen

You will:
• Strengthen your understanding with practice.

Using tables

1 Copy this table of instruments played by students at a boys' school and students at a girls' school.

	Flute	Violin	Trumpet	Total
Girls	13	10	6	ii
Boys	12	i	iv	iii
Total		18	v	53

  a How many girls play the flute?
  b How many boys play the flute?
  c How many students in total play the flute?
    Write your answer in the correct space in the table.
  d Find the number 6 in this table.
    Copy and complete: '6 .... play the ....'
  e Find the number 18 in the table. What does this number tell you?
  f Work out the rest of the values in the table in the order i, ii, iii, iv, v, and write them in.
  g How many boys play the trumpet?
  h How many students play the flute, violin or trumpet?

> **Q1e hint**
> You could begin: '18 students ...'

2 This two-way table shows information about the animals medically treated in a vet's surgery.

	Male	Female	Total
Rabbit	4		10
Cat		8	
Parrot	6		13
Total	15		

  a Copy the table and fill in the missing values.
  b How many cats were treated?
  c What is the total number of animals treated?
  d What fraction of the total number of animals treated were cats?
  e What fraction of the animals treated were male parrots?
  f **Reasoning** Jack says, 'The same number of cats and parrots were treated.' Is he correct? Explain your answer.

> **Q2a hint**
> Look for a row or column with only one value missing.

> **Q2d hint**
> $\dfrac{\text{number of cats treated}}{\text{total number of animals treated}}$

3 **Real** The frequency table shows the numbers of children in families in another street.

Number of children	Frequency
0	3
1	6
2	10
3	4
4	1

  a How many families have no children?
  b How many families have more than two children?
  c How many families are there altogether?
  d Find the mode.
  e Work out the range in the number of children.

> **Q3b hint**
> Add the number with three children and the number with four children.

> **Q3d hint**
> The mode means the most common number of children. What is the highest frequency? What number of children has this frequency?

f Copy and complete this table.

Number of children	Frequency	Total number of children
0	3	0 × 3 = 0 children
1	6	
2	10	2 × 10 = 20 children
3	4	
4	1	
	Total number of families ☐	Total number of children ☐

g Work out the mean number of children for each family.

4 Which of these distances, d (km), are in the set $5 \leqslant d < 10$?
6 km, 3.5 km, 4 km, 6.5 km, 10 km, 9 km, 5 km, 10.5 km

Q3f hint

Ten families have two children each. This makes 20 children in those families.

Q4 hint

Remember ≤ means 'less than or **equal to**'.

5 A zookeeper records the masses (in kilograms) of the baboon monkeys at her zoo.
10.5, 15.2, 16.0, 14.7, 11.0, 10.9, 14.0, 13.2, 15.9, 17.5

Mass, m (kg)	Tally	Frequency
$10 \leqslant m < 12$		
$12 \leqslant m < 14$		
$14 \leqslant m < 16$		
$16 \leqslant m < 18$		

a What does $10 \leqslant m < 12$ kg mean?
b Copy the table. Tally the masses into it and complete the frequency column.
c Which is the modal class?

Q5c hint

Write the class like this:
☐ kg ≤ m < kg

Presenting and comparing data

1 **Real / Problem-solving** Here are Aya's and Jad's marks for their maths homeworks this term.
  a Work out the median mark and range for
    i Aya
    ii Jad.
  b Write a sentence to compare the medians.
  c Write a sentence to compare the ranges.
  d **Reasoning** Who would be the better person to help you with your maths homework? Explain your answer.

Aya	8	2	9	6	10	1	3	10
Jad	7	8	7	7	6	7	8	8

Q1c hint

Who had the smaller range and the more consistent marks?

2 Here are some heights of sunflower seedlings (in mm).
  35 28 22 41 33 19 55 48 29 31
  49 30 18 25 50 39 21 47 38 39
  a Draw a stem and leaf diagram for this data.
  b Use your diagram to answer these questions.
    i How many of the seedlings were more than 35 mm tall?
    ii What percentage of the seedlings were less than 25 mm tall?

Q2a hint

Use the tens digit as the stem. Remember the key.

3 The stem and leaf diagram shows the ages of people using a swimming pool one day.
   a What does 4 | 0 mean?
   b How many people in their 40s were in the pool?
   c How old was the youngest person in the pool?
   d What was the mode?
   e How many people were in the swimming pool?
   f Imagine all the people lined up in age order, holding numbers 1, 2, 3, 4, 5, …
      What number would the 'middle' person be holding?
   g Use your answer to part **f** to help you to find the median age from the stem and leaf diagram.

```
2 | 2, 7, 9
3 | 3, 4, 5, 7
4 | 0, 5, 6, 7, 8
5 | 1, 1, 1, 4, 6, 7
6 | 0, 3, 5, 5, 7,
7 | 1, 3
```
Key: 3 | 8 means 38

Q3b hint

How many values are in the 4 | … row?

Q3d hint

The mode is one of the ages.

Q3f hint

The 1st person is 22, the 2nd person is 27 and so on.

4 A travel company asked 180 people where they went for their holiday. The table shows their answers.

Holiday	Frequency
UK	100
Spain	45
India	20
USA	15
Total	180

   a When you divide a circle into equal sectors to show 180 people, how many degrees represent one person?
   b Copy and complete, to work out the angle for 100 people:

```
        ☐° for 1 person
×100 ⟋                ⟍ ×100
        ☐° for 100 people
```

   c Work out the angles for 45, 20 and 15 people.
   d Draw a pie chart to show the holiday data.

Q4a Literacy hint

A sector is like a slice of the pie.

Q4a hint

There are 360° at the centre of a circle: 360° ÷ ☐ = ☐

Q4d hint

Draw a circle. Draw a vertical line from the centre to the top edge. Draw the first angle. Move your protractor round to the edge of your first sector. Draw the next angle.

5 80 boys and 60 girls choose their favourite topics in maths. The pie chart shows the results for boys.
   a Which is the boys' favourite topic?
   b Copy and complete the two-way table.

	Number	Algebra	Statistics	Geometry
Boys				
Girls	20	10	20	10

   c Draw a pie chart for the girls.
   d Nadia says that as the same number of students like Geometry it must have the same angle in both pie charts.
      Is Nadia right? Give a reason for your answer.

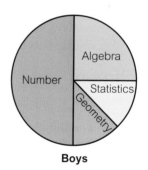

Boys

Scatter graphs

1 The scatter graph shows the mass of a bear cub at different ages.
   a How much did the bear cub weigh when it was 2 weeks old?
   b How old was it when it weighed 1.8 kg?
   c Describe the relationship between the mass of the cub and its age.

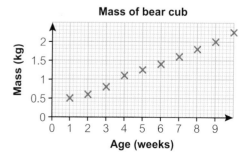

Mass of bear cub

2 For each graph, decide whether it shows positive correlation, negative correlation or no correlation.

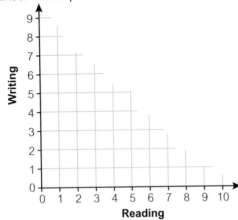

A   B   C   D   E

3 A group of students took tests in French reading and writing. The table shows their results.

Student	Dave	Jim	Hassan	Will	Ali	Paul	Raj	Gavin	Chris
Reading	4	2	5	6	7	7	8	10	10
Writing	6	3	4	6	8	5	7	10	9

a Copy the axes. Plot a point for each student.

b What is the missing word from this sentence?
Choose from: 'positive', 'negative', 'no'.
There is .... correlation between the students' reading and writing results.

c Draw a straight line of best fit.

d Use your line of best fit to estimate
  i the reading score of a student who scored 4 on the writing test.
  ii the writing score of a student who scored 8 on the reading test.

Enrichment

1 a Design a data collection sheet to record the shoe size and hand span of people in your class.
  b Collect the information from 10 people.
  c Draw a scatter graph of the shoe size and hand span.
  d Describe any patterns that you notice.

2 Reflect For these Strengthen lessons, copy and complete these sentences.
I found questions .... easiest. They were on .... (List the topics.)
I found questions .... most difficult. I still need help with .... (List of topics.)

10 Extend

You will:
- Extend your understanding with problem-solving.

1 **Real** Here are the boy's and men's times, in seconds, in a swimming race.

Men	47.52	47.53	47.80	47.84	47.88	47.92	48.04	48.44
Boys	53.00	53.38	53.44	53.47	53.64	53.66	53.75	53.02

a Work out
  i the mean
  ii the median
  iii the range
  for the boys' and men's times.

b Compare the men's and boys' times.

2 **Reasoning / Problem-solving** Here are some records from a running club's 100 m sprint.

Name	Gender	Time, t (seconds)
Jones	F	11.9
Peters	F	12.2
Clarke	M	12.0
Scott	M	12.5
Lee	F	12.0
Smith	F	12.8
Akbar	M	13.6
Ford	M	11.4

Name	Gender	Time, t (seconds)
Pitt	F	12.9
Wang	M	12.5
Henry	M	11.8
Moss	F	13.0
Campbell	F	12.8
Khalid	F	13.1
Lott	M	13.2

a Copy and complete this two-way table to record the times.

	$11 < t \leqslant 12$	$12 < t \leqslant 13$	$13 < t \leqslant 14$	Total
Male				
Female				
Total				

b How many female runners were there?
c How many male runners had a time of more than 13 seconds?
d How many female runners had a time of $11 < t \leqslant 13$ seconds?
Discussion Are male runners faster than female runners? How else could you use this data to investigate this question?

3 Real The tables show the goals scored by Real Madrid and Manchester United during the same period.

Real Madrid	
Goals	Frequency
0	4
1	4
2	7
3	4
4	1

Manchester United	
Goals	Frequency
0	7
1	5
2	4
3	2
4	1
5	1

Which team scored the most goals, on average?

Q3 hint

Compare the means of the two teams.

4 Problem-solving For his geography project, Lee asked shoppers in the town centre how far they had travelled to the shops that day.

Distance travelled, d (km)	Frequency
$0 \leqslant d < 3$	9
$3 \leqslant d < 6$	5
$6 \leqslant d < 9$	4
$9 \leqslant d < 12$	2

a Draw a pie chart to show his data.
b Complete these sentences from Lee's report.
  i The modal distance travelled to the shops is ....
  ii Fewer than half the shoppers had travelled less than ....
  iii Just over 25% of shoppers had travelled more than ....

Q4 hint

The pie chart will have 4 sectors. Work out the total frequency first.

5 Problem-solving This table shows the numbers of members of a hockey club.

	Beginner	Intermediate	Advanced	Total
Girls	6	20		38
Boys			10	34
Women	2		13	25
Men		6		23
Total	21	50		

a Copy and complete the table.
b How many members does the hockey club have?
c Draw pie charts to show
  i the proportions of members that are boys, girls, women and men
  ii the levels of the members.

6 A group of students were tested on their knowledge of countries of the world before and after watching a film.
This back-to-back stem and leaf diagram shows the results.
a Work out the median and range before and after the students watched the film.
b Write two sentences comparing the median and range for before and after.

Before film		After film
8, 5, 3, 2	1	2
9, 6, 6, 4, 1, 0	2	1, 7, 9
2, 0	3	0, 6, 7, 7, 8
8, 4, 3	4	2, 2, 5, 9
	5	0, 0

Key
2 | 3 means 32

Key
3 | 6 means 36

7 **STEM / Modelling** To test how a copper tank would expand
in high temperatures in a power station, a copper bar 10 m long
was heated. Its length was recorded at different temperatures.
The results were plotted on this scatter graph.

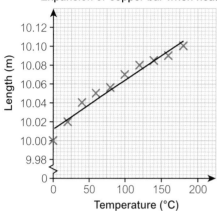

a Describe the correlation shown by the graph.
b What happens to the length of the copper bar as the
temperature increases?
c Use the line of best fit to predict the length of the bar at
   i 20 °C
   ii 110 °C.
d Using your answers from part **c**, estimate how much the
bar would increase in length when heated from room
temperature (20 °C) to 110 °C.

8 Here are the numbers of pages in the books entered for a literature
prize.
125, 200, 316, 412, 517, 627, 196, 256, 358, 420, 464, 562,
446, 376, 137, 294, 327, 488, 534, 496, 382, 584, 367, 578
a Draw a stem and leaf diagram for the data.
   Use the key '1 | 25 means 125 pages'.
b How many books were entered for the prize?
c What percentage of the books had over 500 pages?
d Draw a grouped frequency table for this data. Use the classes
   $100 \leqslant p < 200$, $200 \leqslant p < 300$ etc.
e Use the stem and leaf diagram and your frequency table to find
   i the median number of pages
   ii the mean number of pages
   iii the range
   iv the modal class(es).

9 Modelling Some Year 9 students took two English assessments –
writing and comprehension.
Here are their results.

Student	A	B	C	D	E	F	G	H	I	J	K	L	M
Writing	64	59	78	82	42	76	43	absent	15	38	45	68	72
Comprehension	60	absent	72	88	36	80	49	85	27	37	51	65	76

a Draw a scatter graph for this data. Put writing marks on the
horizontal axis and comprehension marks on the vertical axis.
Ignore the data for students B and H.
b Draw a line of best fit on your graph.
c Describe the relationship between the marks for writing and the
marks for comprehension.
d Use your line of best fit to predict
  i the comprehension marks for student B
  ii the writing marks for student H.

10 Problem-solving Lars and 9 other students measured their left- and
right-hand grip strength.

Student	Lars	Dan	Phil	Hamad	Tom	Marcus	Derek	Jack	Mason	Rafiq
Left-hand strength (kg)	25	17	34	20	24	48	32	41	33	26
Right-hand strength (kg)	27	14	31	16	22	50	36	39	38	25

Lars did hand exercises for the next 6 months. At the end of each
month, he recorded the strength of his right hand. The results are
shown below.

Month	Mar	Apr	May	Jun	Jul	Aug
Right-hand strength (kg)	26	28	28	30	35	37

a Draw a suitable graph for each table of data.
b Use your graphs to estimate the strength of Lars' left hand at the
end of August.

Q10b hint

Draw a line of best fit and use it to
make an estimate.

11 Reflect In this unit you have been introduced to different topics
such as line graphs, median and range.
List all the other maths topics you have used in these Extend
lessons.
How might town planners use these maths topics too?

10 Unit test

1 The pie chart shows the different birds seen in a garden one day.
   In total 72 birds were seen.
   How many of them were
   a starlings
   b sparrows
   c goldfinches?

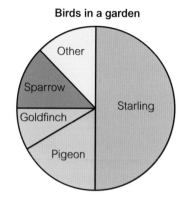

Birds in a garden

2 A survey about shopping habits asked people how many items they
   had bought online that week.
   The table shows the results.

Items bought online	Frequency
0	5
1	8
2	12
3	10
4	8
5	2

   a Work out the range.
   b What is the mode?
   c Work out the mean. Give your answer to one decimal place.

3 The table shows the amounts two families spent on their weekly food
   shop over one year.

	Mean	Median	Range
Smith family	£85	£82.50	£38
Jones family	£75	£81	£24

   a Write two sentences comparing the amounts the two families spent
     on food.
   b Explain why there is unlikely to be a modal value for a family's
     weekly food shop.

4 Draw a pie chart to show the online shopping data in Q2.

5 Two pans of hot water were left to cool to room temperature.
   One pan had a lid. The graph shows the recorded temperatures.
   a What was the temperature of the water in the pan with the lid after
     20 minutes?
   b What was room temperature?
   c Compare the times it took the pans to reach room temperature.
   d What was the difference in the temperatures after 30 minutes?

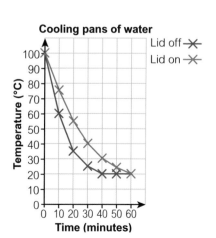

Cooling pans of water
Lid off ✕
Lid on ✕

6 A chicken farmer recorded the mass (in grams) of eggs produced one morning.
58.5, 61.3, 55.2, 58.6, 49.1, 45.2, 64.7, 61.2, 55.0, 59.5
Copy and complete the grouped frequency table for the data.

Mass, m (g)	Tally	Frequency
$45 \leqslant m < 50$		

7 The table shows the number of people playing tennis, hockey and badminton at a leisure centre one morning.
  a Copy and complete the two-way table.
  b How many people were playing tennis?
  c How many people were playing hockey?

	Tennis	Hockey	Badminton	Total
Females	20		15	67
Males		26		70
Total	44		35	

8 A driving instructor tests how long her students take to make an emergency stop. The stem and leaf diagram shows some learner drivers' reaction times in the test.
  a What is the range?
  b What is the median?

10	5, 7
11	0, 4, 9
12	6, 6, 8, 9
13	2, 5, 5, 6, 8
14	1, 3, 3

Key: 10 | 7 means 10.7 seconds

9 The table shows the wingspan and leg length, in cm, of some peregrine falcons.

Wingspan (cm)	102	120	117	112	132	111	126	118	121	107
Leg length (cm)	40	47	45	44	54	45	50	43	50	47

  a Draw a scatter graph for the data using these axes.
  b Describe the correlation between wingspan and leg length.
  c Draw a line of best fit.
  d Use your line of best fit to estimate
    i the leg length of a falcon with a wingspan of 124 cm
    ii the wingspan of a falcon with leg length 45 cm.

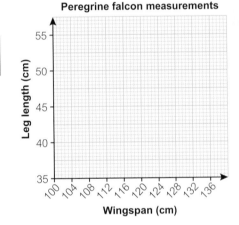

Peregrine falcon measurements

Challenge

10 Real / Modelling

> 75% of 5–18 year olds get pocket money

> Average pocket money is £5.75 per week.

> Approximately 10 million children aged 5–18 in the UK

Source: http://www.aviva.com/

Use these facts to estimate the total amount of pocket money given by UK parents per week.

11 Reflect Think back to when you have struggled to answer a question in a maths test.
  a Write two words that describe how you felt.
  b Write two things you could do when you're finding it hard to answer a question in a maths test.
  c Imagine you have another maths test and you do the two things you wrote in your answer to part **b**.
    How do you think you might feel then?

Q11 hint

Look back at the questions in this test, or in previous tests as a reminder.

Reflect

11.1 Plotting linear graphs

You will learn to:
- Plot straight-line graphs.
- Find the y-intercept of a straight-line graph.

Why learn this?
Straight-line graphs can be used to convert between different currencies.

Fluency
What are the coordinates of these points?

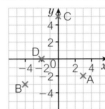

Explore
Can you predict where a line will cross the axes?

Exercise 11.1

1 Work out $y = 2x - 3$ when
  a $x = 4$ **b** $x = 0$ **c** $x = -3$

2 Write the equations of the lines.
  Discussion How many points do you need to plot to draw a straight-line graph?

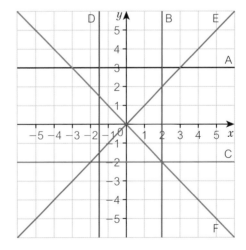

3 a Copy and complete the table of values for the equation $y = 3x - 4$.

x	-2	-1	0	1	2
y					

  b Draw a pair of axes and plot the graph of $y = 3x - 4$.

4 Plot and label these graphs. Use axes from -10 to $+10$.
  a $y = 5 + x$ **b** $y = 4 - 2x$ **c** $y = \frac{1}{2}x$

Q4 hint

Draw a table of values like the one in Q3. Choose at least three x-values. Make sure the coordinates will be on your grid.

Warm up

Topic links: Using formulae, Conversions

Worked example

Plot the graph of $2y + 3x = 8$.

When $x = 0$:

$2y + 3 \times 0 = 8$

$2y = 8$

$y = 4$

> To find the **y-intercept**, substitute $x = 0$ into the equation. Solve to find the value of y.

When $y = 0$:

$2 \times 0 + 3x = 8$

$3x = 8$

$x = \dfrac{8}{3}$

$x = 2\dfrac{2}{3}$

> To find the **x-intercept**, substitute $y = 0$ into the equation. Solve to find the value of x.

x	0	$2\frac{2}{3}$
y	4	0

> Draw a table of values with $x = 0$ and $y = 0$.

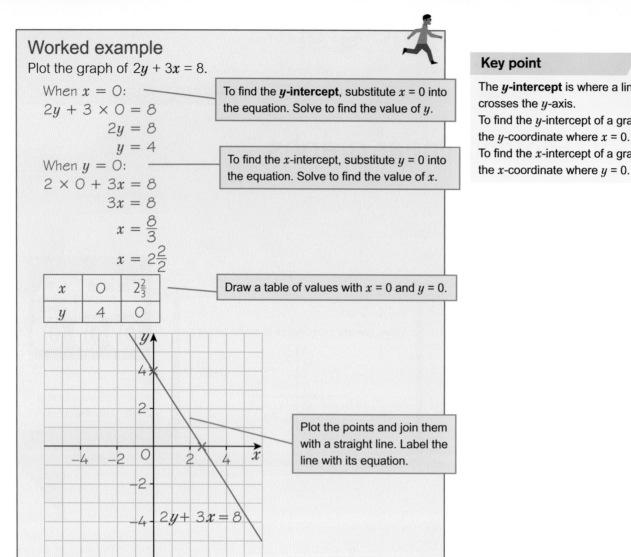

> Plot the points and join them with a straight line. Label the line with its equation.

Key point

The **y-intercept** is where a line crosses the y-axis.

To find the y-intercept of a graph, find the y-coordinate where $x = 0$.

To find the x-intercept of a graph, find the x-coordinate where $y = 0$.

5 The equation of a line is $3y - 8x = 12$.

   a Work out y when $x = 0$.

   b Work out x when $y = 0$.

   c Write down the coordinate pairs and then plot the graph.

6 On separate axes plot the graphs of

   a $x + y = 4$

   b $x - y = 5$

   c $2x + 5y + 9 = 0$

   d $7y - 11x = 18$

Discussion Look at the equation in part **a**.

Where do you think the graph of $x + y = -3$ will cross the axes?

> **Q6 hint**
>
> You could use a graph-plotting package to plot the graphs.

Investigation

Problem-solving

Draw a pair of axes from −5 to 5.

1 On the axes plot and label the graphs

   a $y = x$ **b** $y = x + 1$ **c** $y = x + 3$

   d $y = x - 1$ **e** $y = x - 2$

2 Write the coordinates of the points where each line crosses the y-axis.

3 Compare your answer to Q2 to the equation of the line. What do you notice?

4 Where do you think the graph of $y = x + 2$ will cross the y-axis? Plot it to check.

7 Work out the *y*-intercept for each line.

a $y = 3x - 4$ **b** $y = 2x + 1$ **c** $y = x - 3$
d $y = -2x + 1$ **e** $y = -3x - 4$ **f** $y = -x - 5$
g $y = x$ **h** $y = -x$ **i** $y = \frac{1}{3}x + 1$
j $y = \frac{2}{3}x - 4$

Discussion How did you work out your answers?

8 **Reasoning** Match the equations to their graphs.

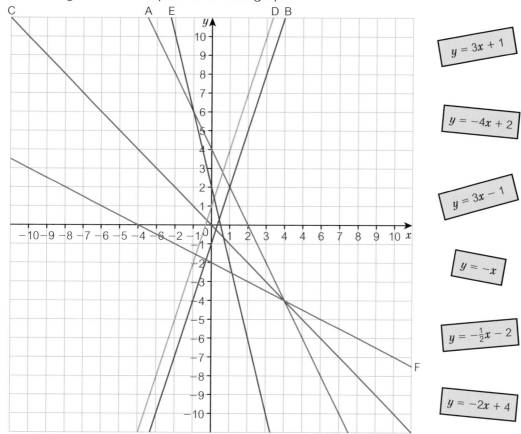

$y = 3x + 1$

$y = -4x + 2$

$y = 3x - 1$

$y = -x$

$y = -\frac{1}{2}x - 2$

$y = -2x + 4$

9 **Problem-solving** Write the equations of three lines that go through the point (0, 5).

Q9 hint

The equations all need to start $y =$

10 **Real / Modelling** A company uses a graph of this equation to work out the monthly pay for staff:
$$y = 20x + 1750$$
where *x* is the number of new clients and *y* is the total monthly pay (£).
a Draw the graph of this equation.
The pay includes a basic payment (£), and then an amount (£) for every new client.
b What is the basic payment?

Q10b hint

What is the pay when there are no new clients?

11 **Explore** Can you predict where a line will cross the axes? What have you learned in this lesson to help you to answer this question? What other information do you need?

12 **Reflect** Write down what you think 'linear' means.
$y = mx + c$ is a linear equation.
Write, in your own words, what *m* and *c* stand for.
Write a hint to yourself so you can remember what they stand for.

Q12 Literacy hint

Some say the *m* comes from the French word 'monter', meaning 'to climb'.

Explore

Reflect

11.2 The gradient

You will learn to:
- Find the gradient of a straight-line graph.
- Plot graphs using the gradient and *y*-intercept.

Why learn this?
Economists use graphs to help predict profit.

Fluency
What is
- 3 × 0
- 3 × 0 + 4
- 3 × 0 – 7?

Explore
What does a 'Gradient 12%' road sign mean?

Confidence

Warm up

Exercise 11.2

1 Find the *y*-intercept of each line.

  a $y = 2x + 4$ **b** $y = -3x + 1$ **c** $y = 2x - 5$ **d** $y = -3x - 2$

2 Which is the steepest graph?

Key point

The steepness of the graph is called the **gradient**.

Worked example
Find the **gradient** of the line.

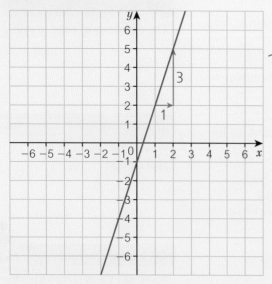

Choose a point on the line.
Draw a horizontal line 1 unit in the *x*-direction.
Draw a vertical line to the graph line.
When the *x*-value increases by 1, the *y*-value increases by 3.

Gradient = 3

3 Work out the gradient of each line.

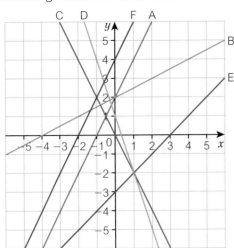

To find the gradient, work out how many units the graph goes up for every 1 unit across.

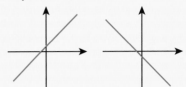

Gradients are positive (/, uphill) or negative (\, downhill).
The larger the value, the steeper the gradient.

Investigation

Draw a coordinate grid from −10 to 10 on both axes.

Problem-solving

1 Plot and label these graphs.

   a $y = x$

   b $y = 2x$

   c $y = 4x$

   d $y = -x$

   e $y = -2x$

> **Hint**
>
> You could use a graph-plotting package to plot the graphs.

2 Where do the lines intersect the y-axis?

3 Work out the gradient of each line.

4 Compare your answer to Q3 to the equation of the line. What do you notice?

5 Where do you think the graph of $y = 3x$ will be on your grid? Plot it to check.

4 Alfie is calculating the gradient of a line.
He works out that for an increase of 2 in the x-direction, the y-value increases by 6.
What is the gradient of the line?

5 Draw lines on squared paper with these gradients.

   a 5   **b** −3

   c $\frac{1}{2}$ **d** −0.25

To find the gradient of a line
calculate $\dfrac{\text{change in } y}{\text{change in } x}$

6 Work out the gradient of each of these graphs.

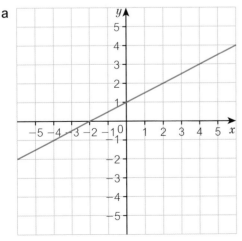

7 Plot these graphs. Fill in the gradient and y-intercept in the table.

Equation of line	Gradient	y-intercept
$y = 2x - 5$		
$y = x + 1$		
$y = 3x + 4$		
$y = -x + 2$		
$y = -2x - 7$		
$y = \frac{1}{3}x + 1$		

Discussion How can you find the gradient and y-intercept of a line without plotting the graph?

8 **Real / Modelling** An advertising company uses a graph of this equation to work out the cost of making an advert:

$y = 10 + 0.5x$

where x is the number of words and y is the total cost of the bill in pounds.

a Where does the line intercept the y-axis?

b How much is the bill when there are no words in the advert?

c What is the gradient of the line?

d How much does each word cost?

9 **Real / Modelling** Naima rents a room to teach English to x people. She uses this equation to work out her profit, y, in pounds:

$y = 10x - 50$

a Draw the graph of the line $y = 10x - 50$.

b i What is her profit when 0 people attend the class?

ii What does the y-intercept represent?

c How much does each person pay for the class?

Q9 hint

Think about the axes you need to use.

10 **Explore** What does a 'Gradient 12%' road sign mean? Look back at the maths you have learned in this lesson. How can you use it to answer this question?

11 **Reflect** Write, in your own words, as many facts as you can about gradients of straight lines. Compare your facts with your classmates' facts.

Explore

Reflect

11.3 $y = mx + c$

You will learn to:
- Use $y = mx + c$.
- Find the equation of a straight-line graph.

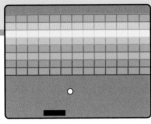

Why learn this?
Computer games designers specify how a character moves across the screen by giving the equations of the lines they follow.

Fluency
What is the inverse of
- +3
- −2
- ×5
- ÷4
- +2x
- −3y?

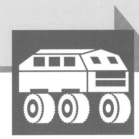

Explore
Can graphs help you to solve algebraic problems?

Exercise 11.3

1 On squared paper, draw a line with gradient −2.

2 $y = 3x - 6$
   a Work out the value of y when
     i $x = 3$ **ii** $x = -2$ **iii** $x = 0$
   b Work out the value of x when
     i $y = 6$ **ii** $y = -3$ **iii** $y = 0$

Key point

The equation of a straight-line graph can always be written in the form
$y = mx + c$.
m is the gradient and c is the y-intercept.

3 Write the gradient and y-intercept of each line.
   a $y = 2x - 5$ **b** $y = 3x$ **c** $y = -\dfrac{1}{2}x + 4$ **d** $y = -x$

4 a Work out the gradient of the line on the right.
   b Where does the line intercept the y-axis?
   c Write the equation of the line in the form **$y = mx + c$.**

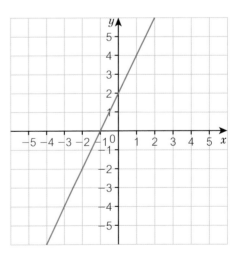

5 Match the equations to the graphs.

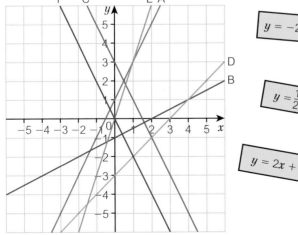

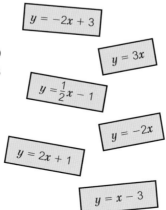

$y = -2x + 3$

$y = 3x$

$y = \dfrac{1}{2}x - 1$

$y = -2x$

$y = 2x + 1$

$y = x - 3$

6 Write the equations of these graphs in order of steepness.

A $y = x + 5$ **B** $y = 3x + 1$ **C** $y = 0.7x + 12$

7 Draw a pair of axes from −10 to +10. A line has equation $y = 3x − 1$.

  a What is its y-intercept? Plot it on your axes.

  b What is its gradient?

  c Start at the y-intercept. Draw a straight line with this gradient. Extend your line to both edges of the grid.

8 Use the method in Q7 to plot these graphs.

  a $y = 2x + 1$

  b $y = x − 5$

  c $y = −2x − 3$

  d $y = \dfrac{1}{3}x$

9 **Problem-solving** Which of these are equations of straight lines?

  A $y = 2x + 5$ **B** $y = x^2$

  C $y = \dfrac{2}{x}$ **D** $y = -\dfrac{1}{2}x + 4$

  E $y = 3x^2 + 7$

Car sales and monthly salary

10 **Real** The graph shows the relationship between the number of cars sold and the monthly salary of a car salesman.

  a How much does he earn if he doesn't sell any cars?

  b How much does the salesman earn for each car he sells?

  c Write the equation of the line that links salary (y) to number of sales (x).

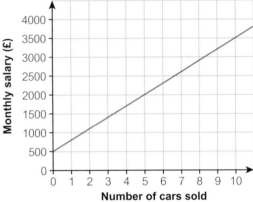

11 $y = 2x + 5$

  a Work out the value of y when $x = 3$. Write the coordinates $(3, \square)$.

  b Does the point $(1, 9)$ lie on the line $y = 2x + 5$? Explain.

Q11b hint

Substitute $x = 1$ into the equation of the line.

12 **Problem-solving** Which of these points lie on each line?

  A $(3, −7)$ B $(0, 5)$ C $(−5, −15)$ D $(1, −1)$

  E $(3, 12)$ F $(−1, 5)$ G $(10, 0)$ H $(3, 4)$

  a $y = 2x − 5$

  b $y = x − 10$

  c $2y = 4x − 8$

  d $2y + 6x = 4$

13 **Explore** Can graphs help you to solve algebraic problems? Is it easier to explore this question now that you have completed the lesson? What further information do you need to be able to answer this?

14 **Reflect** Samina says, 'I can work out any point on a straight line just from knowing the gradient and one point on the line.' Max says, 'I can work out any point on a straight line from the equation of the line.' Whose method do you prefer? How are the methods different? How are they the same?

11 Check up

Straight-line graphs

1 Draw a coordinate grid from −10 to 10 on both axes.
Draw the graph of $2x + y = 8$.

2 The equation of a line is $2x + 3y + 6 = 0$
  a Work out the value of y, when $x = 0$
  b Work out the value of x, when $y = 0$
  c Draw a grid −5 to 5 and use parts **a** and **b** to draw the line for the equation.

3 Match the equations to their graphs.

$y = 2x - 1$

$y = 5 - x$

$y = \frac{1}{2}x$

$y = -2x - 3$

$y = 2x + 3$

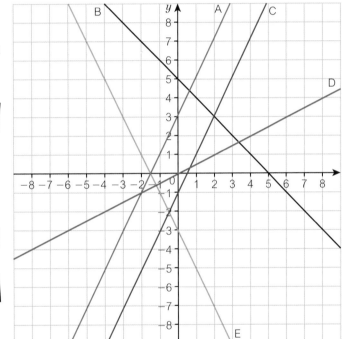

4 Write down the equations of two lines that pass through the coordinate $(0, -2)$.

5 Which of the points lie on the line $y = \frac{1}{2}x + 3$?
  A $(0, -3.5)$ B $(11, 8.5)$

Gradients

6 Find the gradient of this line segment.

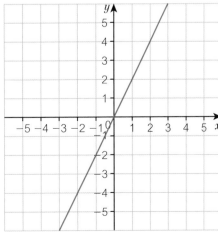

7 Copy and complete the table.

Equation	Gradient	y-intercept
$y = 5x - 2$		
$y = x + 1$		
$y = \frac{1}{3}x$		
$y = 5 - 3x$		

8 Draw a grid −10 to 10 and draw the line with an equation $y = 5x - 2$.

9 Husna hires a studio and runs a photography class for x girls. She uses the equation $y = 15x - 40$ to work out her profit, y, in dollars.
   a Draw the graph of the line $y = 15x - 40$.
   b What does the y-intercept represent?
   c What does the gradient represent?
   d How many students does Husna need to start to make a profit?

Finding the equation of a line

10 For each line write the y-intercept and the gradient.
   a $y = 2x - 4$ **b** $y = \frac{1}{2}x$

11 Find the equation of this line.

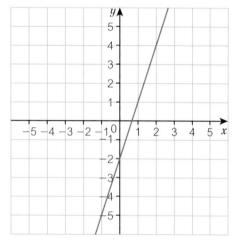

12 Reflect How sure are you of your answers? Were you mostly
   😦 Just guessing   😐 Feeling doubtful   🙂 Confident
   What next? Use your results to decide whether to strengthen or extend your learning.

Challenge

13 Write the equations of four different lines which pass through the point (2, 4) and have a positive gradient.

11 Strengthen

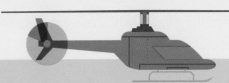

You will:
- Strengthen your understanding with practice.

Straight-line graphs

1 a Copy and complete the table of values for $y = \frac{1}{2}x + 3$.

x	−3	−2	−1	0	1	2	3
$\frac{1}{2}x$							
$+3$							
y							

Q1b hint

What are the smallest and largest values of x and y in your table?
Use these to help you decide on your axes.

b Draw the graph of $y = \frac{1}{2}x + 3$.

2 a Copy and complete the table of values for $x + 2y = 7$.

x	−3	−2	−1	0	1	2	3
$-x + 7$	10						
$2y$	10						
y	5						

b Draw the graph of $x + 2y = 7$.

3 a Draw a coordinate grid from −5 to 5 on both axes.
On your grid, draw these graphs.
Line A: $y = 2x$
Line B: $y = x - 2$
Line C: $4y + x = 4$

b Write down the coordinates of the point that lies on both line A and line B.

4 The equation of a line is $y = 2x - 1$.
a When x is 1, what is y?
b Fill in the missing coordinate: $(2, \square)$.
c When y is 7, what is x?
d Fill in the missing coordinate: $(\square, 9)$.

Q7b hint

When x is 2, what is y?

5 The equation of a straight line is $y = x + 5$.
a Does the point $(2, 5)$ lie on the line $y = x + 5$?
b Which of these points lie on the line $y = x + 5$?
A $(0, 5)$ B $(1, 7)$ C $(2, 8)$ D $(3, 9)$ E $(4, 9)$

Q5a hint

When x is 2, does $y = 5$?

Gradients

1 a Are the gradients of these lines positive or negative?

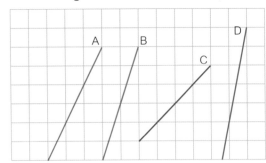

Q1b hint

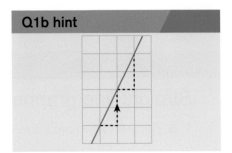

b Choose a point on line A.
Move your finger one square across (to the right).
How many squares does your finger move up to meet line A again?

c Repeat part **b** to work out the gradients of lines B, C and D.

2 a Are the gradients of these lines positive or negative?

b Choose a point on line E. Move your finger one square across (to the right). How many squares do you have to move your finger down to meet line E again?

c Repeat part **b** to work out the gradients of lines F and G.

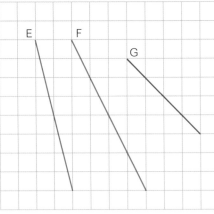

Q2b hint

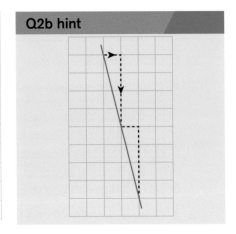

3 Work out the gradients of these graphs by counting the squares up and dividing by the squares across.

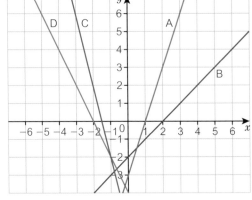

4 These lines have gradients that are fractions.

Write down the gradient of each line.

259

5 a Which of these lines has the steepest gradient?

A $y = x$

B $y = 2x$

C $y = 3x$

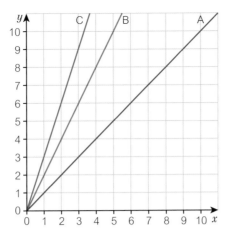

b Nico finds the gradient of the line of $y = x$ by moving 1 square horizontally and counting how many squares he must move vertically to get back to the line.
Copy and complete:
The gradient of $y = x$ is ....

c Find the gradients of lines A, B and C in part **a** using Nico's method.

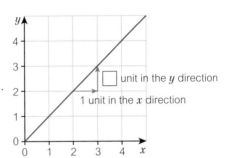

6 The diagram shows the graph of $y = 3x + 1$.
The points (1, 4) and (3, 10) have been marked.
Copy and complete the calculation to find the gradient.

Gradient $= \dfrac{\text{units in } y\text{-direction}}{\text{units in } x\text{-direction}} = \dfrac{\Box}{\Box}$

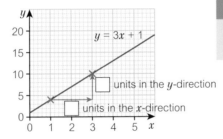

7 a Copy the graph.

b Mark two points on the graph line with whole-number coordinates.

c Draw horizontal and vertical lines similar to the red lines in Q6.

d Find the gradient of the line.

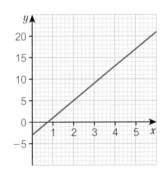

Finding the equation of a line

1 Write the coordinates where each line crosses the y-axis.

a $y = 10x - 7$ **b** $y = 2x - 5$ **c** $y = -x + 1$

d $y = \dfrac{1}{2}x + 7$ **e** $y = 3x - 2$ **f** $y = 4x$

2 Copy and complete this table.

Equation	Gradient	y-intercept
a $y = 3x + 1$	3	$(0, \Box)$
b $y = 2x$		$(0, 0)$
c $y = x + 5$		$(0, \Box)$
d $y = 2x - 3$		$(\Box, -3)$
e $y = 5x - 7$		
f $y = -2x + 4$	-2	
g $y = -5x - 2$		
h $y = -x + 7$		

Q5a hint

Imagine you are walking up the hill from left to right – which is the steepest hill?

Q5b hint

The gradient is the number of units moved in the y-direction when you have moved 1 unit in the x-direction.

Q6 hint

Look carefully at the scales on the x- and y-axes.

Q1a hint

c is the y-intercept.
$y = mx + c$
$y = 10x - 7$

Q2 hint

For the y-intercept look back at Q1.
m is the gradient.
$y = mx + c$
$y = 3x + 1$

3 a Work out the gradient of this line.
   b Write down the y-intercept.
   c Copy and complete the equation of the line.
      $y = \square x \quad + \quad \square$
      gradient y-intercept

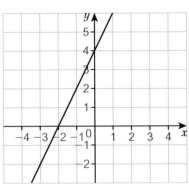

4 Write down the equations of these lines.

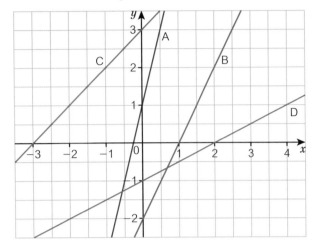

5 Work out the equation of this line.

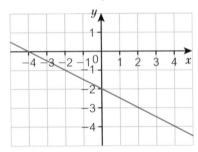

Q5 hint

The line goes downhill \, so the
gradient is negative.

Enrichment

1 $y = x$ goes through the point (0, 0).
   Write the equations of five other lines that go through the **origin**.

2 Which is the odd one out? Explain why.

   A $y = 2x$ **B** $y = 2x - 3$ **C** $y = 3x + 1$

   D $y = 2x + 7$ **E** $y - 2x = 4$

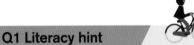

Q1 Literacy hint

The **origin** is the point (0, 0).

Q2 hint

There is more than one answer to
the question – you must explain your
answer!

3 **Reflect** Look back at the questions you got wrong in the Check up.
   Now look back at the Strengthen questions you answered.
   Write down one thing you now understand better.
   Is there anything you still need help with?
   Ask a friend or your teacher to help you with it.

Reflect

11 Extend

You will:
- Extend your understanding with problem-solving.

1 Work out the gradients of these lines.

Q1 hint

gradient = $\dfrac{\text{change in } y}{\text{change in } x}$

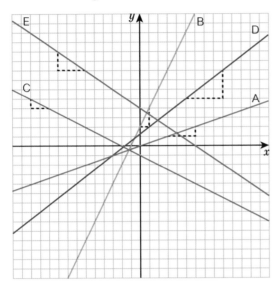

2 **a** Work out the gradient of this line.
 b Write the equation of the line in the form $y = mx + c$.

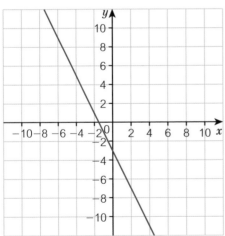

3 A line has gradient 3. It goes through the point $(-2, 4)$.
 a Write the equation of the line in the form $y = mx + c$.
 Substitute the value for m.
 b Substitute the values of x and y for the point $(-2, 4)$.
 c Solve the equation you got in part **b** to find the value of c.
 d Write the equation of the line.

4 A line has gradient −2. It goes through the point (1, 3).
What is the equation of the line?

5 Find the gradient of the line joining each pair of points.
   a (1, 3) and (4, 9)
   b (3, 5) and (5, 11)
   c (4, 8) and (3, 10)
   d (−3, 5) and (1, 9).

6 A straight line goes through the points (0, 6) and (1, 9).
Write the equation of the line.

7 **Problem-solving** A line has gradient 2.
It goes through the point (1, 4) and the point (2, a).
What is the value of a?

8 Here are the coordinates of a graph
entered into a spreadsheet package.
What is the equation of the line?

	A	B
1	x	y
2	2	15
3	5	24

9 **Problem-solving** The coordinates of the endpoints of a line
segment are (1, b) and (3, 5).
Work out the value of b when the gradient is
   a 2   **b** 3   **c** 1
   d −1   **e** −2   **f** $\frac{1}{2}$

10 **Problem-solving**
   a Draw a coordinate grid and plot the points (3, 5) and (1, −1).
   b Join the points with a straight line. Extend it to the edge of the grid.
   c Write the equation of the line in the form $y = mx + c$.

11 **Real** To convert from pounds (P) to rupees (R), a bank uses the
equation $R = 100P − 2000$.

   a How many rupees would you get for £50?
   This graph shows the exchange rate

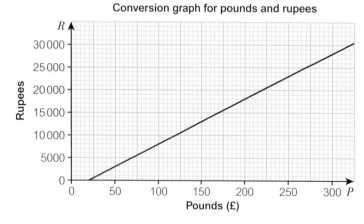

Conversion graph for pounds and rupees

   b Use the graph to work out the cost of 10 000 rupees.
   c What is the gradient of the line?
   d Explain in words what the gradient represents.
   e Why can the graph only be used for amounts over £20?

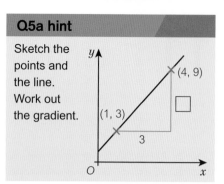

Q5a hint

Sketch the
points and
the line.
Work out
the gradient.

Q6 hint

Work out the gradient.
Use the y-intercept.

Q7 hint

Sketch the line with gradient 2 from
the point (1, 4).

Q9 hint

Sketch the lines.
Label the coordinates.

12 An arithmetic sequence starts: 1, 4, 7, 10, …

  a Copy this graph of the sequence.
    Extend it to include as many terms as you can.

  b Write the equation of the line.

  c Work out the nth term of the sequence
    1, 4, 7, 10, …
    What do you notice?

  d What will the 20th term of the sequence be?

  e Is 23 a term in the sequence?
    Explain.

Graph of an arithmetic sequence

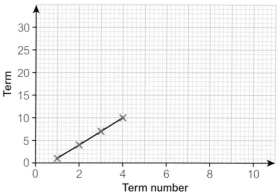

13 **Real / STEM** The scatter graph below shows the
average height and age of 20 plants over 15 weeks.

Plant height

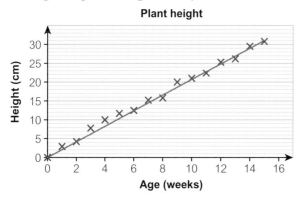

  a Work out the equation of the line of best fit.

  b Use the equation to work out the height of a 10-week-old plant.

14 This graph converts centimetres to feet.

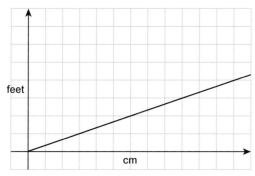

1 foot = 30 cm

  a Are cm and feet in direct proportion?

  b Work out the gradient of the line.

  c Write down the equation of the line.

  d 1 foot = 30 cm.
    How does the equation show this relationship (which in reality is
    an approximation)?

15 In which of these equations are x and y in direct proportion?

  a $y = 2x - 5$ **b** $y = -4x$ **c** $y = 3x$

  d $y = \dfrac{1}{3}\,x$ **e** $y = -\dfrac{1}{2}\,x + 2$

> **Q12d hint**
>
> Substitute $n = 20$ into the equation of
> the line.

> **Key point**
>
> When the 2 quantities A and B
> are in direct proportion,
> $A = $ (a number) $\times B$

> **Q15 hint**
>
> When two quantities are in direct
> proportion, what does their graph
> look like?

16 Problem-solving The rectangle is made using four straight lines.

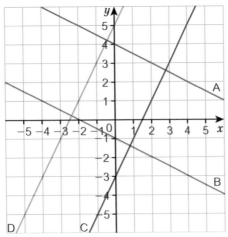

a Which of the lines have the same gradient?

b Write the equations of the four straight lines.

Enrichment

17 a On a coordinate grid from −10 to +10 on both axes, draw a line in the first quadrant.

b Reflect your line in the y-axis.

c Reflect both lines in the x-axis.

d Do any of the lines have the same gradient?

e Do any of the lines intersect with each other?

f Write the equation of each line.

Q17 hint

The first quadrant is the top right quadrant, and has positive x and y coordinates.

18 Reflect Larry enters pairs of coordinates in a spreadsheet like this.

	A	B
1	x	y
2	4	7
3	3	5
4		

In cell B4, he types in the formula   **=slope(B2:B3, A2:A3)**

Use what you know about gradients to explain what this spreadsheet formula does.

What answer does Larry get? Test it for yourself in a spreadsheet.

Q18 hint

What does 'slope' mean? What do you think B2:B3 means? What do you think A2:A3 means?

11 Unit test

1 Draw a coordinate grid with x- and y-coordinates from -10 to 10.
Draw the graph of $3x + 2y = 1$.

2 a Which lines pass through the origin?

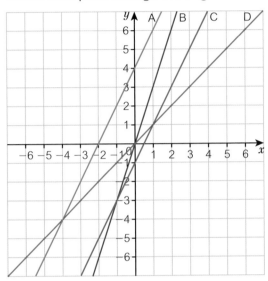

b Which line is the steepest?
c Which two lines have the same gradient?
d Match each line to an equation.

$y = x$ $y = 2x + 4$

$y = 3x$ $y = 2x - 1$

3 a Work out the gradient of each line.

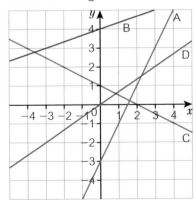

b Work out the equation of each line.

4 Write the equation of this line.

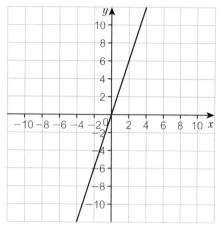

5 a Where does the line $y = 3x - 5$ cross the y-axis?
   b What is the gradient of the line $y = -2x + 7$?

6 A line has gradient 4 and intersects the y-axis at $(0, -3)$.
   Write the equation of the line.

7 Does the point $(6, 2)$ lie on the line $y = 2x - 14$?
   Show working to explain.

8 Work out the equation of each line.

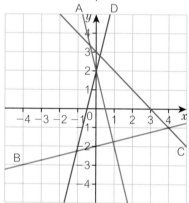

Challenge

9 A graph has equation $y = mx + c$.
   Given that it goes through the point $(1, 3)$ what is the relationship between the possible values of m and c?

Q9 hint

Work out a couple of possible equations of the line.
Then look at the relationship between m and c.

10 Reflect Look back at the questions you answered in this unit test.
   • Which took the shortest time to answer? Why?
   • Which took the longest time to answer? Why?
   • Which took the most thought to answer? Why?

Reflect

Index